COMMUNICATIONS AND NETWORKING IN EDUCATION

IFIP - The International Federation for Information Processing

IFIP was founded in 1960 under the auspices of UNESCO, following the First World Computer Congress held in Paris the previous year. An umbrella organization for societies working in information processing, IFIP's aim is two-fold: to support information processing within its member countries and to encourage technology transfer to developing nations. As its mission statement clearly states,

IFIP's mission is to be the leading, truly international, apolitical organization which encourages and assists in the development, exploitation and application of information technology for the benefit of all people.

IFIP is a non-profitmaking organization, run almost solely by 2500 volunteers. It operates through a number of technical committees, which organize events and publications. IFIP's events range from an international congress to local seminars, but the most important are:

- The IFIP World Computer Congress, held every second year;
- open conferences;
- working conferences.

The flagship event is the IFIP World Computer Congress, at which both invited and contributed papers are presented. Contributed papers are rigorously refereed and the rejection rate is high.

As with the Congress, participation in the open conferences is open to all and papers may be invited or submitted. Again, submitted papers are stringently refereed.

The working conferences are structured differently. They are usually run by a working group and attendance is small and by invitation only. Their purpose is to create an atmosphere conducive to innovation and development. Refereeing is less rigorous and papers are subjected to extensive group discussion.

Publications arising from IFIP events vary. The papers presented at the IFIP World Computer Congress and at open conferences are published as conference proceedings, while the results of the working conferences are often published as collections of selected and edited papers.

Any national society whose primary activity is in information may apply to become a full member of IFIP, although full membership is restricted to one society per country. Full members are entitled to vote at the annual General Assembly, National societies preferring a less committed involvement may apply for associate or corresponding membership. Associate members enjoy the same benefits as full members, but without voting rights. Corresponding members are not represented in IFIP bodies. Affiliated membership is open to non-national societies, and individual and honorary membership schemes are also offered.

COMMUNICATIONS AND NETWORKING IN EDUCATION:

Learning in a Networked Society

IFIP TC3 WG3.1/3.5 Open Conference on Communications and Networking in Education June 13-18, 1999, Aulanko, Finland

Edited by

Deryn M. Watson
King's College London
UK

Toni Downes
University of Western Sydney
Australia

KLUWER ACADEMIC PUBLISHERS
BOSTON / DORDRECHT / LONDON

Distributors for North, Central and South America:
Kluwer Academic Publishers
101 Philip Drive
Assinippi Park
Norwell, Massachusetts 02061 USA
Telephone (781) 871-6600
Fax (781) 871-6528
E-Mail <kluwer@wkap.com>

Distributors for all other countries:
Kluwer Academic Publishers Group
Distribution Centre
Post Office Box 322
3300 AH Dordrecht, THE NETHERLANDS
Telephone 31 78 6392 392
Fax 31 78 6546 474
E-Mail <services@wkap.nl>

Electronic Services <http://www.wkap.nl>

Library of Congress Cataloging-in-Publication Data

IFIP TC3 WG3.1/3.5 Open Conference on Communications and Networking in Education (1999 : Aulanko, Finland)
Communications and networking in education : learning in a networked society: IFIP TC3 WG3.1/3.5 Open Conference on Communications and Networking in Education, June 13-18, 1999, Aulanko, Finland / edited by Deryn Watson, Toni Downes.
p. cm. — (International Federation for Information Processing; 35)
Includes bibliographical references and index.
ISBN 0-7923-7760-5
1. Internet (Computer network) in education—Congresses. 2. Computer-assisted instruction—Congresses. 3. Information technology—Congresses. I. Watson, Deryn. II. Downes, Toni. III. International Federation for Information Processing. IV. Title. V. International Federation for Information Processing (Series); 35.

LB1044.87 .I45 2000
371.33'4—dc21 99-088176

Printed on acid-free paper.

Printed in the United States of America.

Contents

Part 4: Cognition and learning

Part 5: National and system-wide programmes

Part 6: Reflections on research in ICT and learning

Preface

This book has been compiled from a refereed selection of papers and discussions that occurred during an international conference in Aulanko, Finland in the summer of 1999. Communications and Networking in Education: Learning in a Networked Society (ComNEd 99) was an International Federation of Information Processing (IFIP) Education event, organised by the Working Groups in Primary (WG 3.5) and Secondary (WG 3.1) Education, and in affiliation with Distance Learning (WG 3.6).

Information and Communication Technologies (ICT) have already had a significant impact on education in many countries in the world. In most schools the dominant supporting technology has been either the stand-alone personal computer or a modest local network. The situation however is changing rapidly as a rising number of schools provide access to the Internet for their staff and pupils. Thus when the Director of the ICT Learning Centre at the University of Helsinki, offered to host an IFIP Education conference, it was clear that the topic should be on the new forms of communication and networks and their potential for education. Such a topic was not only timely, but particularly appropriate for one to be held in Finland – not just the home of the mobile phone, but the location of many innovative projects for the use of ICT in developing new networks and forms of distance learning.

A major strength of IFIP Education conferences is the valuable opportunity provided when practitioners, evaluators, lecturers, teachers and researchers come together to share and discuss their experiences. The occasion attracted over 250 delegates from 33 different nations – from Iceland, Chile and Estonia to India, The United States and Japan. This size, and the fact that all delegates stayed in the same location, were ideal for ensuring involvement of all attendees in the conference – and heavy social schedule. And so in perfect mid-summer weather among the lakes and forests of Finland, a sense of occasion developed through the conjunction of the timeliness of the topic, the range of interesting papers and debates, and the development of a human network through being at Aulanko. This book, of refereed selected papers, the three keynote addresses – one of which was given through video-conferencing, and reported discussions, is thus a record of the scholarly focus of this event.

The sense of occasion was reinforced by the opening addresses to the conference and the organisational infrastructure that ensured it happened.

1. OPENING ADDRESS

Olli-Pekka Heinonen
Minister of Transport and Communications of Finland

I was asked to open this conference when I was Minister of Education under the previous government. Although now Minister of Transport and Communications, there is no reason to then cancel, as the theme of the conference is well chosen and still relates to my work. Communications, communications technology and media play a key role in our ministry and will continue to do so into the next century.

The impressive number of international representatives at this conference shows that the programme is already a success. It is tempting to stay and follow the debates amongst the international community of people who have developed information and communications technology for educational purposes. Finland is an excellent forum for this. We have recently been building up our profile as a laboratory for the advance of the information society. Social experiments involve risks and they often have a bad reputation. But, the progress of ICT and in globalisation of the economy is so rapid that it would be a much greater risk to fall behind. In my opinion, this is something that a small country in particular, cannot afford. Rather, the only way we can succeed is to anticipate the direction of development and to react to the changes faster than others. There may be misjudgments and mistakes, but sensitivity to change will help to overcome them. Besides, change in the field of education and research is painfully slow, which is yet another reason why waiting is not an option.

The development of ICT for educational purposes started in Finland in upper secondary schools and in vocational training about ten years ago. In other words we started our national programme a few years later than, for example, Great Britain. The emphasis then was to organise the teaching of information technology. Its development was interrupted for a few years by the recession, until 1995 when a national information strategy for education and research was completed and this was resolutely implemented during my period as minister of education.

Parliament has also focused its attention several times on the pivotal role of education and research in the development and discussions on the information society. An example is the recent extensive assessment of the impact of ICT on education commissioned by Parliament's Committee for the Future. The results were well timed as background material for the new working group that I appointed. The group's task was to prepare a new strategy to extend the existing one. During the strategy period 1995 to 1999 steps were taken towards an information society. These steps forward form an impressive list. Our country has undertaken a number of excellent experimental and development projects. People are extremely interested in and committed to development. However, the introduction of new technology in education has not always been smooth. There are still many things to be completed. Advancement has also been very uneven.

The challenge now is to gather together effective practices and put them into common use. The organisation for implementing the new strategy is currently being created. Costs are estimated to be slightly greater than those of the previous strategy. Although many parts of the previous strategy have to be included, there are differences of emphasis. Attention must be shifted from technology to its real, pedagogically justified and effective use, from metal to content, from networks to networking in education, from a means of communication to communications itself, from knowledge to know-how. There are real dangers of dark corners in the information society. Education must repel threatening social replacement based on technological 'know-how'. Navigation in the information society requires a new focusing on ethic co-ordinates and new fixed points on a national and international level.

IFIP, created under the auspices of UNESCO, has proved to be a responsible and successful agent in finding solutions for the social and educational issues in the use of ICT. I am delighted Finland is able to serve the international community of teachers, researchers and development workers by being the host of the conference, and hope that in return, we will receive feedback on our own operations in advancing education. I would like to thank the various IFIP education working groups and the local organisers for putting this conference together. I wish the ComNEd 99 Conference every success.

2. WELCOME FROM PROGRAMME CHAIR

Bernard Cornu
IFIP WG 3.1 Chairman.

As the chairman of IFIP Working Group 3.1, and on behalf of my colleague Anton Knierzinger, chairman of IFIP WG 3.5, it is my pleasure to welcome each of you at ComNEd 99. Thank you Minister, for your kind words. We know how you, when Minister of Education, have been involved in the integration of ICT into education. Your country is one of the most advanced in that integration, and we are very honoured to have you with us today. And 'the day' has arrived! For many months we have prepared for this conference. The programme committee has selected a set of papers and has designed the structure and the content of the conference. The local organising committee has prepared everything so that we have an excellent week, not only for work but also for enjoying the venue and the Finnish environment. Many thanks to both committees.

IFIP has a long tradition of international co-operation in the field of ICT. The Education Committee (TC3) and its working groups, are especially active, producing publications, such as the international Journal Education and Information Technologies, a series of guidelines for good practice, and a curriculum for Informatics in secondary schools. We organise international conferences, from which we publish books of selected papers. The more recent were in Harare (Zimbabwe): 'Capacity Building for IT in Education in Developing Countries'; in Kiryat Anavim (Israel): 'IT: Supporting Change through teacher education'; and in Barcelona (Spain): 'Integrating IT into Education'. We participate in the IFIP congresses, and organise the World Congress on Computers in Education: the last one was in Birmingham (1995): 'Liberating the learner', and the next will be in Copenhagen (2001): 'Networking the learner'. Themes in progress include the role of the teacher and teacher education, ICT and lifelong learning, and the school of the future.

The computer has been our main object of interest for last 20 years – as a tool for teaching, and as an aid for learning. But while information technologies were developing, so communication technologies also developed, and the merging into ICT has led to new developments in education. Our conference focuses on Communications and Networks. We will examine how it changes teaching and learning, how it leads to new pedagogical environments and strategies. ICT are influencing our societies very profoundly. Knowledge itself is changed, different subjects to be taught are evolving. The means to access knowledge is becoming different. And therefore, the role of the school is changing, the role of the teacher is changing. These topics will be central in our conference.

A conference in Finland is not simply a nice environmental opportunity This country is especially advanced in the domains of ICT in education, and we will profit from the experience and expertise of our Finnish colleagues. Networking is common in Finnish schools, and work on their content and use. But the beauty of your country, the special spirit provided by the 24 hours daylight, by your lakes, by your trees, will inspire us. Let us share your 'sisu', this special Finnish character which makes you so efficient and powerful. This conference will be a strong human experience: we come from 33 different countries, we have a lot of expertise to share, we have a lot of contacts to establish. Many thanks to our Finnish hosts, many thanks to all those who made this event possible; I wish to all of you a very pleasant and fruitful conference, ComNEd 99.

3. CONFERENCE ORGANISATION

All conferences take a substantial amount of organisation, and those of the IFIP educational community are no exception. Conferences usually take at least two years' work from initial planning to the event. All is done by volunteer members of the local organising and international programme committees. A particular feature is the strong and friendly working relationship which develops between these committees; without them the conferences would not occur. This book records with thanks the work of those who ensured the conference and thus the publication happened. Thanks are also due to the Organising Institutions, without whose financial and other support, the conference could not have taken place.

3.1 International Programme Committee

Chairs: Bernard CORNU, FR
Anton KNIERZINGER, AT
Members: David Benzie, UK
Peter Bollerslev, DK
Toni Downes, AU
Raymond Morel, CH
Sindre Røsvik, NO
Brian Samways, UK
Matti Sinko, FI
Deryn Watson, UK

3.2 Local Organising Committee – Finland

Chair: Matti Sinko, Ministry of Education
Members: Mikko Horila, Summer University of Häme
Ella Kiesi, National Board of Education
Jari Koivisto, National Board of Education
Varpu Kuuliala, Summer University of Häme
Eero Pekkarinen, Kemi-Tornio Polytechnic
Marianna Niemi, National Board of Education
Eero Pekkarinen, Kemi-Tornio Polytechnic
Martti Piipari, University of Tampere
Timo Portimojärvi, University of Tampere
Riitta Rinta-Filppula, National Board of Education
Eva Forssén (1997-98)
Maria Salonen (1998-99), University of Helsinki
Martti Siekkinen, University of Joensuu
Jari Tiainen, Summer University of Häme
Marja-Terttu Tyynelä (1997-98)
Leena Merisaari (1999), Finnish I.P.A.
Leena Vainio, ICT Centre / University of Helsinki
Jarmo Viteli, Finnish I.P.A. University of Tampere

Eeva-Liisa Tomi-Kö, Maria Salonen, Päivi Saarinen and Matti Sinko were technical editors of the conference proceedings for Aulanko.

3.3 Organising Institutions

The International Federation for Information Processing (IFIP)
University of Helsinki, Centre for Continuing Education / ICT Learning Centre
Finnish Information Processing Association (I.P.A.)
Summer University of Häme
Finnish National Board of Education
Finnish Ministry of Education

PART 1

THE GLOBAL CONTEXT

Communications in an era of networks

Projects, models and visions challenged by a complex reality

Deryn Watson and Toni Downes
Kings College London, Franklin-Wilkins Building, London SE1 8WA, UK.
deryn.watson@kcl.ac.uk;
University of Western Sydney, Macarthur, Australia.

1. INTRODUCTION

For those who have been involved for several decades in efforts to integrate new information and communication technologies into education, or to re-think the purposes and forms of education in ways that harness of the power of new technologies, there is much still that reminds us of a dual track we tread. Each new wave of technologies, both more powerful and different from those before, lures politicians and educators into thinking that 'this time' the new technologies promise education a liberation, a definite advance towards change. And yet our understanding and evidence also suggests that the relationship between education, new technologies and change is far from simple. Indeed we are often still attempting to unravel the complex issues and problems that have emerged with using technologies in education, while at the same time welcome and prepare for the new.

This book reflects this complexity. The conference had a responsibility of developing further the vision of how these new technologies, and in particular the facility to network and communicate in ways not achievable hitherto, could indeed improve and transform aspects of education. Yet in parallel it was equally charged to ask serious questions about the realities of an interface between the social, cultural and pedagogical contexts of education and the actual affordances that these new information and communication technologies offer. The chapters in this book provide a heady mix of foreseeing and practical reporting, of planning for the future but at the same time respecting the problems education already has with current technologies.

The richness of the points presented here in this book stems in part from the range of experience of the international authors – from academics and administrators, to teachers and curriculum designers. This mix ensures that the central questions which are addressed are considered not simply from a variety of personal perspectives, but also from different cultural and environmental experiences. And yet interest also lies in the commonality of reporting and discussion based on activity in the field. All the contributions draw heavily on research and experience in devising and running projects and experimental activities in a range of schools and teacher training institutions and environments. The opinions expressed are thus grounded in knowledge gained from work embedded in the reality of today's educational settings. This must be the only sound base upon which to consider the issues of the future.

2. QUESTIONS TO BE ASKED

There is a strong perception that information and communication technologies (ICT) have already had an impact on education in many countries around the world; often at issue is the substance and nature of this impact. There is little doubt that during the course of the introduction of information technologies into schools a number of interesting questions have emerged with respect to the style and nature of learning, the complex relationship with teaching, pedagogy and the curriculum, appropriate resourcing and support, and the training and professional development of existing and future teachers with a technological environment in mind. In most schools during this debate, the dominant supporting technology has been either the stand-alone personal computer or a modest local area network.

The situation however is changing rapidly as a rising number of schools provide access to the Internet for their staff and students. The growth of communications technologies and the networks they can open mean that a further range of questions need to be addressed. The issues related to this change can be grouped into six themes: learning processes and IT; supporting autonomous learners; the changing role of the teacher; the school of the future; school systems in a networked society; and the social context of learning. It is these themes, broken into a range of subordinate questions, that the papers in this book address.

2.1 Learning processes and IT

The availability of ICT provides us with a new dimension to the challenge to understand the process of learning. Historically many models of the learning process have been offered but are they robust enough for the ways in which students learn about and with ICT? More specifically:

- How do students learn with and about ICT?
- What is knowledge in an ICT dominated world?
- Can ICT be used to support any pedagogy?
- Do traditional models of cognition adequately account for learning in an ICT rich environment?
- What are the consequences for the learning environment of our understanding of how learning occurs when ICT are available?

2.2 Supporting autonomous learners

Many have claimed that in future an individual's ability to manage their own learning will be seen as a key skill. The ability of an individual to manage their own learning is also seen as a critical attribute for effective lifelong learning. It has also been claimed that ICT can make a distinctive and effective contribution to the development and support of autonomous learners. Consequently:

- What are the key attributes of an autonomous learner?
- How can ICT be used to support the development of these attributes?
- How can ICT be used to enable groups of autonomous learners to collaborate and support one another?

2.3 The changing role of the teacher

Individual teachers play the most significant role in shaping the learning environment for students. ICT are often associated with changes in both learning activities and learning objectives for students and this has an inevitable impact on the role that the teacher is asked to play. However new teaching strategies are far from self-evident and so teachers themselves need the opportunity to develop new classroom skills whilst receiving support. Thus against this background:

- What is the role of the teacher in an ICT rich environment?
- What is the impact on pedagogy?
- How can we motivate and support teachers as they develop new skills?
- Can ICT be used to support teacher communities and hence facilitate change?

2.4 Creating the school of the future

Schools are still organised in very traditional ways. The subject structure of the curriculum would largely be recognisable to students from past generations, and teaching generally proceeds with the assumption that all relevant information can be provided by the teacher together with the few books that can be made available in school. ICT present a challenge to these assumptions by creating the possibility of alternative, or at least modified, patterns of activity. But what exactly are these challenges? For instance:

- What should we be aiming for when creating 21st century schools?
- What are the consequences of ICT for curriculum organisation?
- How can we manage change associated with the introduction of ICT in school?

2.5 School systems in a networked society

Schools are generally seen as discrete institutions where students and teachers meet at fixed times. ICT create the possibility for greater community involvement in education, for students to work and learn at times and places that are unconstrained by timetables and geography, and for widespread co-operation in education. The challenge therefore presented to school systems can be explored by asking:

- Is the virtual school, possible? If so, is it desirable?
- Does schooling have to take place at fixed times with all students present?
- How can we use ICT to involve the wider community in school education?
- What are the implications of ICT for an organisation of school education at global, national and regional levels?

2.6 The social context of learning

ICT provide unconstrained access to vast collections of information but that access has costs and dangers associated with it. Cultural and language domination is a serious possibility and there are significant equity issues associated with access to the technology. It is essential that all in the community consider:

- Can ICT be used to help students to respect and value cultural and linguistic diversity?
- What can schools do to ensure that all students have the opportunity to become capable users of ICT?

– What value systems are we implicitly promoting through our use of ICT in schools?

3. ADDRESSING THESE QUESTIONS

It is inevitable that these questions cannot be asked in isolation. Not only are they are inter-related, but the very nature of educational environments, with their multi-layered webs of activity and focus ensure that work reported here covered a range of concerns when considering these issues. For the same reason, issues cannot necessarily be addressed within the neat category of themes.

Thus the papers that make up the bulk of this book have been linked not by the themes, but rather the focus within which some answers are located. We have considered these as Sections. And it is important to understand the dynamic nature of the conference is also represented in this book. Firstly, the keynote address by Margaret Riel was actually a real-time video-conference presentation followed by a live discussion between the presenter in the United States and the participants in Finland. And secondly, the conference included active discussion panels. The debates considered in some detail issues that had been raised, and a synopsis of these discussions are presented here as two further chapters.

The first section, Global Issues, is made up of our first two keynote addresses. This is followed by a section called Networked Learning in Action. Here are grouped papers that cover a range of examples of networking from a range of perspectives, but each nevertheless focuses on the questions and issues, as well as results, of such networking. The third section, Models and Issues in Networked Learning, groups together those papers which probe a model – such as that of learning or teacher education. The papers in this section do collide, or rather lead into, those in the next section where the title speaks for itself, Cognition and Learning. The fourth section, Nation-wide and System-Wide Programmes, collects together those chapters which address whole institutions, cities or countries and their use of networks. The final section consists of only one chapter, that of the closing keynote paper from Erno Lehtinen. It does reflect the development of our current understanding on the area – indeed his subtitle, 'Desires, promises and obstacles', encapsulates the fundamental writing in this book.

The book concludes where we started, by re-iterating the notion of a dual track – or exploring the new while reminding ourselves of the issues and understandings learnt, sometimes painfully from the present. We cannot leap uncritically into the future. We must be aware that many of the questions we ask are still unresolved. While education has been coping for some time with the notion of the role of new technologies, we are moving into an era where this must be seen within the broader social and cultural perspective. All segments of our social and cultural lives are being influenced by the new communication technologies, and the influence they have on the information available to us and how we handle it. Thus the relationship with our wide communities, not simply those of education, has moved into the spotlight. And this raises questions of equity and cultural imperialism in ways not perceived hitherto. The reality of schools and their work must now be re-considered within this more panoptic sense. The next timely debate of this IFIP education community is on 'The School of the Future'.

BIOGRAPHIES

Deryn Watson is Professor of Information Technologies and Education at the School of Education, King's College, London University. During the 1970s and 1980s she was actively engaged in the research and development of computer assisted learning materials in the humanities and languages, with concerns for both models of software development and the potential for interactive learning to stimulate the exercise and development of process skills amongst learners in the classroom. Her research interests lie in the impact of IT on children's achievements, the issues embedded in understanding teachers' use of IT, training and professional development in an arena of innovation and change, and the reality behind the policy rhetoric for ICT.

Toni Downes is the Associate Dean of the Faculty of Education and Languages at the University of Western Sydney, Macarthur. Her teaching responsibilities include educational computing, leadership and technology. Her two broad areas of research interests are on the use of new information and communication technologies for teaching and learning, administration and leadership; and paradigms for researching children's lives. Her current research projects and consultancies span from early childhood education to university education. They include the development of an online course in quality leadership and technology, the investigation of the educational use of the Internet with young children, the changing nature of literacy, and the use of computers for teaching and learning in educational settings.

The future of technology and education: Where are we heading?

A report of a video-conferenced keynote address

Margaret Riel
Center for Collaborative Research in Education, University of California, 2001 Berekely Place, Irvine, CA 92697. mriel@uci.edu

Key words: future, history, technology, technology, integration, communication

Abstract: Technology is shared minds made visible. It connects people through time and across distances. Our shared past is divided into five periods which are based on the intellectual puzzles that have dominated our collective minds in terms of communication. These puzzles are discussed by focusing on how they have been transformed by technology in the past and will continue to be transformed by technology in the future. The 21st Century will be the Age of Communities because of the rapid expansion of what is possible in terms of shared values, goals and actions by people who can communicate over time and distances in ways not previously conceived. The four C's for the future of education are: Community, Collaboration, Curriculum, and Creativity. Each of these is used to organise a discussion of where we are heading in education during the Age of Communities.

1. INTRODUCTION

The question that I pose today is: The future of technology and education – Where are we heading? I have used the verb 'to head' on purpose. A soundbite summary of my talk is 'technology is shared minds made visible'. I pair this with a quote from the, the walls at UCLA's Royce Hall that I believe is from the philosopher, Royce. 'Education is learning to use the tools which the human race has found indispensable'. With the current attention on Y2K problems and fears that our world may stop functioning if the computers are confused over the date, it should be clear technology is essential to our society. The important question is not if we should use computers, but how we should be using this technology.

All technology is shared minds made visible but I will focus on the technology that enables sharing knowledge across distances and across time. Across time we need to save our wisdom so that we can compare the past to the present, make predictions and adapt our behaviour to the next cycle, to establish and protect rights and responsibilities, as well as to solve puzzles, celebrate successes and inspire new ideas. Now we also want to share across distances, to extend the range of our communication. We communicate across time to co-ordinate behaviour, to provide for group needs, to announce events or share information or observations, and to warn others when we are in harm's way. I will show you technologies that we have evolved for communicating across time and distances.

2. HISTORY OF INFORMATION TECHNOLOGIES

One way of lookinmg forward is to look behind us at where we have come from. I will show five periods of time characterised by different technologies for making our shared minds visible. I will discuss:

- Pictorial representation in the Age of Pictographs
- Representations of speech in the Age of Alphabets
- Access to literacy in the Age of Print
- Multi-sensory Recording in the Age of Graphics
- Multi sensory interaction in the Age of Communication
- And the future which I am calling – The Age of Communities.

2.1 The Age of Pictographs

We begin with pictorial representations in the earliest time, the Age of Pictographs (Figure 1). Early humans wrote on cave walls saving important information across time. For more portable messages, they carved and drew on bones and later on their portable cave walls – clay tablets. In 2500BC we appears the first form of paper, papyrus.

Early humans communicated across distances by shouting and whistling. They made flutes which could have been used as signals as well as for music; they could have used drums and signals from fire, torches, and smoke. By 2000 BC the domestication of horses and the invention of the wheel made it possible to send messages across greater distances at faster speeds. So we have always put information in public spaces from cave walls, palace walls, church walls, billboards to neon signs. Jim Sphorer and Sonny Kirkley are currently working on an Internet markup language to take the web out of the box and place it in the world. They will attach websites to a specific latitude, longitude and altitude. Information could also be attached to objects and people through the use of bar codes, radio frequency tags or small transmitters embedded in objects. Then using portable wearable devices such as watches, palmpilots, glasses, or headgear people can experience information tied to places.

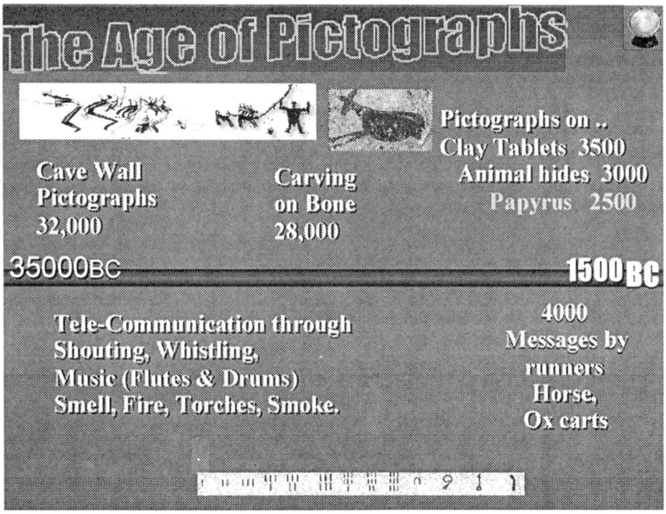

Figure 1. The Age of Pictographs

An example is a bike rider with a key pad that enables him to project virtual road signs computed for his purposes. These virtual signposts can tell him how far he has travelled, his speed, the time, and when to turn left, as well as other useful information about his journey. Instead of finding the route information on the Internet, printing it and trying to read a map folded over the handlebars, the rider sees the map superimposed on the pavement indicating when a right or left turn is needed to reach the specific destination. The rider can use the keypad to call up information about weather, hotels, restaurants or attractions. The information appears on virtual road signs only visible when they are needed. The rest of the time the rider can enjoy natural sights without the clutter of road signs.

In Museums, digital guide devices will allow for flexible use. You could programme a special tour around your interests and the time available and follow the purple footsteps that suddenly appear on the ground, or you can wander. Objects can have radio tags so at an exhibit you can see information about it in the language you select. Transparent markers temporarily appear to help guide you. Any one exhibit can be linked to infinite information on the Web so the choice of how much to learn will be a visitor decision, not one determined by exhibit designers.

Students going on field trips could explore more freely as they will be in less danger of becoming lost. Small devices will report their location and provide regular contact with the teacher. Information about an object, animal, plant, place, or process will not need a person to stand by the group and explain over the sounds that children make. Students could access the information and search for answers to their particular questions. They can collect information or measurements at a location. Graphs could show the results in real time as they collect it. The information that each child brings back from the field trip will not be identical and increase the value of having students work together; for more information consult Worldboards (www.worldboards.org).

2.2 The Age of Alphabets

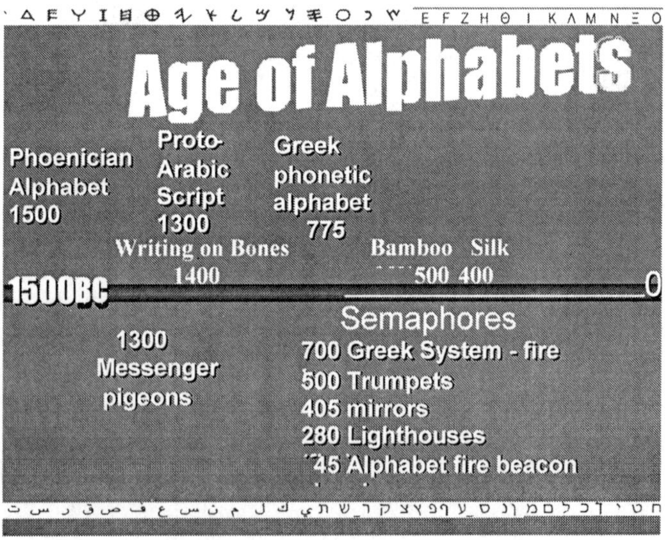

Figure 2. The Age of Alphabets

The Age of Alphabets was dominated by the task of inventing ways of coding our spoken language into a written language; in this period eight different scripts for coding language were created. In Figure 2 I have listed a number of different kinds of signal systems, or semaphores. In 45BC there is evidence of using the fire signals combined with a code to transmit verbal messages. The alphabet letters were divided into five groups of five. A system of sending fire signals was devised that involved sending two numbers for each letter (one for the group and one for the position in the group). This was the telegraph system; see Figure 4. If we fast forward, how are we continuing to solve the problem of saving our ideas in text over time? Of course, the printing press, the typewriter and the computer are part of this story. The QWERTY typewriter is not one of our most efficient tools; but all keyboards may soon find themselves on closet shelves. We are very close to talking instead of typing with our computers.

Increasingly we will have devices that will allow us to project images, hear speech and interpret our words. When we approach our house or car, our voice will operate like a fingerprint unlocking the door. We will have smart appliances that respond to verbal commands. As one gives a talk, the written record will be recorded in text making it possible for us to really listen, watch and worry less about taking notes. Linguistic barriers may not divide us as strongly as they do today. While translation programmes today are still far from adequate, they do project an image of the way in which we might move flexibly across languages.

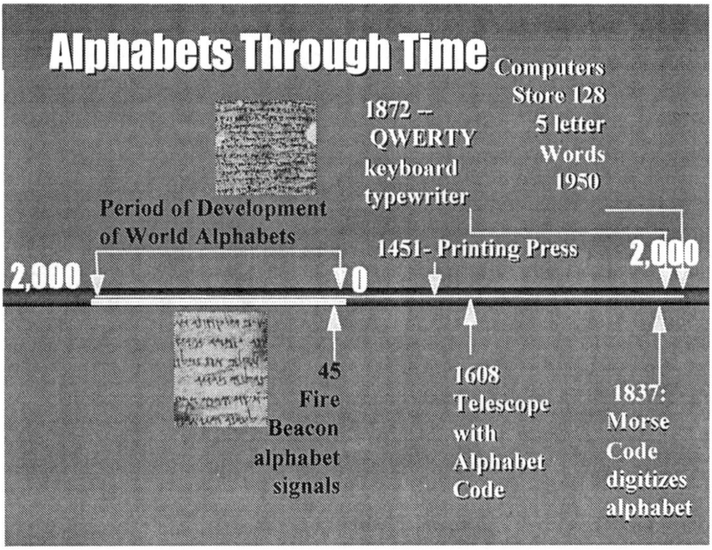

Figure 3. Alphabets through time

Here are a few scenes from a video created by a team of visionaries from AT&T Bell Labs (now Lucent Technologies), called *Connections.* Note there are no keyboards, all the machines are interactive, with personal agents that keep track of work. The use of the picture window as a computer screen is similar to the conception of Worldboards that I discussed earlier – the ability to project information anywhere.

2.3 The Age of Print

In the Age of Print the invention that dominated was the printing press. It was the time that we also figured out how to make the paper necessary for the printing press. At the beginning of this period, quills were used for writing. In 1565 we invented pencils, and later steel point pens. If we look below the timeline in Figure 4, we see that we are continuing to find ways to extend our ability to communicate over distances. Calling post messengers was a sequence of people positioned shouting distance apart. One person would shout the message to the next who would shout it to the next; they could get a message 153 miles from sunrise to sunset by this means. This led to ideas about how to use vision with using various signals which included flags.

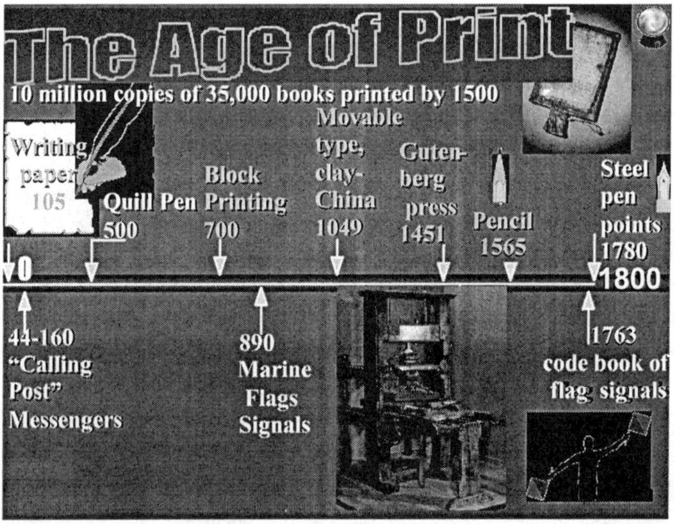

Figure 4. The Age of Print

Let us consider the pencil (Figure 5). It took 300 years to create the modern pencil with an attached eraser. I don't know why that is. I wonder if we were so excited about being able to write things down, that the idea of erasing them was not a high priority. But with the eraser came the ability to write, erase and rewrite. Current cutting edge technology is electronic paper for printing books that we can erase as easily as marks from a pencil. The printing press let us create thousands of copies of the same book as easily as we created a single copy in the past. But we have not before thought about unprinting a book.

Below is an extract from an article by Bennett Davis, to help you think about what digital paper might look like. Not a screen – at Xerox and MIT, scientists are designing digital paper with the look and feel of paper and ink – as thin, flexible, portable and crisply readable as paper:

> *Stack these electronic pages together, flick a switch and you can have any book you want: Hamlet, the latest John Grisham or the proceedings from the conference you attended last week. As with any other book, the print and pictures will remain in place for years without drawing electrical power. The one big difference is that when you want something else to read, the old text vanishes and the new replaces it. From newspapers and magazines to fax machines and advertising hoardings, the possibilities for electronic paper are endless. Already, posters made from electronic paper are hanging in a store near Boston. Within a couple of years, the inventors expect, they will have spread to supermarkets, airports and other public places. By 2006, the researchers predict that they will have mastered the subtleties of colour, and electronic paper will begin to replace the displays on pagers, machinery, calculators, digital clocks and even computer screens. Twenty years from now your groaning bookshelves could be replaced by a single electronic book.*

http://newscientist.com/ns/19990515/papergoese.html

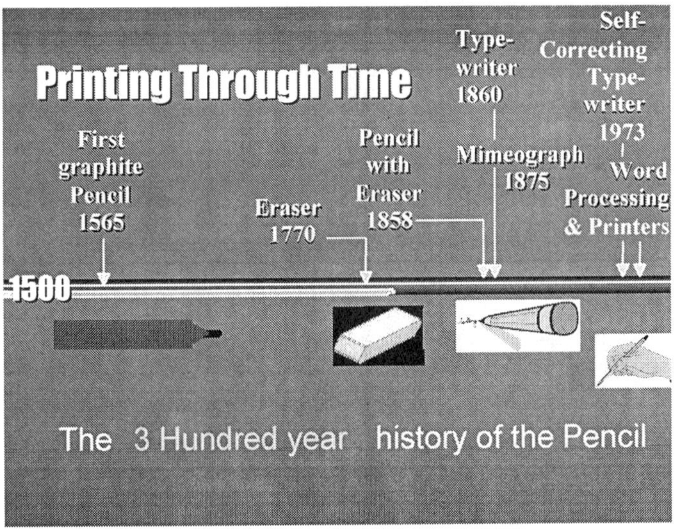

Figure 5. The 300 year history of the pencil

The quality of print on electronic paper is similar to the output of laser printers, and does not lessen over time. An average 250-page novel takes up 1 megabyte of storage space, so with existing technology 100 books could be squeezed into tiny chips embedded in an electronic book's spine. Some new technology for storing information will make it possible for a digital book to change into thousands of different books. E-Ink's electronic paper can change the image on a page as often as 20 times a second. Digital paper will be used in signs, books, cards, and newspapers. In this last case, we will no longer need to recycle huge piles of newspapers. Your 'news-paper' will stay wherever you like to read it. It will be reprinting all the time so that when you pick it up to read it, it will be current. The change will be analogous to that of the evening news to CNN on television. Stories may be similar over a short period, changing when the news changes. So as an event unfolds, the story will be updated as the reporter sends in new information. Either linked by phone lines or radio transmissions, your 'news-paper' will let you read the most current news at any time.

I highlighted the pencil of the last period for another reason. This writing 'lead' was given its current name Graphite at the end of the 18th century. This word *graphien* from the Greek to write or draw, serves as a metaphor for this next century of inventions. Notice the ending of most of the inventions of this time period. They end in this same stem-graphic or graphy – the lithograph, the photograph, the mimeograph, (school printing press), kinematograph, the radiograph, the telegraph. Why are they so named? I think because we wanted to write down, to record our multi-sensory experiences. We had already found ways to represent what was said in print; the typewriter is part of the progress of the Age of Print. But now we recorded exactly what our eyes saw and what our ears heard. At first these recordings were separate and static. But they enabled us to save what was seen and heard; to view or listen to sights and sounds as we please tomorrow, next month or in years to come. On the bottom half of Figure 6, is the telegraph, the transition technology to the communication age. How have we moved forward in our ability to record our experiences?

If we fast forward from the 19th century our ability to save and store sensory information increases in capacity while getting smaller in size. An article on IBM by John Markoff about magnetic storage capacity, describes how 100 books could be embedded in an electronic book's spine or covers. In a few years, with only the weight of single book, our students will be able to carry whole school libraries, in readable form, in their backpack in a book weighing far less then an average textbook of today. You could highlight text, underline or add code words and the content saved in your personal database with reference of the source and links to the original article. Now that is connected information!

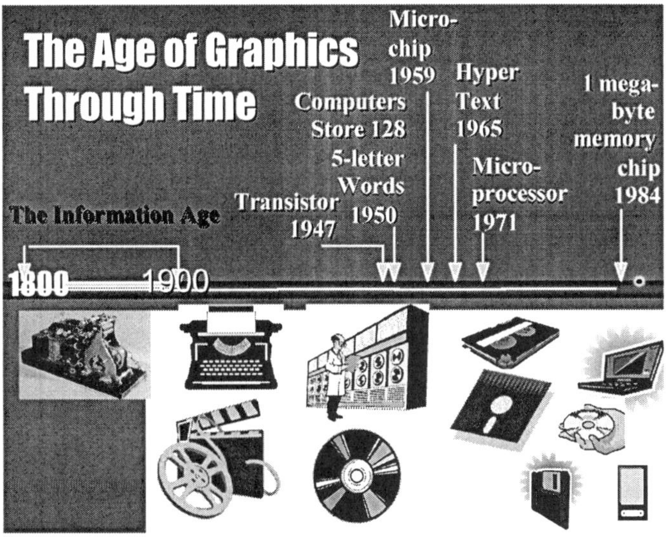

Figure 6. The Age of Graphics through time

2.4 The Age of Communication

Finally, we arrive at the Age of Communication (Figure 7). One point is that it becomes more difficult to decide what to put above or below the line. Most technologies for communication through time can also be used across distances. Is television about transmitting information live across distances or making entertainment to last? With digital communication, information can be transmitted, saved and recorded. It makes no sense to ask if a computer is a storage or communication device. I call the last century the Age of Communication rather than the Information Age because it is not just about new ways to store information, a task that continues from the past. The imagination of this century was focussed on communication and connections *over distances*. I would point out the use of the prefix 'tele' just as I highlighted the suffix 'graphic' in the previous century. The telegraph is the transition technology from the 19th century as it contains both the prefix and suffix. It is followed by the television, telephone, telerobotics, and teletype; we talk about activities such as tele-teaching and tele-mentoring in telecourses, and tele-conferencing, and tele-marketing in telecommunities. Another common stem is 'cyber' as in cybernetics or cybercafes, a reference to the helmsman again emphasising finding our way across the distance.

Intel, the company that developed the microchip that made personal computers possible, did not build a personal computer. Gordon Moore, co-founder of Intel, reports that the idea was discussed but they could not think of any use for a personal computer in the home. The only use the designer could imagine was having his wife store recipes on it! Without a vision of what it would be used for, they did not build it. (PBS, Triumph of the Nerds, http://www. pbs.org/nerds/transcript.html). The first personal computer was an Altair 8800, the idea of an ex-airforce officer, Ed Roberts, who conceived of this kit to keep his calculator company from collapsing. The Altair did little; it was a box with switches as input devices and lights as output. You had to build it yourself and many did not work. But it inspired Steve Wozniak to build the Apple 1 computer kit. This was little more of a computer than the Altair, a single circuit board with neither case nor keyboard. Still, Steve Jobs sold 50. That indicated there was a market for personal computers; the Apple II appeared 2 years later with a monitor and keyboard and printer giving rise to a new industry.

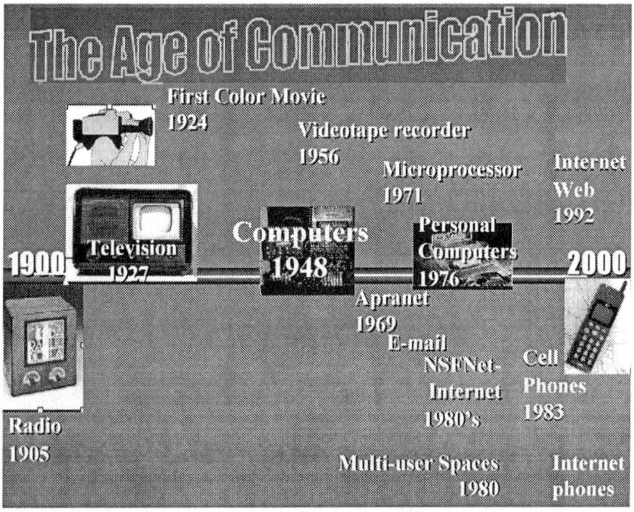

Figure 7. The Age of Communication

At the same time, Vint Cerf was considering an Internet protocol to make it possible for computers to exchange information and share processing power. This insight lead to the development of a world-wide Internet. To understand how we will be moving forward with each of these developments, we need only to look at the plans for Internet II, the tele-immersion project at Advanced Network and Services (http://www.advanced.org/).

2.5 The Age of Communities

In the 21st century we will be able to access, project and store information wherever we go without having to go to the computer. We will have devices that can project the information we need using the world as a screen (Figure 8). We will be able to talk to our tools using natural language to facilitate many of the things that require manual inputs now. Working across languages will become easier as the need to becomes more critical. The book we carry with us will display libraries of information at our fingertips without wires. We will be connected to whomever we want and we will be able to leave computer agents to take care of the interactions that we cannot handle. Physically we will be in one location but we will have the sense of being in multiple spaces mentally. We will share these informational spaces with others who are working on similar goals and interests.

The communities we form will be virtual and they will be the way we come to see ourselves and others, contributing to our identity. We identify ourselves by our name, occupation, generation, geographic location, nation, nationality and perhaps religion. In the future we may also include where we homestead on the net. Finally incorporating all of these inventions for sharing minds, the students at the University of California, Santa Cruz have created a glimpse of what learning environments on the web will soon look like. This extract is drawn from a shared Active World environment, Touring Virtual University of California, Santa Cruz that students have created working with Bonnie DeVarco. This active world construction is being developed as a different way of creating online educational and social contexts.

> *Welcome to the virtual UCSC campus, a 21st century university. Hi, I'm Anna and I'm a fine art major for the college, I'll be your virtual guide for the next few minutes. This is not really me of course, this is my avatar, my persona in cyberspace. I'm sitting in front of my computer but with my avatar I can take you on a virtual tour of our campus. Just kick back in front of your screen and I'll show you the ropes ...We just warped over to the campus teleport map. UCSC students built this campus, I think that's pretty cool. And they did it as a summer project with world class 3-D designers, living in other countries. Many of our team members haven't even met each other in person but it doesn't really matter. Why not? Because our campus is a shared virtual space. We can all meet here but be physically located anywhere on the planet.*

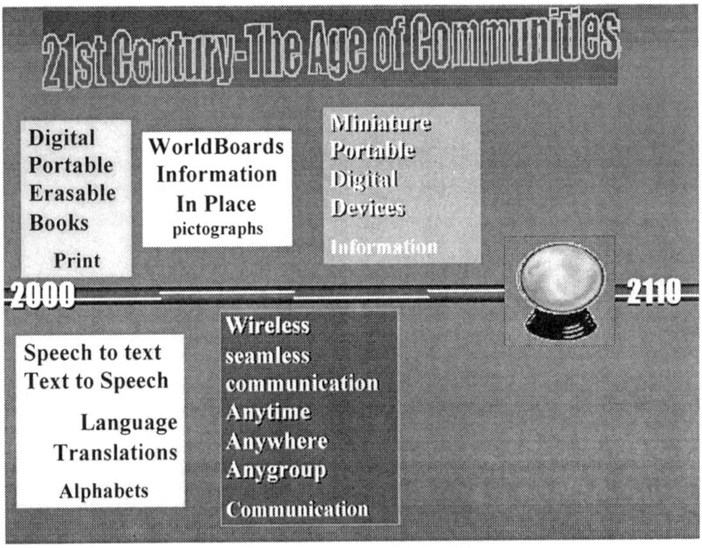

Figure 8. The 21st century: The Age of Communities

For more information see Avatar 98 Virtual Education (http://www.cruzio.com/~devarco/av98edu.htm). For examples of new technologies and images of the future, explore – Learning Spaces in the Networlds of Tomorrow (2http://www.iearn.org/webtour/2).

3. THE FUTURE

If I am right about the next century, education as well as work will be much more collaborative. I want to consider a business card from a new organisation – the Center for Innovative Learning Technologies. Notice this business card has a hole in the middle; if you flip it over you see that it is a circle with a square in it. This card has 13 megabytes of information stored on it and will play in any CD-ROM machine. The message is from CILT, a collaboration of research centres from across the US, who are exploring ways in which technology is changing teaching and learning. They are organised into research themes and encourage a new level of partnership that may lead to important research findings. In the introduction of their business card are quotes form a number of people making predictions about the future. Examples include: I foresee an analytical machine that can not only foresee, but can act on that foresight (Charles Baggage, Envisioned the computer, 1834); I foresee that the analytic machine might compose music and graphics of any degree of complexity or extent (Lady Ada Bryon Lovelace, Wrote the first computer program, 1843); I foresee a world market for maybe 5 computers. (Thomas Watson, Chairman of IBM, 1943); I foresee a time when computers may weigh no more than one and a half tons. (Popular Mechanics, 1949); and I foresee no reason for people to have a computer in their home (Ken Olson, President, Digital Equipment Corporation, 1977).

So it is not always easy to guess where we are heading. Where are we heading? Can I foresee the future? I know I can 4-C the future, using Community, Collaboration, Curriculum, and Creativity.

3.1 Community

The Center for Innovative Learning Technology (www.cilt.org) (US) and the TeleLearning Centre of Excellence (www.telelearn.ca) (CA) are research communities that believe that community research efforts are more powerful than individual ones. Researchers work together with their unique perspectives and different populations to create better understanding of common results. With the changes in education involving working worldwide, it does not make sense to work alone any more. Institutions providing professional development to teachers are working in larger coalitions (explore the Tapped In community (tappedin.sri.com)). Here teachers and support agencies from across the United States come together in a social online environment for teacher professional development. At the school level, world-wide communities are helping students work with their peers around the world in problems they share. A good example is the International Education and Resource Network (www.iearn.org).

3.2 Collaboration

Here is a list of groups to illustrate the level of collaboration that I see happening in the near and distant future:

- Virtual Canyon (www.virtual-canyon.org)
- ThinkQuest org (www.thinkquest.net)
- IEARN Learning Circles & Projects (www.iearn.org/projects)
- Passport to Knowledge (passport.ivv.nasa.gov)
- Knowledge Forum (learn.motion.com/lim/kf/KF1.html)
- Globe (www.globe.gov)
- Virtual High School -Concord (concord.org)
- The George Lucas Education Foundation (www.glef.org)

The Virtual Canyon Project, Monterey Bay, (www.virtual-canyon.org) shows you what this collaboration will mean for teaching and learning. Using a web site to explore Monterey Bay on the research institute's boat, students pose and test questions in a proper investigative fashion. One student then commented:

> *I've always wanted to work with the scientists because I really admire them and really look up to them with all of their work that they've put into it and just being with them it makes me feel like you know, that I'm part of this and not just some little kid that they're teaching ...*

This is what we are working towards, for children to feel such motivation, partnership, collaboration and community around good content.

I also want to mention some research I'm doing with, Hank Becker (who is here tonight with me providing me a local audience along with Mike Miller who I want to also thank for all of this technical support). I was surprised to learn from a national survey of teachers that the number of teachers in this country who are engaged in these exciting projects is less than 10% (www.crito.uci.edu/tlc). So while we celebrate the accomplishments of the these few classrooms, we need to think about how to make it possible for more students to engage in this type of learning., We are learning from the teacher's professional role orientation, and collaborative schools culture, that the position of teachers in the educational community mirrors the position of students in the classroom community (Becker and Riel, 1999). Teachers who have been making the types of shifts that I have been describing have classrooms in which students are encouraged to play leadership roles. However this data indicates that 55% of American teachers are engaged in what we call private practice, isolated and insulated from the changes that are part of our world. They are missing the benefits of shared minds.

3.3 Curriculum

What we teach is important, and we are beginning to address this question world-wide in the area of mathematics and science. The Third International Math and Science Study (nces.ed.gov/timss/) is not just looking at test scores, but also looking at what is taught and how the curriculum is organised in different countries. While using performance on standardised tests might not be the best outcome measures for this form of comparison, the analysis of curriculum decisions worldwide should help us make decisions about the best content. It is important for students to learn what has come before so that they can look forward from the perspective you get standing on the shoulders of giants. What they see into the future will shape the world. Creative tension is needed between what they learn and how they use this content to see in new ways. I also want to mention the collaborative curriculum building tools that Stone Wiske at Harvard is developing (learnweb.harvard.edu/ent/). They are helping to create teacher dialogues around curriculum building.

3.4 Creativity

I recommend the book: How children learn, brain, mind experience in school; read it online at (www.nap.edu/books/0309065577/html/). I urge you to read the chapter on the relationship of brain development to learning. The way in which the brain develops is dependent upon the form and process of shaping understandings. Very young children overbuild an extensive neural network, and this system of pathways is used to link experiences that a child encounters. Those pathways that are not used are eliminated. So the brain is shaped by the experiences that students encounter in and beyond school. This new line of research may be able to provide a strong incentive for constructivist learning which has long been one of the dominant psychological theories of learning.

I am going to end with an example to illustrate why we need to pay attention to what students are doing creatively with their minds rather than focus narrowly on conformity. I am fearful that high test performance is going to create a strong pull toward conformity and restrict a focus on creativity. Children learning the alphabet and their numbers, often reverse them. Some students have a lot of trouble with the J and Z and the 5 and 6. We don't ask why. We are not curious about why they reverse these letters and focus our teaching energies on getting them to form the letters correctly. But if we were to look at what kids really do and pay much more attention to how they are thinking, we would see that, there's actually something funny about the J and the Z and the 5 and the 6. In fact, reversing these letters is a sign of students who are not just copying what they see but really thinking.

Look at capital letters. Ignore those that are symmetrical like the O and H and notice that all of the other letters, well all but two, orient to the right. The two of course are the J and the Z. Now look at numbers, ignore the symmetrical ones, and you will see a different pattern. They all orient to the left with two exceptions. Now I'm not suggesting we should switch the J with the 6 or the 5 with the Z to make the pattern perfect. But I am suggesting that we should look very carefully at what children are doing, because hidden in these errors is evidence of thoughtful analysis — finding a pattern and applying that pattern to new constructions. Early learning is directed by using experience to find patterns and then applying those patterns or rules to the evidence. We see this same process of rule application in the language learning of young children if we look at their errors. A child who says "he goed to the store" understands something about present and past tense and is not just repeating what was heard. Children also discover exceptions to rules but how we react to these errors may shape their future behaviour. Students that are rewarded for thinking will continue to think accepting errors as a natural process of learning. Students who are only rewarded for correct answers will learn to distrust thinking and focus on memorisation as the major learning tool. Memorisation will help students learn what everyone else knows and this conformity is rewarded on standardised multiple choice tests. However real thinking means taking risks. It means sometimes being wrong but understanding why and trusting your minds to create new ideas.

In the research with Hank Becker, teachers who made a shift to more constructivist teaching practices reflected on what caused the change. The most common response was changes in the way they see their students learning. And while they do not often list computers as the major reason for change, it turns out that computer use is high in the group of teachers who make this shift and focus more on student learning. This is evidence that collaboration and community supported by computers and networks will help us pay more attention to student creativity. In conclusion, the message for the future is to pay more attention to what children are doing, to help them develop their brains, develop their minds and share their minds with others. I think that the 21st century will be about community building because we have all the tools in place and I think these are the tools that we need for the 21st century. So I end with my beginning: Technology is shared minds made visible.

BIOGRAPHY

Margaret Riel is the Associate Director of the Center for Collaborative Research in Education, at the University of California, Irvine. She has developed and researched models of network learning, particularly cross-classroom collaboration designs. She has written a number of research reports and articles (www.crito.uci.edu). Her recent research involves helping educators pursue their own professional. Her online office is found at www.gse.uci.edu/mriel.html.

Technology in transforming education

The Opening keynote address

Alexei L. Semenov
Institute of New Technologies, 10, N. Radishevskaya, Moscow, 109004, Russia. alsemenov@mtu-net.r

Key words: Societal needs, mathematics, co-operative teaching, information skills, emerging technologies

Abstract: This paper addresses the relationship between societal needs and ICT. In particular it identifies how society now has different goals and needs because of the new technologies. These include a recognition of the change in mathematics and the language of reason; thus discrete processes, such as approximation, will be more important than arithmetic. And yet change can be threatening for teachers, even those who are innovative. It will be important that the best of new technologies are harnessed for Information Processing by learners. But also new curriculum projects such as building an address book, should be devised for learning about information and information handling. A model for change is proposed based on co-operation, which builds on willing teachers, who are paired with a technology teacher for certain lessons. Help from the Internet and links with traditional educational ideas, such as the role of the teacher, should lay the foundation for open-ended change.

1. INTRODUCTION

For the last fifteen years I have been involved in the introduction of IT in Soviet Russia, from the different positions of school teacher to purely a bureaucrat and official. From this perspective I will try to elaborate some reflections on what is happening and what I hope will happen in the field in future years.

In preparing this paper, I searched the Mamamedia site for recent publications of Seymour Papert. I found a paper published in Technos magazine in which Seymour mentioned a question from his closing speech to the Sixth World Congress on Computers and Education in 1990. The question was: Why do we refer to *computers* in the name of our conference; others do not call their conferences *paper-based* educational events? I looked at the title of this conference and discovered that it is not about computers, but about *Communication* and *Networking* and we all agree that communication and networking are crucially important for education. In the title of this paper, *Technology* is compensated by ambiguity.

I have a serious problem with translating the non-linearity of my keynote presentation into a linear paper. So, I will present a site-map of it. There is some correlation between the content of my paper and IFIP/UNESCO recommendations on Informatics in Primary Education. I will start with a general outline on the topic of what influences transformations in schools, the needs of society and individuals, and how they influence the goals for education. Then I will concentrate on changes to the mathematics curricula which lie at the core of our school education. I will then discuss the importance of information communication technologies, the high speed of changes, the question of what is appropriate for schools and some general studies of implementation and cost. I will follow this with reflections on what is happening with respect to learning through the Internet and the role of the teacher and traditional institutions.

2. CHANGES INFLUENCED BY ICT

Let us start with the general goals of education and in particular the emerging needs of society and individuals with the introduction of ICT, and how these goals are or will change schools. An average primary school in Russia today is still attached to the goals of teaching writing, reading and arithmetic in the same way as it was in the 19th century. At that time, the acquisition of these skills was important for the most prestigious jobs. Now, or in the near future, the needs of society and individuals will be both much less, and much more.

2.1 New needs

Let us consider the new needs. There is a greater emphasis on needing the abilities to search, collect, analyse, organise, present and communicate all kinds of information, to design objects and processes, and to implement plans. We need more independence, self-confidence and responsibility. We need less routine information processing skills, like handwriting skills, and less mental arithmetic. In an educational perspective, this means that self-discovery of the multiplication table is more important that memorising it. There is nothing wrong in memorising, but it is best when used deliberately, as a conscious act, and not as a pre-requisite.

This shift in needs, and consequently, in the educational goals, is happening now as the result of global changes in civilisation, but especially due to the progress of ICT. Text input, spell-checking, outlining, technical drawing, as well as arithmetic and algebra are now done with a computer. Literally, computers can 'do' the old skills of reading, writing, and arithmetic; progress in speech recognition over last years has completed the picture.

The whole situation implies changes in the content of education and the curriculum structure which are deeper and more long-lasting then just using today's ICT. Let us consider the changes in mathematics and language. This also gives as a new view on the theme of the conference. In essence I propose a new literacy – mathematics and languages for the next century.

2.2 A change of mathematical focus

Traditional primary school mathematics is oriented towards numbers, while in the secondary school this includes continuous and infinite objects. The contemporary 'high-end', adult mathematics is much broader and its focus is different. The applications of current ICT exploit mostly discrete, finite objects.

The place of numbers is taken by finite strings (words). In this sense, numbers are taken to also be words. The realm of human languages and reasoning is one of the major environments for mathematical studies. At the same time human language is one of the major realities surrounding the child from their very first days. To study its logic and mathematics is both more interesting and adequate for the future applications than traditional arithmetical problems. I am suggesting that although arithmetic should not disappear, an ability to estimate roughly the value of a complex expression, or the number of seeds in a jar will be more important than long multiplication.

Hyper-text and other hyper-structures of the information objects were always quite natural for human thinking. Children find them in fairy-tales and construct in their own drawings and writings. But only the advent of ICT into adult business practice gives hyper-structures a chance to become legitimate subjects in the primary school both in mathematics and language arts.

Mathematics and science in our schools is concerned with processes. In the 19th century, it was continuous processes, described by differential equations. In the 21st century, it will be discrete processes. These processes do describe many social and natural phenomena; approximate continuous processes are essential for computer science. Approximation is associated with a very general type of discrete system in which global behaviour is determined by local laws of evolution. A classic example is heat transfer and its discrete approximation. The most impressive and famous example is the Life game. As you remember, the game is the process of evolution of an infinite, or big enough, squared plane. The laws of the evolution are:

- Any cell of the plane can be in two states – living or empty.
- Each cell has eight neighbours.
- The living cell which has two or three living neighbours stays alive.
- The empty cell which has exactly three living neighbours becomes live.
- All other cells become empty.
- In each step this happens for all cells simultaneously.

By iterating steps we can observe the process of global evolution of the initial configuration, that is, a set of living cells. You can choose an initial configuration and see what is happening on the computer screen. It can be done on paper as well, but only with a huge amount of work.

Children would start with some simple small configurations: one, two, etc. cells. First they find configurations which disappear (die) soon, then those, which behave periodically (in life cycle). If they draw arbitrary configurations of living cells they probably will discover soon a non-cyclic configuration – they find movement which appears in the evolution of different configurations. Then they can discover or design configurations which generate moving things ad infinitum – so this is a replication. Then an interaction between moving creatures and streams of them can be investigated. At the end of the day we find that the game is as complex and universal as any computer. You can call it consciousness. It is amazing how complex behaviour can appear out of an initial configuration of five cells only (the genetic code).

Generally, the mathematics needed for practical life and for child development in the next century is more real, visible, palpable, and audible than mathematics of the past. To decide how to compare two bags of LEGO bricks is a mathematical task which gives to a primary school student more insight into future mathematics than working on dozens of long divisions and 'word problems'.

2.3 The reaction to changes

As you can see here we are discussing not what is usually called 'content', but also what is called 'method'. This latter, in our understanding, is a very important part of the content that is acquired by a student in the process of learning. Both the content and the method are now changing, influenced by ICT. The general direction for changes was outlined by Jean Piaget. Most of the teachers and administrators of education consider this direction, the constructivist approach, in a positive light. The problem is – how it is reflected in their practice?

Here is a story from our own practice in Moscow. We were looking an elementary-school teacher in a good school in Moscow to work with us. We found a young, progressive, intelligent one. We discussed with her different aspects of the educational process and agreed that there should be more freedom in the classroom. In the process of implementation we changed the arrangement of tables in the classroom. We made a square out of them, with the teacher's position closer to students inside the square. She tried to work in this new arrangement and gave up. We asked her "Why?"; she answered "I do not feel myself as the master and the leader, I do not have control over the situation." We exclaimed "But weren't we talking about freedom?". She replied "Yes, but not to that extent!".

3. WHY ICT ARE RELEVANT FOR EDUCATION?

3.1 Educational applicability

Information and Communication Technologies (ICT) are constructed not for education, they are designed for 'serious' jobs, that is business applications. But most of the activities in school are information processing activities. Although as an aside, this is not so good; perhaps we need more physical, practical, hands-on activities. However, the reasons why adult technologies are relevant for education are:

- Any computer is universal – it is a finite approximation of a universal mathematical machine, a Turing machine, which, by a given programme, can do any IP (Information Processing, not just Internet Protocol) job.
- The human mind is universal by its very nature; we use the same hard and soft-ware for different kinds of IP, including learning.
- The human interface with the outside world is universal; we use the same senses all the time, and connection with this machine interface is universal also.

– ICT make human IP more effective and creative.

A recent example: computers provided a non-linear tool-kit (HTML, etc.) for non-linear human IP. The consequence of this is that using ICT for IP in learning is inevitable.

It explains also why all technological advances have immediate educational applications. What is interesting, is that such advances influence even schools which do not have access to them. So, one of the issues I address is: What is the level of technology appropriate for the process of school transformation today, and in what manner does the high-end technology influence the low-end school?

3.2 What level of technology is needed?

Here is an example of what could be called scale-down of technology and its influence on content. In some Russian schools the very first school year for the six-year old students starts differently. They come to school and receive badges with their names, as do their teacher and the school principal. It is promoting the concept of name tag, which is a part of the information society culture and of mathematics as well. The children sit at computers and try to input something about themselves: name, parents' names, place where they live, favourite song. Now the information about all children from the class is collected in a computer network, or just in the only computer in the classroom. Then it is printed out in the form of loose pages for an address book. Each child in the class receives a set of these pages and makes their first nice address book, with a needle and colouring pencils. For the children it is one of the lessons on an information culture, both in the traditional sense of an address book, and in a very advanced sense of a Net metaphor. Indeed, each child tells the computers about themselves only, but gets back the information about everybody in the class. The address book project is the beginning of an expanding set of educational activities to learn about your body, your family, place where you live, the Earth, the History. Some of the information can be found by a child in the Net and placed into the Net, to constitute shared knowledge.

3.3 Do we need new and emerging technologies?

Are computers for schools today really different from the computers we had five years ago? Here are the dimensions of this difference: adequacy to human interface; connectivity; price and size; peripherals; software; general applications; information sources; virtual construction kits; and tutors, such as touch-typing, languages.

This means that we are arriving at computers with the picture quality approaching the limits of the human eye, which can sound human and store enough of sound, which can recognise basic things you are saying to them, and use full-scale GUI on new Windows or Mac. These computers can easily access the world information which is coming into the Net. Video-conferencing for schools is almost real; inside school we can use radio and infrared networking.

The computers are small, they do not require a special school desk, are not noisy, and do not need special cooling. They are notebooks you can carry easily. You can attach to a computer all sensors, digital cameras, colour printers, and bright projectors to work in daylight. All this is relevant for school applications.

4. A STRATEGY FOR CHANGE

4.1 Use only willing teachers

So we associate technology with a radical educational transformation. Only a minority of schools and teachers are ready for this. We cannot expect many teachers today to use computers effectively. We do not even expect many teachers to use computers at all. But which teachers actually transform school today who become originators of the future school? Many of them use ICT naturally and ICT constitutes the context of this transformation. The transformation itself is not about computers; it is progressing along the lines available for centuries.

So the simplest strategy, and the most rare in practice, is to give technology to those who can use it and want to do so. There are many aspects determining this readiness and willingness, including results achieved in the past, previous training, ability to plan, and team work. As an oversimplified solution I suggest some contexts should use, as a quantitative indicator, a percentage of teachers in school who learned touch-typing in the last two years. More seriously, we can use a Vygotskian term 'zone of proximal developmen', not only for learners but for such developing social entities as schools. So we are speaking of providing adequate support and social interaction for schools in accordance with their zone of proximal development.

There are also many teachers who are innovative enough to think about new ways of learning with computers, but responsible enough to expect serious difficulties along the way. There are several approaches to this. One is to introduce ICT not into the regular classes but into out-of-class activities, like preparation of presentations, components of websites, and other materials by teachers or a homework student. For this we need, of course, computers outside the classrooms. Computers in homes (maybe notebooks) is one approach. Having enough computers in the school library, teachers' room, technology resource centre, and other premises for learning will be especially efficient. The use of the computer by the principal is helpful, both for them and for the whole school.

Another approach is based on co-operation of teachers. Out of class, it can be productively combined with the previously described approach, including team work on environmental and other research projects. In the classroom it generates a productive two-teacher model. This is an officially approved (non-experimental) model for the city of Moscow, with a population of 10 million. In this model two teachers, such as a technology teacher and a language, physics, or history teacher, combine their resources. They use technology hours and language hours to master the technology of text-processing and to apply this technology to language matters. In these hours they come to class together. Both are paid; this is important, not because of material reasons, but because it makes their joint activity automatically legitimate. Then both teachers and their students learn intensively and comfortably. The technology teacher introduces and demonstrates technical skills, provides trouble-shooting and learns what technology is needed for and what problems there are with using it seriously. The language teacher learns how to use it and invents new ways of learning the subject, not depressed by the technicalities. The role of technology teacher can be played by the technology co-ordinator of the school for whom organising and conducting these co-operative activities is a major responsibility.

4.2 Relative cost

There is a disadvantage in this kind of gradual approach because most of the educational and other authorities like simple solutions. "Let us put 13 computers into each school of our district, train all teachers to use MS DOS, or Windows 2000, and teach all students to programme in BASIC." As we know, this approach does not work so well. Even more, it usually causes much negative reaction in public. As an alternative we can give ICT, hardware, software, training, and support, to schools who really need this and are qualified for this. The cost for the educational system to put computers to schools in accordance with their zone of proximal development is relatively small.

We should expect that more and more teachers and schools will communicate and co-operate in the diversified process of school transformation supported with ICT. The different level of ICT gradually coming to schools can be managed by a combination of scaling-down and sharing the most advanced resources. With this approach you can meet the problem of lack of funds in some years. It can be easier to find 10 million dollars once than 10 thousand each year. In some countries it is possible to establish an endowment or to use a respectable private foundation to manage the money issue and provide the constant support and upgrading for technology in schools over several years.

5. LEARNING IN THE NET

One important aspect about using the Net is that we come to it when we need to find something, because we want to do something – to buy a ticket, to make a meal. We learn something and we do it in the way we found out from the Internet. We can extend this situation further from a single action to the ability to act in some way, for example, to speak a foreign language. Then learning starts to dominate over immediate doing, but we should think how to exploit the doing component. The most obvious cases are different kinds of design and performance – such as music, poetry, interiors, and Internet sites. Learning games, like chess can be another type of a balanced activity. Here are some more areas of learning and doing: literacy, international languages, health, first aid, legal advice, tax paying.

The Net can be used as a mirror or a self-portrait of learners, which reflects their dynamically changing personality and their goals and targets to achieve. It is an active mirror providing advice, connections, and follow-up for the process of learning and development. The Net is a genuine environment for co-operative learning and doing. Eventually we are talking about lifestyle and further, the civilisation of learning. There is a strong tendency for more free information on the Net; John Barlow is the most famous and eloquent speaker about this. It includes even sophisticated software (like Finnish LINUX).

In the educational area one possible scenario is that the price of educational services will be determined mostly by the individual interaction between student and teacher. This price policy means that the information resources are free in general. The computer is used to answer typical questions (80%) and to pass the rest (20%) to a human. It is well known about home appliances and some other cases, that the type of advice in this 80% is routine and simple. At the same time to recognise the level of human presence can be a hard task, as in Eliza software.

The Net can be a very good mirror to learn more about yourself, to make more of yourself. The Net can give you advice in different situations or connect with people who will give you advice. Moreover, it can check how you are following the advice and decisions which you and the Net made together. We can see a continuous spectrum of individual involvement of the teacher: vis-a-vis talk, video-conference alive, postponed telecommunication, individually planned computer-supported communication, interactive software with human involvement in evaluation, information resources only.

6. TRADITIONAL EDUCATIONAL INSTITUTIONS AND NEW WAYS OF LEARNING

What can a school – primary, or university, or any other – provide in addition to the Internet? I do not think that school will die in the next century. The situation is not as simple as is implied sometimes from Seymour's statements like "... the presence of digital technologies is rapidly moving us into a period where learners can learn what they need to know on their own agenda rather than on the predetermined agenda of a curriculum. We will soon be able to give up the assembly line model of grade after grade, exercise after exercise." Two things are evidently important, but in different ways: human relations and formal recognition.

6.1 Teacher as the master of leaning and doing

The wish and ability of a human being to learn is not a result of the pure curiosity of an isolated mind. It is a result of constant interaction with other humans, primarily with the mother and hopefully with a teacher. So, the ability of a student to learn depends on the ability to know and to use the knowledge, and the ability of the teacher to learn. So we need the teacher as a partner in learning enterprise, as an advisor, guide, and a source of inspiration and behaviour to follow. The student will learn from the teacher how to learn. The problem is – can we provide enough teachers of this kind? I think many communities still need a socially responsible and paid class of people who will support the children's ability and willingness to learn.

In my country the majority of teachers are not paid their salaries for many months and some years. They come to their schools every morning. In the Soviet time when they were paid regularly they constituted perhaps the only big sector of workers who were doing a real job. The Russian joke about the whole country was that we look like working and they look like paying us. The teachers were working in reality. At the same time I agree with Seymour in his evaluation of children as the driving force of change.

The strategy should involve the whole community in the process of learning and an adequate structuring of priorities.

6.2 Formal recognition

The whole situation with formal exams, diplomas, certificates, and licences will change radically in the next decades. We can expect a whole range of approaches, from traditional Chinese exams and American bar and medical corporations to diploma baking factories and complete inflation. Indeed, testing with no access to information for the student becomes less and less natural and relevant, so testing with access to all information needs to be developed. The most popular Russian educational sites contain essays. It makes more difficult, and possibly kills, one of the methods of evaluation.

7. THE OPEN END

So links have to be constructed to develop an open-ended approach. Poor and weak content of educational resources in the Net needs addressing. Learners themselves will contribute into learning cyberspace; there will be cyber agents and human information managers; there will even be co-operative games and a re-creation of the world and culture. There will be Net forms of lifestyle and a stereotype of continuous learning for what you need. Placing success stories on education on the Net is the start to this open-ended change.

REFERENCES

Papert, S (1990) The Perestroika of epistemological politics. In A. McDougall and C. Dowling (eds.) *Computers in education*. Amsterdam, The Netherlands: North Holland.

Mamamedia site: www. mamamedia.com

BIOGRAPHY

Alexei L. Semenov, graduated from Moscow State University, and worked at the Department of Mathematical Logic in the field of mathematical logic, theory of algorithms and theoretical computer science. He was involved with the introduction of computers into all schools of the Soviet Union in 1985-87. He founded the Institute of New Technologies (INT), Moscow in 1987, and led the team which developed and implemented a course in mathematics, languages, and computer science for primary schools. Since 1993 he has been the Rector of Moscow Institute for

Teacher Development. In 1998 he received the President's Prize for the work of introducing IT into the Moscow region.

PART 2

NETWORKED LEARNING IN ACTION

Interactive distance learning between Japan and Germany

Hisao Koizumi, Takashi Dasai, Klaus-D. Graf, Kiyoshi Yokochi and Seiji Moriya
Dept. of Comp. & Systems Eng., Tokyo Denki University, Ishizaka, Hatoyama, Saitama, 350-0394 Japan. koizumi@k.dendai.ac.jp
Info. Tech. R&D Center, Mitsubishi Electric Corp. Japan.
Emeritus Professor of Yamanashi University, Japan.
Institut fuer Informatik, Freie Universitaet Berlin, Germany.
Faculty of Education, Yamagata University, Japan.

Keywords: distance learning, information technology, multimedia, cultural exchange, ISDN

Abstract: The authors have investigated methods of interactive distance learning which enable the exchange of vivid images and voices, interactively and in real-time, between two remote classrooms connected via ISDN. We believe that such methods will bolster pupils' desire to learn and nurture their creative potential through presentations and discussions between schools with different cultures and customs. In this paper, we propose a new method of distance learning which is conceived specifically for use in international distance learning. We also attempt to evaluate the results obtained from actual distance learning experiments conducted between Japanese and German elementary schools.

1. INTRODUCTION

We have constructed an environment for interactive distance learning based on multimedia communications, video equipment and computers, prepared lessons and teaching materials suitable for use in such an environment, and conducted studies on an interactive distance learning system which combines these elements. This system we have named a CCV (short for the primary components of computer, communication and visual,) educational system. The aims of a CCV educational system are to enable exchanges between mutually unfamiliar pupils at remote sites, and by exposing each group to the reasoning styles and presentations of the creations of the other group, to stimulate the desire to learn and cultivate creative thought.

Based on such aims, we undertook verification experiments on the interactive distance learning system between elementary schools within Japan (Graf and Yokochi 1997; Koizumi, Dasai, Moriya et al. 1997). Interactive distance learning with overseas elementary schools is of great interest from the standpoint of exchanges between different cultures, but a number of problems exist to impede such verification experiments. In addition to language barriers, time differences and problems with communication circuits, there are also such critical issues as co-operation between teachers in designing and preparing lessons. In particular, in light of the practical application and widespread adoption of interactive distance learning, it is desirable that communication circuits should be based on ISDN, which is already a global standard, and should moreover be at 128 kbps, which is more appropriate for transmissions not limited to data.

In this paper, we propose methods for computer and learning support to enable bi-directional real-time distance learning in which a sense of presence or unity is maintained at a communication bandwidth of 128 kbps, together with the verification experiments conducted between an elementary school in Berlin, Germany and an elementary school in Yamanashi prefecture, Japan.

2. METHODOLOGY OF INTERACTIVE DISTANCE LEARNING

2.1 Model of interactive distance learning

Figure 1 shows the model of interactive distance learning based on the CCV educational system. Each classroom consists of not more than 40 pupils and a teacher. Equipment includes audio and video equipment, computers, and large-format screens; these are together referred to as CCV equipment. The audio and video equipment includes cameras to capture images of the classroom and microphones to capture voice signals, which are transmitted to the remote classroom. The computers are used to manage, retrieve and display animations and other teaching materials. The camera images and computer screens are projected onto the large-format screens by projectors installed in the classrooms; the images are shared between the two classes.

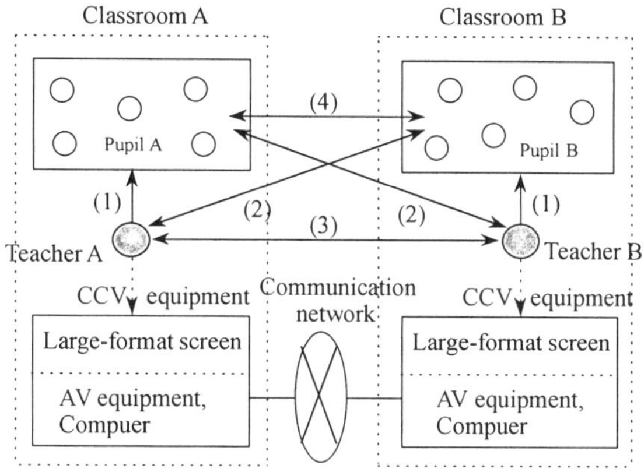

Figure 2. Model of distance learning lessons

In Figure 1, (1) to (4) denote types of interaction in distance learning lessons. Here (1) represents teacher-pupil exchanges within the same classroom (teacher A and pupil A, or teacher B and pupil B); (2) denotes exchanges between a teacher and a pupil in different classrooms (teacher A and pupil B, or teacher B and pupil A); (3) is an exchange between teachers in different classrooms (teacher A and teacher B); and (4) denotes interactions between pupils in different classrooms (pupil A and pupil B). These four types of interaction may occur either individually or in various combinations, according to the lesson content.

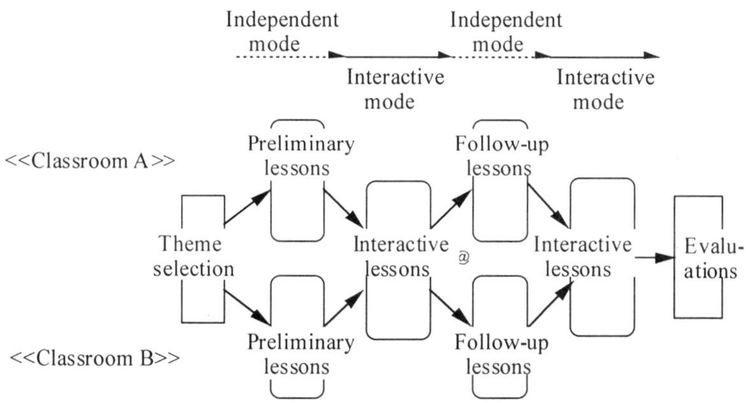

Figure 3. Model of the process of interactive distance learning

The interactive distance learning process is, as indicated in Figure 2, a combination of an interactive mode in which the lesson is conducted with bi-directional communication maintained between the classrooms A and B, and an independent mode, in which studies are conducted independently with no communication between the two sites.

In the interactive distance learning process, first the common problem to be addressed is chosen. This common problem is presented to each of the classes A and B in concrete form, but from different points of view in each case. In preliminary lessons, the problem is solved independently in the classes A and B, and related works are created. At this time, interest in and anticipation of the unfamiliar pupils at the remote site are mingled with the children's lack of confidence in their own solutions, and these amplify their interest in the solution to the problem and spur them to create better works. Interactive lessons of from 60 to 90 minutes are assumed. After the pupils greet each other and introduce themselves, the results of the preliminary lessons are presented and opinions exchanged. At this time children may discover new ideas and techniques they had not thought of before, and this makes them eager to solve the problem or to improve their solutions. In follow-up lessons, the pupils review these new discoveries, and reflect on their own works and problem-solving methods. In the process, their own understanding of and interest in the problem is deepened, and at the same time a sense of competition with the remote-site children spurs them to improve their solutions or creations. As a result, in the next interactive lesson the children can study with a better grasp of the subject matter. Through this teaching procedure the children's desire to learn is stimulated and their creative instincts are encouraged.

2.2 Communication system for distance learning with overseas sites

As means of communication in interactive distance learning, satellite communications or high-speed dedicated circuits may be used to achieve image quality comparable to that of broadcast television (Nemoto, Hamamoto, Suzuki et al. 1997). But in order for bi-directional interactive distance learning to come into widespread use in future, it is desirable that ISDN be used for communication, at a data rate of 128 kbps to hold down communication costs. We propose the following type of communication system for use in interactive distance learning with overseas sites.

1. ISDN circuits at 128 kpbs are adopted for communications. Included in the 128 kbps bandwidth are camera images, audio, images from stand cameras, and computer data.

2. Camera images are images of teachers while teaching and of pupils giving presentations. Computers and stand cameras are used to capture works created by pupils for transmission to the remote-site classroom. Stand cameras are used to capture flat objects; solid or three-dimensional objects are captured using motorised cameras.
3. Audio quality is of prime concern for communication between remote sites. Hence microphones were embedded in the ceiling to clearly capture voices, and 16 kbps of bandwidth was allocated for voice transmissions.

3. CONSTRUCTION OF THE INTERACTIVE LESSONS

Geometry was chosen as the subject for interactive studies; the theme selected for the lessons was 'patterns', because of the chance it afforded to have pupils view images of attractive works and grasp their features. The Japanese class studied the properties of stripe patterns and created works in advance. The patterns themselves were created using computer drawing software, output to a colour printer and then applied to kites, fans and penholders to form completed works. The German class studied the properties of rectangular patterns and composition of motions, and created related works. The German class also used computers to study the features of patterns, and then created works by painting patterns on tiles or postcards.

3.1 Language and time-zone problems

With respect to language problems, it was initially proposed that English be used as a common language; but in view of problems with obtaining accurate translations within the limited time available for interactive lessons, it was decided instead to employ one specialist interpreter at each of the two sites.

The time difference between Germany and Japan is seven hours in summer, eight hours in winter. During summer, 8:00 a.m. in Germany corresponds to 3:00 p.m. in Japan. Taking the circumstances of the children's travel to and from the school, it was decided to hold interactive lessons for 60 minutes, beginning at 8 am in Germany and 3 p.m. in Japan.

3.2 Construction of experimental lessons

The interactive lessons conducted in these experiments will be referred to as DL1, DL2, DL3 and DL4, in the order in which they were held. The relationships between them are illustrated in Figure 3.

In DL1, each class is attended by the teachers and the children. The children first greet each other, and the Japanese children then present works incorporating stripe patterns, while the German children show works which included rectangular patterns. In DL2, only the teachers take part on the German side; the Japanese children present works they had completed as homework, and receive comments and instruction from the German teachers, after which they learn about the approach used in the German class to studying patterns. In DL3, the arrangement is opposite to that of DL2: the German children study the approach to patterns used by the Japanese class. And in DL4, the classes present works which incorporated improvements based on the methods of the other class, and discuss the results. Finally, the two classes discuss future exchanges.

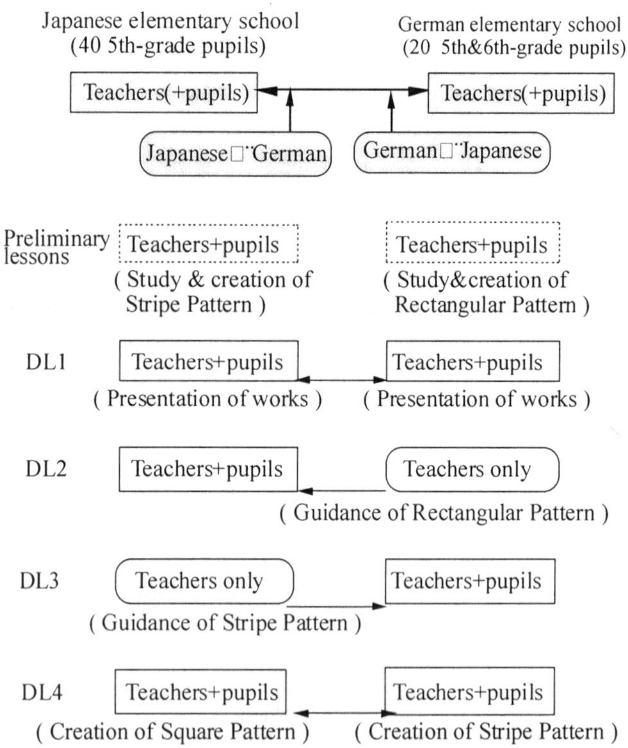

Figure 4. Relation of verification experiments between Japan and Germany

4. EXPERIMENTAL SYSTEM AND RESULTS

Interactive lessons were conducted by two teachers in each classroom, who together taught the lesson and operated the system equipment. Images used in interactive lessons were of two types: images from the TV conferencing system, and computer screen images. Of these, images transmitted via the TV conferencing system consist of images of pupils speaking captured by a motorised camera, scenes of the entire classroom captured by a panoramic camera, enlarged images of pictures and text captured by a stand camera, and video images. These images were shared between the German and Japanese sites via a communication network.

At the Japanese elementary school, these images were projected onto an 80" large-format screen. At the German elementary school, a 42" monitor was used. The communication data rate of the ISDN circuit was 128 kbps, and the H.261 specification was adopted for transmission of TV conferencing images.

4.1 Experiment results

The Japan-Germany interactive distance learning lessons were conducted on the dates indicated below.

a. Prior arrangements
(1) DL1: 17:00-21:00, Sept. 24, 1997(Japanese time)
(2) DL2: 17:00-21:00, Sept. 29, "
(3) DL3: 18:00-20:00, Oct. 20, "
(4) DL4: 17:00-21:00, Nov. 7, "
b. Interactive lessons
(1) DL1: 15:00-16:00, Sept. 25, 1997(Japanese time)
(2) DL2: 15:00-16:00, Sept. 30, "
(3) DL3: 15:00-16:00, Oct. 21, "
(4) DL4: 15:30-16:45, Nov. 10, "
c. Review meetings
(1) DL1: 16:30-17:30, Sept. 25, 1997(Japanese time)
(2) DL2: 16:30-18:45, Sept. 30, "
(3) DL3: 16:30-18:30, Oct. 21, "
(4) DL4: 17:00-18:00, Nov. 10, "

Figure 4 shows some examples of the works presented in DL4 by the German children. Most of the works they presented in DL1 using rectangular patterns were abstract ones. But when they saw the works of stripe patterns created by the Japanese children in DL1, they were interested in various kinds of patterns full of Japanese-like features expressed in them.

They tried to find patterns reflecting German features in their own surroundings. Therefore, their knowledge about the patterns was remarkably increased and their creative potential became heightened. At last, they could create far more complex patterns in their works incorporating their own invention with the knowledge absorbed from the works of the Japanese children. They presented them in DL4. Thus through the mutual stimulation, their works have been considerably improved in quality.

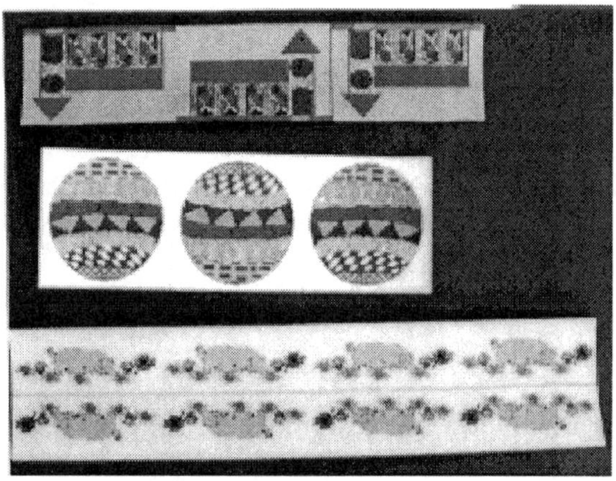

Figure 4. Example of works of German children (Pattern)

5. EVALUATIONS AND DISCUSSION

5.1 Evaluations by the German children

Questionnaires were prepared concerning the desire to learn and attitude of the children during the interactive lessons, the teaching method used, performance of the equipment, and other matters, and the children filled out the questionnaires after each interactive lesson.

The overall evaluation of the lessons was extremely favourable, with pupils agreeing that 'the lesson was enjoyable' and 'I was attached'. Responses to the statement 'I understood everything' indicating depth of understanding of the material was lower for DL4 than for the other lessons. There was insufficient time in DL4 to cover this material in detail. In future it will be necessary to adjust the pace of the lesson to the lesson contents. In response to the statement 'I could follow the lesson' a low score was recorded for DL1 only. This is probably because the German children initially were not accustomed to the lesson format. In response to 'The lesson was boring', the scores for DL1 were low even compared with the other lessons, indicating that they approached DL1 with great enthusiasm.

The responses to the statements 'The Japanese teachers explained well' and 'Our teachers did a good job of teaching' indicated that teaching by both the Japanese and the German teachers was highly regarded by the children. Team teaching by German and Japanese teachers should be possible. In DL3, the score for 'It was easy to understand the presentations and explanations from Japan' was very high. In this lesson, only the teachers were present at the Japanese site, so this indicates that the learning environment provided by the CCV educational system can be said to satisfy the necessary conditions for distance learning in which pupils are instructed by a teacher at a remote site. The score for 'I wanted more explanations' item was negative, but the absolute value was small. This reflects the fact that the natural opportunities children have in a conventional learning environment to raise their hands and ask questions are limited in distance learning. More time is needed for children in order to become accustomed to freely asking questions of a teacher appearing only on a screen. The items relating to the interpretation, 'I understood the translations well' and 'I was very bored while waiting for translations' elicited favourable responses, indicating that even consecutive translation is sufficient for simultaneous bi-directional distance learning.

Responses for all the lessons disagreed with the statements 'The equipment got in the way of studies' and 'The jerky motions of the images interfered', while responses tended to agree that 'The sound quality was good', thus indicating that the learning environment provided by the CCV educational system did not interfere with studies. A bit rate of 128 kbps seems to have been sufficient as well.

5.2 Evaluations by the Japanese children

Overall the evaluations of the Japanese children were more critical. In particular, the Japanese children wanted more detailed explanations from their German counterparts, and thought that explanations were insufficient. They also felt that the interactive lessons were special types of lessons. With respect to the equipment, they noted that motions were unnatural, and that voices were difficult to understand. There were more children in the Japanese class, and so probably more noise near the children's seats, making it difficult to hear what was said at the remote site.

5.3 The lesson content

In DL4, an attempt was made to have the children study together to solve a single problem. However, the teachers would like to have the pupils present works of their own creation during interactive lessons, so that an excessive amount of time is spent in presenting works. Some innovations are needed here.

Because of the differences in culture, considerable time is required to make arrangements. Some two and a half hours or so were spent making arrangements for each hour of lesson time. Exchanges between the children were affected by the extent of exchanges between the teachers before and after the interactive lesson. The key to lesson progress for the teachers is to place sincere trust in each other. Through a relationship of trust, the timing of the lesson progress, the assignment of roles to different teachers, and other aspects of the lesson go smoothly.

5.4 The communication system

In general, it is not possible to exchange clear images at a transmission rate of 128 kbps. But these experiments demonstrated that if a combination of camera images, stand camera images, and computer data is exchanged as in the present system, the objects of camera shots are limited, and in effect 128 kbps becomes viable. It is also thought that the teachers, pupils and classroom scenes that are captured in camera images are familiar to persons with past experience of interactive lessons, so that such persons will unconsciously tend to augment the quality of the images.

6. CONCLUSION

A teaching method was proposed whereby, through interactive distance learning, the desire to learn of pupils is stimulated and their creative abilities are nurtured. Experiments to verify the proposed method were conducted centred on geometric lessons between elementary school children in Japan and Germany. Exchanges with unfamiliar children were observed to induce a heightened desire to learn and an increase in creative thought, and it was confirmed that the method can be applied to distance learning with overseas sites. However, numerous interesting problems such as the problem of language barriers require further study in order to facilitate intercultural exchanges. We intend to continue our research in this area, building on the results of these verification experiments.

ACKNOWLEDGEMENTS

The authors are grateful to all those who have worked in the series of distance learning experiments. Especially they would like to thank Mrs A. Leukert and Mrs E. Teige of Peter-Witte Schule, Berlin, Germany, Mr P. M. Lischka of Hildegard-Wegscheider Schule, Berlin, Germany, and Mr K. Okuyama of Yamanashi University Attached Elementary School, Kofu, Japan, for their generous co-operation and assistance.

REFERENCES

Graf, K.D. and Yokochi, K. (1997) Educational experiments of distance learning and reorganisation of mathematics education. In *Proceedings of the IFIP WG3.1 Working Conference,* Villard sur Lan, France 26th-31st October, 1997, 21.1-21.8.

Koizumi, K., Dasai, T. S., Moriya S., et al. (1997) Proposal of an interactive distance learning of CCV educational system and verification experiments. In *Proceedings of the International Conference for Computer Communications* (ICCC'97), 19th-21st November 1997, 107-114.

Nemoto, Y., Hamamoto, N., Suzuki, R., et al. (1997) Construction and utilisation experiment of multimedia education systems using Satellite ETS-V and Internet, *IEICE, Trans.Inf.&Syst.*, E80D(2) 162-169.

BIOGRAPHIES

Hisao Koizumi is a professor of Tokyo Denki. Since 1970, he has been engaged in the research and development of operating systems, software engineering and computer communication system design. He is a member of the Information Processing Society of Japan, the Institute of Electrical Engineers of Japan and Japan Society of Mechanical Engineers.

Takashi joined Mitsubishi Electric Corporation in 1969. Since then, he has been engaged in the R&D of computer language processors, knowledge information processing and educational materials. He is a member of the Information Processing Society of Japan, the Institute of Electronics, Information and Communication Engineers and Japanese Society for Information and Systems in Education.

Kiyoshi Yokochi has held professional posts at Wako University, Yamanashi and Tokai Universities before becoming guest professor at Beijing Normal University in 1985. He has been president of the Mathematical Education Society of Japan since 1986, organiser of the Five Nations Conference on Mathematics Education since 1986 and organiser of the International Conference on Cultural History of Mathematics since 1991. His special fields include mathematics, mathematics education, informatics, cultural history of mathematics and kindergarten education.

Klaus-D. Graf was a research assistant at the University of Illinois and the California Institute of Technology in 1963 becoming assistant professor in cybernetics at the University of Mainz. He became professor in mathematics and mathematics education in 1971, and subsequently in cybernetics, computer science and computer science education at Freie Universitaet Berlin. In 1987 he was visiting professor at the National Central University in Taiwan. He specialises in applications of IT in mathematics and mathematics education, history of computer science, and international and intercultural co-operation. He is an active member of IFIP working groups and ICMI activities.

Seiji Moriya's current interests include the utilisation of computers in mathematics education. He is a member of the Mathematics Education Society of Japan, Japan Society of Educational Technology and National Association for the Study of Educational Methods.

Creativity, visual literacy and information and communications technology

Avril M. Loveless
University of Brighton, Falmer, Brighton, BN1 9PH, UK. a.m.loveless@brighton.ac.uk

Keywords: ICT, visual literacy, artists, pedagogy, art curriculum

Abstract: ICT can be a catalyst for an interaction between practising artists, learners and teachers facing the challenges of developing pedagogy appropriate to new aspects of subject knowledge. This paper focuses on the ways the wider community can make a contribution to the ongoing curriculum, and provide insights into how ICT can extend the cultural experiences of children. It addresses some questions about the contribution of ICT to children's learning in the visual arts when artists bring their knowledge, understanding and practice into and beyond the school environment.

1. FOREWORD

"It is my view that the production of powerful and meaningful art work is made possible through a long term development of ideas and their visual representation. It is the representation of meaning that is the key that elevates production to a position beyond the merely decorative. My experience as an image maker has led me to conclude that this is achieved by entering into a 'dialogue' with the work. By dialogue, I mean the dynamic and creative cognitive processes involved when encoding and decoding meaning in visual texts. The meanings encoded are not necessarily known completely before a piece is produced. A powerful piece of work simultaneously represents less and more than the artist intends. The meaning and its representation in a visual form resolve themselves through a working method – a dialogue where the maker produces and the work responds. This takes time and a continuation of intention and cannot be achieved by ad hoc projects based on mechanical processes." (Taylor, 1998)

2. INTRODUCTION

Our young people perceive and use ICT as a cultural artefact in their world. Probing the potential involvement of the community in school education may also provide new insights into how ICT can change and extend the cultural experience of young people. This paper addresses some questions about the contribution that ICT can make to children's experience of the visual arts when digital artists bring their knowledge, understanding and practice into – and beyond – the school environment.

Children can be creators and collaborators with ICT – not just consumers and collectors of information. This is an exciting thought for teachers involved in the developments in the use of ICT in education, in which the UK National Grid for Learning claims to connect learners to a physical network, a resource network and a human network (DfEE 1997). Easy access to information does not automatically lead to learning – any more than the availability of educational TV programmes does not transform a couch potato into a scholar. As teachers, we need to explore and be explicit about, the ways we can help children become learners who use a wealth of resources to assist them in the construction of their own knowledge and understanding. We also need to think about how we can encourage children to be active learners, using ICT to represent ways of knowing which have not been available to them with other technologies.

In an Information Society, meanings are communicated in a range of media – from the presentation of the weather forecast, to the packaging of a breakfast cereal or the conventions of the animated cartoon. Visual literacy plays a key role in our ability to decode and encode meanings, both to establish communication and to express our ideas to others. In helping children to develop literacies appropriate to our modern society, we must provide them with informed choices about the media they select to explore and express their visual ideas. What might ICT contribute to developing a visual literacy which is creative and collaborative?

A busy teacher might well argue that the use of ICT in the visual arts is inappropriate in an overfull curriculum using hard pressed resources. The argument is not based on evidence of children's actual use of ICT in their informal learning and culture. An increasing number of children have access to multimedia computers at home and can use them in creative ways. Teachers and parents do not seem to know how their children use computers, videos and games. They express concerns about games or inappropriate material found on the Internet, yet have a laissez–faire approach to children's experience in a world which is not understood or mediated by adults (Sanger et al, 1997). Even when children have access to technology which enables them to make, save and display visual work, they often find themselves producing visual images or animations which are incomplete and lack an audience for the presentation, development or exhibition of work (Sefton-Green and Buckingham 1998).

Teachers and artists are in a position to provide a framework for children which gives them confidence and skills to extend the boundaries of their creative experience. They can offer opportunities to children to develop processes of visual literacy, practise techniques with different tools and resources, and provide a range of audiences, separated in time and space, communicating through electronic networks.

2.1 Adding to children's experience of visual arts?

ICT's contribution is through the medium, approaches to working and the display of work. Digital data can be considered as a distinctive medium for 'making marks with mathematics', contrasting with other media, such as paint, clay, textiles and photographic emulsions. It is early days for understanding the distinctive expressive qualities of this medium (Mitchell 1994; Loveless 1997). There are many possible approaches. Mimicking the techniques and processes of other tools can produce lively and interesting images. But the ability to take an image apart, manipulate it, merge it with other images or use elements of it as starting points for new ideas, opens up a range of processes not easily available to children using traditional media. The form in which the image is to be displayed will influence the ways in which the audience views and interacts with the image. The children have to make choices about the appropriate ways in which to show and share work – from printers to Web pages.

2.2 A contribution to developing visual literacy?

Creative visual literacy can be described as a long term and tentative, development of dialogue between the artist and the work. This requires exploration, taking risks, engaging with new techniques and processes, taking time for evaluation and making the most of the unexpected. The characteristics of the digital can provide children with opportunities to develop this dialogue between maker and made. The provisionality of ICT enables them explore visual ideas, try things out, and re-work without the discouragement of 'spoiling'. Ideas can be saved, recalled and changed with a choice to delete previous ideas, or leave a trail of different images saved, to show how the ideas developed from the start. Nothing need be final, images can displayed and passed on to others to develop. The interactivity of ICT supports this exploratory way of working, giving feedback on the consequences of decisions and offering chances to undo, change or extend ideas and actions. ICT can enable the children to save complex images as digital information and communicate and exhibit their ideas in a variety of forms across space and time.

2.3 ICT in the art curriculum

ICT presents new challenges to teachers' understanding of subject knowledge in art in order to underpin the children's experience with focused learning intentions in a meaningful context. The National Curriculum for Art in England and Wales requires that students should develop visual literacy to communicate ideas, feelings and meanings; that they should be taught about the visual elements of pattern and texture, colour, line and tone, shape, form and space; that they should be given opportunities to explore and use a range of media working on a variety of scales and be able to respond to and evaluate art, including their own and others' work (DFE 1995). ICT offers opportunities to develop these in contrast with other media and offer unique processes and experiences.

2.4 The role of the teacher

Teachers need to reflect on teaching strategies and organisation to facilitate such learning and how these may contrast with more familiar strategies. The teacher plays a role in giving children access to wider audiences, whether by leading a critical discussion with peers at the end of the day, displaying work around the school, collaborating with children in other schools, or exhibiting work on the school website.

2.5 Artists in residence

What do artists bring to this situation in which children and teachers are encountering new learning experiences? How do they support teacher development in the nature of art as a subject, in the technical skills required, in the ways of working as individuals and with others, in the opportunities to share and develop work with an audience, and in the dynamic process of developing visual literacy as a dialogue between maker and made? The artist in residence can be stimulating, encouraging and provoking, bringing new ways of looking and working to be built upon by teachers, children and artists as a powerful learning experience for all. There is a danger that the work of artists, both in their own right and with children, takes place outside the classroom and its curriculum concerns, so not touching the development of teachers or learners.

3. TWO CASE STUDIES

In each project the artists worked with ICT to exploit its potential to allow children to construct visual images; develop them immediately and dynamically; display them in a number of forms to different audiences and develop their ideas over time. Each project illustrates how the interaction between the learners, teachers, artist and ICT provoked debate about the purpose and practicalities of such activities in the classroom. These discussions highlight ways forward for children to use tools to help them express visual ideas in sophisticated ways and engage in ways of working which challenge the development of teachers' subject knowledge and pedagogical strategies.

3.1 Access: The Brighton Media Arts Project

This project for teacher development took place in three primary schools, where teachers had little experience of using ICT in their art work. A three day course was provided to meet and work with the artist, Terry Taylor; provide some technical training with the ICT resources and suggest ways forward in curriculum planning and classroom practice.

Terry's own work raised questions about notions of contrast and difference between the natural and the manufactured, using space and positioning in the images to create surprising, curious or seemingly impossible juxtapositions of elements of the image. The children were fascinated, drawn in by the prospect of meeting with a 'live' artist. The children's work developed in different ways, initially using traditional techniques and then developing the children's ideas using digital cameras and graphics software. What contribution did ICT make to the development of visual literacy in these activities?

In each activity the children came to a point where they needed to construct their own images. The themes were abstract and sometimes difficult for the children to express and they needed the opportunity to try out their ideas, discard those they did not like and develop those that came closer to that which they were trying to express. Using the digital camera they were able to 'frame' a picture which could be used to develop a more complex image. Viewing it on the computer screen, the children could make decisions about whether they had managed to capture some of their ideas in ways which could be worked upon, or whether they needed to go out to look for and construct another image.

The key issues raised related to the ways in which ICT enabled the children to develop a 'dialogue' between themselves and the images they were making. The interactivity, provisionality and capacity of ICT gave them opportunities to look at, think about, refine and evaluate their work with immediate feedback and reassurance that mistakes would not frustrate their ideas. The digital camera enabled the children and teachers to build upon work developed with photography in framing and capturing images from the immediate surroundings. The graphics software let them develop these images with their imagination, using the variety of tools to present their ideas in different forms. The digital medium provided access to techniques and effects which could not be produced easily with more traditional processes and resources.

3.2 The Bristol Internet Project

This project focused on features of ICT to enable children to collaborate with others in their creative work. The ICT facilities were simple to use, but the processes in which the children were able to engage were powerful. Two artists worked in two schools in different parts of the city, which has a multicultural population, but in which communities were sometimes isolated or confrontational. The children in the schools represented two different communities with little opportunity to meet and work together. One of the aims of the project was to use art and ICT to set up communication between the groups of six year old children who could work with each other over space and time to produce visual images.

In each school, the children talked with the artist about activities that they liked or would like to do – driving a racing car, flying, playing basketball or sleeping and reading. They worked in pairs to construct images of themselves acting out these activities, thinking about how they would present themselves and instructing their friends on how to frame and capture that image using a digital camera. The children were asked to use a simple graphics package to work on their image – changing colours or cutting out irrelevant backgrounds. Again, the features of ICT were used to support this creative process – constructing, developing and presenting visual ideas which conveyed meaning.

The next stage in the project took forward the presentation of these ideas. The images were attached to an email message, and sent to children in the other school, requesting that they look at the pictures, think about what the activities might be, develop and complete the pictures using a graphics package, and send back their ideas with another email. A boy who sent a picture of himself 'flying' over the camera, returned portrayed as Superman. Another child who sent a cut-out of himself in a contorted position, received a picture of himself jumping up to a basket ball hoop. The children at each end of the Internet link were able to communicate with each other through text and visual images, think about what their partner was trying to say to them, and respond by developing their visual ideas. They used straightforward graphics techniques to interpret and complete the pictures – from painting, drawing, cutting, and pasting, to using the 'dropper' to pick up and use a subtle range of colours from the clothes of the child in the picture.

ICT made two particular, unique contributions to the collaboration. The first was the ease, speed and informality of the communication over the Internet, covering gaps in space, time and culture. The second was the ways in which the children could alter and develop the piece itself, working with the digital medium to produce an image which was the result of more than one person's imagination, but leaving a trail of saved images which traced the development of ideas between those people.

Issues raised about the use of ICT in these activities related to both the unique facilities of the resources and the limitations imposed by the tools and techniques. The nature of the communication and exchange of ideas between the two groups of children were facilitated by the technology, from the digital cameras to the email links. Questions were raised about the 'origin' and 'ownership' of the shared images and the shifting roles of 'authors' and 'audiences' in such as activity. Some of the children, however, were disappointed by the clumsiness of the graphics tools.

4. CONCLUSIONS

Both projects demonstrated ways in which artists could work with children and teachers to contribute their expertise and experience to the art curriculum. They focused on meaningful ways for children to express and communicate their visual ideas to others. Within this context they used a range of media, techniques and processes to support and extend the children's capabilities. ICT features provided the children with a new medium for work, a range of techniques, an immediacy in the processes and the opportunity to explore, refine and express their visual ideas in creative and collaborative ways. ICT assisted the artists and teachers in setting up and maintaining a 'dialogue' between the children, their work and their audience and challenged the teachers to analyse the nature of this interaction and practice in order to develop their own pedagogy.

REFERENCES

DFE (1995) *Art in the National Curriculum.* London: Her Majesty's Stationery Office.

DfEE (1997) *Connecting the Learning Society: National Grid for Learning. Consultation Paper.* London: Department for Education and Employment.

Loveless, A. (1995) *The Role of IT: Practical Issues for Primary Teachers.* London: Cassell.

Loveless, A. (1997) Working with images, developing ideas. In A. McFarlane, A. (ed.) *Information Technology and Authentic Learning: Realising the Potential of Computers in the Primary Classroom.* London: Routledge.

Mitchell, W.J. (1994) *The Reconfigured Eye: Visual Truth in the Post-Photographic Era.* Cambridge: MIT Press.

Sanger, J., Willson, J., Davies, B., and Whittaker, R. (1997) *Young Children, Videos and Computer Games: Issues for Teachers and Parents.* London: Falmer Press.

Sefton-Green, J. and Buckingham, D. (1998) Digital visions: Children's 'creative' uses of multimedia technologies. In Sefton-Green, J. (ed.) *Digital Diversions.* London: UCL Press

Taylor, T. (1998) *The Access Project.* An unpublished report to the Arts Council of England. UK: The University of Brighton.

ACKNOWLEDGEMENTS

Thanks to Terry Taylor, the artist working in the projects described, Access: The Brighton Media Arts Project was funded and supported by the Arts Council of England, the University of Brighton, South East Arts and Lighthouse, the Brighton Media Centre. The Bristol Internet Project was funded and supported by the Arts Council of England, Watershed Media Centre, Bristol, and Netgates Internet Service Provider, Bristol.

BIOGRAPHY

Avril Loveless is a Senior Lecturer in IT in Education at the University of Brighton, UK. She has taught in primary schools and worked as advisory teacher. Her research focuses on issues of culture, pedagogy and curriculum and the creative use of communication technologies.

Collaborative teacher training through telematics

Giampaolo Chiappini, Augusto Chioccariello and Camillo Gibelli
Istituto per la Matematica Applicata, Consiglio Nazionale delle Ricerche, Via de Marini 6, 16149 Genova, Italy. chiappini@ima.ge.cnr.it
Istituto per le Tecnologie Didattiche, Italy.
Don Milani Lower Secondary School, Italy.

Keywords: distance teacher training, computer supported co-operative learning, experience-based learning, collaborative training

Abstract: The traditional approach to in-service teacher training is based on a transmissive model and on a hierarchical relationship between experts and trainees. By contrast, our work centres on collaborative training in workgroups and experience-based learning. In our model, knowledge building is the result of trainees interacting with an environment; the creation of interactive trainee communities dedicated to projects conducted in schools stimulates the emergence of shared knowledge. In this framework, we have developed a computer network infrastructure that integrates communication and collaboration, providing an efficient solution to distance workgroup activities in teacher training. Both the methodology and the tools developed are currently being tested in a national project funded by the Italian Ministry of Education.

1. INTRODUCTION

Reforms currently being introduced in the Italian education system (OECD 98) are aimed at fundamentally restructuring the school cycle and developing school autonomy, innovations that are significant from both the technological and curricular viewpoints. In order for these reforms to take effect, the Italian education system must be ready not so much to modernise but rather to rebuild itself. This means being able to redefine the cultural and epistemological framework, trying out new models for the organisation of teaching, and updating contents and teaching methods.

In order to be effective, any change made within individual schools must build upon the educational developments already actuated within the school itself. In addition, prior consideration must be made about the nature of problems arising in educational management and about the nature of educational and organisational variables involved in each problem. This process cannot be imposed bureaucratically from the outside, entailing as it does the re-elaboration of previous experience and, at the same time, planning and decision-making regarding changes in the system of constraints surrounding the teaching/learning process. Reform requires all the actors within the education system to become involved and take responsibility. The underlying objective of the project described in this paper is to foster schools' educational and organisational autonomy. This is to be done using network technology to improve communication and collaboration between the various actors in the education system, helping schools to re-elaborate previous projects and develop collaborative planning skills.

2. ASSUMPTIONS AND CONTEXT OF THE RESEARCH

Copernicus is a Ministry of Education training project designed to foster the autonomy of schools. It is based around six centres located throughout Italy and involves collaboration with universities and research organisations. Each centre gathers together twelve primary, lower- and upper-secondary schools, and within each school there are five representatives (the principal, three teachers and head of administration).

Each centre has its own specific research and training theme regarding school autonomy. The theme in Genoa is 'distance co-operation and collaboration to support school autonomy'. The pedagogical philosophy guiding the development of our segment of the Copernicus network is to promote an active, participatory and collaborative learning process, as defined by socio-cultural philosophy (Vygotsky 1962; Cole 1985; Engeström 1987). Copernicus is a collaborative training project designed to transfer knowledge and develop skills through group interaction. This approach to training is in stark contrast with the transmissive model that still dominates present-day schooling in Italy. The training model adopted in the Genoa section of the Copernicus network is based on four assumptions.

- Recent pilot projects have led to the development of professional skills within schools and these can and must be mobilised and used for training within those same schools.
- Actors in the education system (directors, teachers and administrative staff) must be considered active players in their own training process,

and training itself should be seen as a social process of construction and appropriation of new ideas and methods. Training ought to be based on the *description*, *comparison* and *re-elaboration* of the experiences conducted in schools, and on assisted testing of the new educational and organisational approaches shared by all.

- The research contribution must no longer be limited to the transmission of academic knowledge or the dissemination of research results. A new kind of relationship between research, training and educational/administrative innovation must begin to take shape. The first step is the realisation that there are no pre-set roles, authorities or responsibilities in the relationship between the research world and schools involved in training; these must be subject to ongoing negotiation (Bottino and Chiappini 1998).
- Technology in general and computers and computer networks in particular can be used to actuate the training processes underlying the above assumptions. Nowadays, collaborative training in workgroups and experience-based learning are pedagogical training methods that can be supported and integrated using ICT. The former promotes learning through active communication among members in a workgroup, while the latter consolidates training concepts through the description, comparison and re-elaboration of experiences developed in schools.

3. THEORETICAL FRAMEWORK OF THE RESEARCH

Underlying our experience is the conviction that in order to foster collaborative training in workgroups and experience-based learning, the computer/network infrastructure adopted for the training course must provide for the construction of a social space that satisfies the professional and training needs of those involved.

The notion of social space is taken from anthropology and has been elaborated by Fortes: "An individual's social space is a product of that segment of the social structure and that segment of the habitat with which he or she is in effective contact. To put it in another way, the social space is the society in its ecological setting seen from the individual's point of view. The individual creates his social space and is in turn formed by it. On the one hand, his range of experiences and behaviour are controlled by his social space, and on the other, everything he learns causes it to expand and become more differentiated. In the lifetime of the individual it changes *pari passu* with his psycho-physical and social development... In the evolution of an individual's social space we have a measure of his educational development." (Fortes 1973).

For our purposes the social space can be defined as the area where trainees interact with groups of colleagues in a learning-by-doing process. Engaging in activities, the trainees encounter and help elaborate meanings that characterise the social culture of the group. In this framework, an information and communication structure (ICS) can help to shape the trainees' social space if they recognise it as a useful tool for their production and communication activities. In other words, an ICS is useful to the trainees if it can support the motivational, social and interpersonal process of the workgroup and create three things: a concrete interdependence among the members of a group performing a task; a commitment to mutual assistance; and responsibility for the group and its objectives. Only under these conditions can an ICS provide "the crucial match between a support system in the social environment and an acquisition process in the learner" (Bruner 1985), i.e. contribute to expand and differentiate the individual's social space.

4. COLLABORATIVE LEARNING IN WORKGROUPS

Our experience underlines the strict correlation between evolution in the ICS made available to the trainees from one phase to the next, and the characteristics of the social space that develops in the training context with the mediation of the technological tools on offer. Three phases can be identified.

4.1 Phase 1: Contact

This can be defined as the contact phase, that of exploring the potential of network-based social interaction for setting up discussion groups.

At the outset of our training programme, the actors' competence in the use of computer and network technology differed enormously, as did the computer equipment available in each school. The upper-secondary schools had computers linked up in networks, whereas in the primary schools computer labs had only been up and running for a few months, and Internet connections were still being installed. None of the schools had previous experience with ICT-based training courses.

The technology employed in this early phase was email and mailing lists. At this stage the groups were merely virtual, having no actual identity. The communication structure was not arranged according to the groups' specific communication requirements but was general in nature, designed to foster interpersonal contact and exploration of the potential that multipoint network communication offers. The shift towards increasingly 'creative' output reveals that individuals are beginning to see themselves as group members. From the very outset, participants are called upon not just to share their experience with others, but to re-evaluate that experience and work in collaboration to formulate new responses and new solutions to the problems faced. While there is growing discussion at this stage on various issues of interest to the participants, it gradually becomes clear that the communication structure on offer is inadequate. It is too general and thus unable to meet the communication demands made of it.

At the same time, the effort of researchers focuses increasingly on the design of new environments, tailoring them to the particular needs of each group as it emerges from its anonymity and seeks out new technological solutions. In this loose beginning, hints emerge of new communication possibilities. In some cases, network interaction is uneven, suffering from structural and organisational difficulties.

As things progress, the majority of participants begin to demonstrate an effective need for an improved communication environment, and some even play a part in its design. At the same time, participant identity begins to take shape through the setting of objectives and issues for collective online discussion. However, we should note that even at this stage some of the participants are incapable of joining in productively.

4.2 Phase 2: Growth of group identity

In this phase, growth in group identity is reflected in the multiplicity of common objectives and more advanced exchanges between participants. Group development reaches completion in all its facets, and the need arises for a more organised space to manage communication within the group, to control group dynamics and to trace the thread of discussion. In addition, group members need to have some way of retracing the group's communication history in order to reflect on the group's activity and at the same time discuss and compare viewpoints and solutions deriving from other experiences. For this purpose, a specially designed environment for communication and network discussion is provided. This new communication tool was created using Lotus Notes, and entails the construction of eight mailing lists that can be accessed via a simple interface. All participants are free to browse any of the lists on a read-only basis, while only those who have chosen to subscribe to a given list can exercise writing privileges. The various list functions are described below.

Together with standard computer conferencing functions, the environment features the possibility to manage the breakdown of roles among group members and non-members. In addition, participants can store messages using either a commonly agreed classification scheme or freely chosen **Keywords**. This message classification is personal and therefore cannot be seen by other participants, not even by fellow group members. The introduction of the new communication structure calls for changes in groupware management. Two new roles are created: the group co-ordinator, chosen by their fellow group members, and a facilitator appointed from among the project staff.

Table 1. Copernicus conferencing system functions

Contribute (group members)	Contribute (members of other groups)	Read	Classify
Send a message Reply to a message Attach files to a message	Send a message	Sort messages by: • date • author • thread List: • unread messages • non-members' messages • message readers	According to a shared taxonomy Free text

The new opportunities offered by the communication structure together with the new groupware management permitted the various groups in Copernicus to bring their objectives into sharper focus. A balance was struck between requirements, viewpoints, different relationship forms and communication modes, all directed towards the common goal of bringing innovation and enhancement to the experiences undertaken in schools. In this respect, we note that while there was overall improvement in the quantity and quality of message exchange, reference to previous experiences remained somewhat in the background, even though documents were at hand to be sent as attachments. Nevertheless, at this stage there was no common model for documenting the experiences. This made it difficult for the participants to get a feel for the various experiences, as they did not have the means to take them apart and understand fully the reasons, methods and conditions behind their creation, not to mention the problems in their management. Consequently, group members discussed and compared their knowledge, values and personal judgement on an individual basis, rather than setting the debate within the described experiences in order to re-elaborate them.

4.3 Phase 3: Re-elaboration of the experiences

This can be described as the phase of full maturity in group identity, where the experiences conducted in schools were re-elaborated and improved using the new information and communication tool, which offers the possibility of integrated communication and production.

The intense social interaction that developed in the mailing lists during Phase 2 has led to a new embodiment of common needs, ones that cannot find an effective response through use of the communication tools in play. This new embodiment has opened the way to a structured environment for the free formation of working groups so that the experiences carried out in schools can be discussed. This should lead to testing in a social context and consequent re-elaboration of the experiences themselves, hopefully bringing them more closely into line with actual training needs in education. It should be pointed out here that this new embodiment is consistent with the assumptions made by the project staff and, more importantly, that it is the result of expansion and development of the participants' social space. The latter is an outcome of the vigorous online exchange of opinion and debate that took place in earlier phases. Hence, they were not needs imposed from outside, but rather those arising from the social structure within the training process in Phases 1 and 2.

All this led to the remodelling of the information and communication structure to be used by participants. This task was performed by the project staff, who drew on the latest groupware management systems used in the business environment, tailoring their functions in response to specific project requirements. The actual systems adopted were Lotus Notes and Domino, which are used throughout the business world to allow people to work together in a faster, more efficient and productive way. We used the functionalities of these packages to develop tools we consider innovative with respect to those generally adopted in distance training for teachers. These tools broaden and further diversify the social space in response to the common needs that emerge.

Using a standard network browser, the new information structure adopted in Phase 3 allows the participants to do the following.

- Freely and autonomously *create and manage* the formation of workgroups that will describe experiences conducted in schools and store these in a special database. The system will automatically assign these groups reading and writing privileges for the experiences that they want to describe and share online; other Copernicus participants will only have reading rights. As they work, group members will always have the possibility to modify group composition; the responsibility for this task lies with the members themselves.

- *Fill in* three specially designed forms describing an experience and create a database of HTML documents that can be seamlessly and automatically linked to those forms. Re-editing functions allow group members to update experience description in an on-going manner. The forms are designed to collect information about the background of the experience, its main characteristics and the issues that it raised. In addition, the system allows the group to link up its own experience with another in the database it deems similar.
- *Consult* the database of experiences using a variety of access modes. The experience document contains links to similar experiences, together with related attachments and a list of contributors who have discussed that experience (see next point).
- *Discuss* the experiences in the database via mailing list, with the possibility of establishing a seamless link with the one or more experiences under discussion. These links will automatically appear in the related experience documents. The result is close integration of the experience database and the mailing list, as it is possible to call up an experience and then access any comments that have been made about it and vice versa.
- *Consult* the various contributions in the mailing list using a variety of access modes.
- *Use* functions that show who has read a message sent to a mailing list or accessed an experience in the database.

At the time of writing, Phase 3 is in full progress, so it is still too early to give a complete report on changes in the participants' social space arising from use of the information and communication structure described above. We shall thus concentrate on the qualitative changes that have occurred so far.

In this phase of Copernicus, the participants are developing the ability to construct and manage workgroups autonomously, completing the definition of their objectives and acquiring full awareness of the potential and limits of their roles. Against this background, the new environment helps to complete the gelling process between participants and the individual schools. It also fosters construction of a basic common language that clarifies ubiquitous **Keywords** like project and experience, words that are frequently attributed different meanings. This development is essential if the group identity is to reach full maturity.

At this stage the group is transforming itself into a production unit, i.e. an entity that can delve beyond the surface of the experiences, dismantle them and shape their future. This important result is based on the fact that the social conditions have been created whereby the input of experiences for workgroup discussion no longer reflects an individual outlook; the forms for analysing and describing those projects held to be important can at this stage be negotiated beforehand in relation to common goals. Finally, exchange of information about the products has given way to debate about the processes that have generated them. The greater rigidity and complexity of the discussion and storage environment (something which would have been totally out of the question at the outset of the project) is an achievement that is firmly rooted in developments in earlier phases. The tool's complexity and non-neutrality are proportional to the maturity that the subjects acquire during training, both as individuals and as groups.

In this phase, over half the participants have so far achieved these positive results: even though the others followed the group activities, their role was marginal. During this year of work, a number of obstacles were encountered along the path toward a common language and shared group objectives: the involvement of different school levels, which in Italy traditionally suffer from a lack of interaction; and the differences in professional expertise and the variety of cultural backgrounds. Our goal for the second year is to increase the percentage of people achieving the positive results described above.

5. CONCLUSIONS

The experience conducted thus far underlines the close interaction and reciprocal conditioning that occurs between communication technology and the professional and relational contexts of the groups engaged in training. The architectures for information gathering and communication on the one hand and the groups on the other progressively modelled themselves on each other. The information and communication tools, the contents and the forms of co-operation all developed in an ongoing manner, pooling their resources. There was no fixed hierarchy among these elements, but rather a sort of role-play in which turns were taken to put forward work plans for negotiation and testing: at one moment the information and communication structure would take the lead, at others the groups and individual trainees. The whole training path can be seen as a process whereby the training groups and collaboration environment gradually shift out of the blur into ever-sharper focus, the tools used and the social space mediated by those instruments evolving from simplicity towards complexity.

REFERENCES

Bottino, R. M. and Chiappini, G. (1998) Teacher training: New models and tools in the era of communication technologies. In G. Davies (ed.) *Proceedings of the XV IFIP Word Computer Congress, Teleteaching 98*, 31st August-4th September, Vienna-Budapest.

Bruner, J. (1985) *Child's talk: Learning to use language*. New York:W.W. Norton.

Cole, M. (1985) The zone of proximal development: Where culture and cognition create each other. In J. V. Wertsch (ed.) *Culture, communication, and cognition: Vygotskian perspectives*. Cambridge, UK: Cambridge University Press.

Campo-Moltavo, E., Martinez-Orga, V., Medinilla-Martinez, N., and Meziat-Luna, D. (1998) Internet support for collaborative learning in workgroups. In G. Davies (ed.) *Proceedings of the XV IFIP Word Computer Congress, Teleteaching 98*, 31st August - 4th September, Vienna-Budapest.

Fortes, M. (1973) Social and psychological aspects of education in Taleleand. In J. Middeleton (ed) *From child to adult: Studies in the anthropology of education*. New York, Natural History Press.

Engeström Y. (1987) *Learning by expanding. An activity theoretical approach to developmental research*. Helsinki: Oventa Konsulktit.

OECD 98 (1998) *Reviews of National Policies for Education: Italy*. Paris: OECD Publication, [OECD Code 911998061P1].

Vygotsky L.S. (1962) *Thought and language*. Boston, MA: MIT Press.

BIOGRAPHIES

Giampaolo Chiappini is a researcher at the Institute for Applied Mathematics of the Italian National Research Council. His research interests are in educational computing, teacher training and the integration of students with disabilities. He has developed ICT-based systems for mathematics education and experimented with them in school classrooms. He has written many professional papers and participated in national and international projects on teacher education and the didactions of mathematics.

Augusto Chioccariello is a researcher at the Institute for Applied Mathematics of the Italian National Research Council. His main research interests concern both the theory and applications of ICT in education, with particular reference to constructivism in the education of pre-primary school children. He has been involved in many international projects and is currently involved in ESPIRIT CAB Project, on the development of intelligent toys for children.

Camillo Gibelli is a middle school language teacher and long-term collaborator at the Institute for Educational Technology. His main research interests concern the teaching of history and humanities with ICT.

Approaching pedagogical networking through teacher education

Tomi Nummi, Riikka Ristola, Aarno Rönkä and Janne Sariola
Media Education Centre, University of Helsinki, National Board of Education & Ministry of Education, PL 38 (Ratakatu 6 A), 00014 Helsingin, Yliopisto, Finland. riikka.ristola@pp.inet.fi

Keywords: pedagogical networking, teacher education, open and distance learning, virtual school environments, teacher's roles

Abstract: The concept of networking has become one of the key issues in the discussion about the development of schools in Finland. In this article we are outlining the characteristics of pedagogical networking in virtual school environments. Pedagogical networking means above all teachers exploiting decentralised knowledge, creating open, distance and co-operative learning environments and being an active partner in network-based teamwork. Teachers also need network knowledge about maintenance of interaction using various media in a pedagogically meaningful way. These questions are further researched in the LIVE (Learning in a Virtual School Environment) project It aims to develop pedagogical networking models for pre- and in-service teacher education.

1. OUTLINING THE CHARACTERISTICS OF PEDAGOGICAL NETWORKING

During the last few years the concept of networking has become one of the key issues in the discussion about the development of schools, especially where new media are involved. One of the main reasons for this was the reform of the Finnish national curriculum at the beginning of this decade (POPS 1994) which gave schools more freedom to organise their work. It also enabled the growth of various experiments in open and distance learning environments with the aid of the modern information and communication technologies (ICT).

The role of networking can also be seen as a significant natural continuation of open and distance learning (ODL), which was originally based on the idea of a single learner's opportunity to study independent of time and space. The concepts of co-operative learning and virtual learning communities have also been included in ODL through networking.

A wide variety of categories are created by analysing different classifications of networking, depending on the point of view from which networking is being examined. While Helakorpi and Suonperä (1995) classify the networking levels of a school by the property of distance, Tella's (1997) viewpoint is socio-cultural rather than spatial. Since this paper is part of the LIVE project research, we wanted to create a classification of our own to examine networking of schools from a pedagogical point of view, especially through teacher education.

The lowest level of networking is physical networking. This includes the technical infrastructure needed for telematic communication based on telephone lines and computers with Internet connections. A more sophisticated environment may include a complex LAN/WAN network with video conferencing and groupware facilities. More important than the technological progressiveness of this network are the development, maintenance, usability and uniformity of this system throughout the network. No higher level of networking is possible if the infrastructure behind it is unstable or out of use. In Finland we have a very high level of technological infrastructure. The objective of the Ministry of Education to physically network all schools by the year 2000 will be achieved (Ministry of Education 1995). The physical is more concerned with the maintenance of these systems.

We call the second level of networking social networking. It is based on the fact of people knowing each other, having interrelationships and interests in working together. The information society offers people new, complementary communication tools to maintain these relations. Information networks create new types of social structures, virtual communities and means of social participation (Tapper 1998). Social networks promote interaction in telematic networks. The network is a resource to be exploited in the field of education as well. Tella (1997) for example discusses the networking of telematic virtual school environments,.

The third level of networking is an active learning environment, not just a resource. When the interaction in the social network has produced motivation for people to co-operate, we can speak about pedagogical networking. It means above all teachers exploiting decentralised knowledge, creating open, distance and co-operative learning environments and being an active partner in them. Pedagogical networking is an intentional and object-oriented activity by means of media education in an modern ICT-rich environment. Evaluation of different activities, especially learning, is characteristic of pedagogical networking and in that sense it also differs from social networking. One of the challenges of teacher education is to train network educators, virtual teachers who have the skills and abilities in pedagogical networking.

2. NETWORK KNOWLEDGE AND SKILLS

In addition to understanding the structure of pedagogical networking, it is important to consider the teacher's skills and knowledge in relation to the development of the information society. The teacher's network knowledge, which should be developed during pre- or in-service teacher training, forms the foundation of pedagogical networking. Network knowledge can be defined as the teacher's ability to plan and carry out an educational project in open and distance learning environments. To accomplish such a complex task, the teacher also needs to know the curricular content of various educational institutions as well as the characteristics of the various media and how these characteristics effect a learning situation.

The teacher's own interaction skills and flexibility in the planning phase are also important. To maintain and develop the physical network, teachers also need to be familiar with the terminology used by the computer and communication industry. They have to be able to decide which technological choices are suitable for their school. From the viewpoint of administration, networking also requires understanding of the mechanisms of the network economy. Teachers mastering network knowledge can be seen as entities of decentralised expertise, but rather than being individuals, they should be able to combine other expert knowledge (teachers, students, specialists) for the good of their pedagogical network.

To summarise the various aspects of a teacher's network knowledge and skills, it can be said that the most demanding task for a teacher in a pedagogical network is the maintenance of interaction, which should be done at all levels of the network, using various media channels in a pedagogically meaningful way. Through the management (hallinta) of network knowledge and skills teachers can achieve multidimensional mastery of network competence. The challenge in teacher education is to develop tuition and tutoring skills in a complex, multi-mediated pedagogical network, opening future and in-service teachers virtual wormholes to the global networking level.

3. NETWORKING TEACHER EDUCATION – THREE CASES

3.1 Teacher training practice

In this section we describe the phenomena of networking through three cases. Our first example of networked teacher education comes from teacher training practise, where open and distance learning methods have been used by the students as well as in the tutoring process between the student and the lecturer (teacher trainer). In this particular example student teachers were physically separated: one was at the Second University Training School in Helsinki and the other one at Kilpisjärvi about 1300km away. During the interactive phase of teaching the pupils in both schools networked into co-operative groups using LIVE working. Before the teaching session there was a meeting in which the teleteam of teachers (student teachers, local tutoring teachers and a teacher trainer) planned the upcoming work and evaluated the plans using video- and audio-conferencing (Ristola and Rönkä 1998). Helakorpi and Suonperä (1995) refer to an amoeba-like team of teachers which functions flexibly according to pedagogical needs.

In the planning phase the element of openness, creating choice for the pupils, was emphasised. At the same time this session was part of teacher training practice, in other words a simulation of a real classroom situation. A key issue, in educating teachers who have a good command of telematic communication, is giving student teachers real experiences in implementing networking and open and distance learning during part of their studies. In their portfolios students have also raised the question of time as a key factor of networking. The network established during the teacher training period is a short-term, almost a momentary phenomenon, but in the background there is a permanent basic network of teacher training which is constantly maintained.

3.2 In-service course in media education

The second example of networking in teacher education comes from the area of in-service teacher education. Since autumn 1996, the Media Education Centre has been organising a 5 credit (7 ECTS) course in media education. The course is financed by the National Board of Education and is free for all teachers working in primary, secondary and tertiary schools as well as in folk high schools or workers' institutes. The main objective of the National Board of Education has been to give the teachers attending the skills and knowledge to work as pedagogical modern ICT-experts in their own schools. In the courses organised by the Media Education Centre, this aim has been achieved by initiating teachers into the working methods of team- and network-based learning and open learning environments and by giving them facilities for telematic communication through co-operative working.

The main core of the course is a 2 credit (3 ECTS) pedagogical project, which is focused on the development of the pedagogical use of MICT in the teacher's own working environment. For this project the participants are divided into tutor groups of around 15 people. In the first tutor group meeting the group is further divided into 4/5 person teleteams based on their own areas of interest and the subject of their project. The aim is that in every teleteam there is a pair of teachers from two different schools. This enables creation of a team where teachers will be networked inside their own school as well as between schools.

As mentioned before, every teleteam plans and carries out a pedagogical application related to its own area of specialisation. The subject of this application can be, for example, an analysis of the learning material available in the information networks, production of WWW learning materials, a learning module based on video-conferencing technology, or a research-related analysis of distance education. A teleteam is also responsible for deciding the common objectives, working and evaluation methods and criteria for their project. Every teleteam will get feedback from their tutor as well as from other colleagues in the tutor group via email, a web-based discussion forum and during the face-to-face meetings taking place 4-5 times during the four-month course.

The analysis of the feedback gathered from the participants shows that networking of teachers has been an essential part of their learning experience. Having an opportunity to share one's own experiences, problems, frustrations, successes with colleagues of the same background has been seen as important. Tutor group meetings have also been important events for getting feedback on one's own decisions and gaining new ideas when listening and commenting on other people's work. Evaluation of the projects clearly shows that teleteams, which have had clear and common aims and functional communication channels for their project, have been the most successful. The pressure to keep up with the schedule is also stronger, working in a co-operative team where every member has their own task to accomplish. One of the biggest problems of the teleteams has been of a technical nature. Members have not had functional email connections or easy access to web-based discussion, so that the co-operation has been limited. Problems also arise when a teacher comes to the course without a clear picture of their own aims or areas of interest in mind. They might become part of a team whose project does not have a clear connection with their everyday work.

3.3 The LIVE Project

The LIVE project is a three-year research and development project, intended to develop teaching and learning practices in an information-rich and knowledge-intensive virtual school environment with a particular emphasis on mobile communication. This is carried out by increasing the potential for co-operative and experiential learning in teacher education and by using modern information and communication technologies in open and flexible learning environments effectively.

The example of networking in the LIVE project is a development group, which started its work during the first year of the LIVE project. The members of this are all teachers/lecturers in the University training school (an upper and lower secondary school) tutored by the researchers of the LIVE project. The main objective of the work of this development team has been to promote teachers' pedagogical thinking in open and flexible learning environments. Another aim has been to support training school teachers pedagogically and technically when they start using the modern information and communication technologies (ICT) in their work. Teachers taking part in the work of the development group have familiarised themselves with the various phases of LIVE working (Nummi et al. 1998) such as didactic media planning (Sariola 1997, 1998). During the school year 1997-1998 teachers carried out some pilot projects using integrated mobile communicators in their own classes. These projects have been reported to the research group of the LIVE project. The development group has become a part of the research arrangements as well as the objects of the research through these experiments.

From the educational point of view a group of teachers working within one school towards the same set of goals forms the smallest networking unit. Members of the development group establish this kind of network when they plan LIVE working. In the practical implementation of LIVE working the co-operative planning of at least two teachers is needed. The idea of co-operation as a part of networking arises from the theoretical background of the LIVE project (Nummi et al. 1998). In the development group, teachers work co-operatively in a technology-rich environment where planning together is a key issue. Teachers have been able to introduce and develop new ideas together, get support and encouragement from their colleagues and discuss on the values of the use of modern ICT.

A development group is an organic part of the everyday life of a school and its developmental activities. Teachers can establish internal networks (local networking) in schools whenever needed. Through these development teams, the value of the most natural basis of ICT-based networking, the colleague next door, is promoted. At the same time, interaction in the networks also promotes new thinking and new innovative activity (Andersson 1994). By means of LIVE working, local networking can be extended to the surroundings of the school. Authentic information is gathered using portable telecommunication equipment, where it is most naturally available – market places, shopping centres, museums, enterprises, universities. The role of experiential learning as a mean of more effective learning is enhanced through networking.

In their self-evaluations the members of the development teams wrote that there had been efforts towards networking and co-operation in their team. Professional development can also be seen through the development of ideas and innovations within the development teams. Working in the group is seen as in-service education, which supports the theory that in networked organisations in-service education increasingly takes place in working places (Helakorpi and Suonperä 1995).

4. CONCLUSIONS

In many cases physical networks have been used to distribute pedagogical information such as learning and teaching materials, or evaluation data according to the principles of decentralised expertise. The essential features of pedagogical networking, as we see it, are on the one hand the characteristics of high quality learning (De Corte 1995; Jonassen 1995) and on the other hand the clear pedagogical aims of the activities in the network.

Our three cases of the development of teacher education towards open and distance learning clearly indicate that the first, physical level of networking is reached when teachers have access to use technology within a relevant information network and also have the basic ICT skills. In fact, fulfilling those requirements is essential for open and distance learning. Further, the level of social networking requires interaction skills as well as the ability to use the physical network for social interaction. In addition, motivation, i.e. willingness to co-operate, and clearly stated learning aims are needed to reach the level of pedagogical networking. Pedagogical networking can give added value to learning if it helps to create authentic, real-life situations where each learner as a participant has an active role. It is also important to understand how pedagogical networking changes the teacher's pedagogical work. Through co-operative planning and evaluation, the teacher changes from a traditional individual athlete into a team player, from a referee into a quarter back.

Based on our observations, it seems that pedagogical networking is not an easy way for a teacher; it requires much commitment and patience in the searching and testing of the characteristic working models of the network.

The design of learning environments based on the use of modern ICT is often solely focused on open and distance learning and the development of networking skills. This is understandable because various applications of virtual school are often the new aspect of learning enabled by ICT. It becomes problematic if the interaction between the physical learning environment and the virtual classroom is forgotten in the design of learning situations. In the open and distance learning of adults the meaning of the physical environment is not as important as in the classroom-focused distance learning where uniting the virtual classroom and the physical classroom into a common learning space is essential for pedagogical networking.

Another challenge in pedagogical networking is the development of assessment methods. The way of assessment should support the learners' own studying and learning processes and strengthen the cohesion of the learner groups. For these purposes, the latest effort within the LIVE project has been the launching of the development of virtual portfolio in teacher training. It is our belief that, by changing assessment practices, the school culture of teachers and learners can be changed towards the creation of an open, pedagogically networked school.

5. REFERENCES

Andesson, C. (1994) Verkostot ja strateginen oppiminen klustereissa. *Aikuiskasvatus* 14(4) 232-234. (in Finnish).

Helakorpi, S. and Suonperä, M. (1995) Verkostoituva oppimisympäristö – tie Eurooppaan. *Kasvatus* X(5) 475-484. (in Finnish).

Ministry of Education. (1995) *Education, Training and Research in the Information Society: A National Strategy.* Helsinki: Art-Print Painotalo. URL: http://www.minedu.fi/infostrategy.html

Nummi, T., Rönkä, A., and Sariola, J. (1998a) The LIVE Project: Learning in a virtual school environment. In T. Nummi, A. Rönkä and J. Sariola (eds.) *Virtuality and digital nomadism: An ntroduction to the LIVE Project (1997-2000).* Media Education Centre, Department of Teacher Education, University of Helsinki.

Nummi, T., Rönkä, A., and Sariola, J. (eds.) (1998b). *Virtuality and digital nomadism: An introduction to the LIVE Project (1997-2000).* Media Education Centre, Department of Teacher Education, University of Helsinki.

POPS-*Peruskoulun opetussuunnitelman perusteet* (1994). Helsinki: Painatuskeskus. (in Finnish).

Ristola, R. and Rönkä, A. (1998). Findings from the pilot stage of the LIVE Project. In T. Nummi, A.Rönkä and J.Sariola (eds.) *Virtuality and digital nomadism: An introduction to the LIVE Project (1997-2000).* Media Education Centre. Department of Teacher Education. University of Helsinki. Media Education Publications 6.

Sariola, J. (1997). Minustako virtuaaliopettaja? (Virtual Teacher-me?) In Salminen, J. (ed.) *Etäopetus koulussa (Distance Education at School).* University of Helsinki. II University Teacher Training School Publications 1, 72-81. (in Finnish).

Sariola, J. (1998). The planning of an open learning environment and didactic media choice in teacher education. In T.Nummi, A.Rönkä and J.Sariola (eds.) *Virtuality and digital nomadism: An introduction to the LIVE Project (1997-2000).* Media Education Centre. Department of Teacher Education. University of Helsinki. Media Education Publications 6.

Tapper, H. (1998). Information society: Another modernity. Licenciate thesis. Department of Communication. University of Helsinki.

Tella, S. (1997). Verkostuva viestintä- ja tiedonhallintaympäristö opiskelun tukena. In Lehtinen, E. (ed.) Verkkopedagogiikka. Edita: Helsinki, 41-59. (in Finnish).

6. BIOGRAPHIES

Tomi Nummi works as a Senior Adviser in the Finnish National Board of Education. His main area of responsibility is strategic planning and co-ordinating different in-service teacher education programmes. He has also worked as a lecturer in media education courses and is involved in various modern ICT research and development projects such as Euro-Land and LIVE.

Riikka Ristola is a research assistant in Media Education Centre of the Department of Teacher Education, University of Helsinki. Her main area of responsibility is research and developmental work for the LIVE project. She is also a lecturer and tutor in media education courses.

Aarno Rönkä has worked as an English teacher and a teacher trainer at Helsinki Second Teacher Training School since 1976. He has been actively involved in many school projects developing educational applications of ICT. Before the LIVE Project (1997-), he was the training school co-ordinator of the Kilpisjrvi Project (1994-1997), developing classroom-focused distance education using video-conferencing. He has written several articles in educational publications and is also involved in in-service teacher training.

Janne Sariola is Senior Adviser in the Ministry of Education, Finland. He has worked for a long time in both initial and in-service teacher education. His special areas of interest are the co-operative applications of open and distance learning and information and communication strategies in all levels of education.

Lurking, anonymity and participation in computer conferencing

John Pearson
Monash University, Churchill, Victoria 3842, Australia.
john.pearson@education.monash.edu.au

Keywords: computer-mediated communication, electronic networking, pre-service teacher education, computer conferencing

Abstract: This paper presents data from a case study on the use of electronic networking in an initial teacher education course. These data revealed that the network was used extensively for private mail but only to a limited extent for public conferencing except for one conference where trainee teachers were able to use an anonymous account when contributing messages. The reasons for limited participation by trainee teachers in conferences, and the ways in which access to an anonymous account influenced participation on the network, are discussed drawing on interview data from trainee teachers.

1. INTRODUCTION

This paper present data from a case study on the use of electronic networking in the fourth year of an initial teacher education course. A feature of the course was a 'school-based' practicum, developed in partnership with local schools, and one of the innovative features was the provision of an electronic network for individual mail and computer conferencing amongst trainee teachers, classroom teachers and university staff. Data on the nature and extent of usage by trainee teachers are presented. These data revealed that the network was used extensively for private mail but only to a limited extent for public conferencing, except for one conference, Course Comments, containing evaluative comments about the course, where trainee teachers were able to use an anonymous account

Mary Smith when contributing messages. The reasons for limited participation by trainee teachers in all conferences, except Course Comments, are discussed, drawing on interview data collected at the end of the course.

2. THE SCHOOL-BASED COURSE

The 'school-based' course aimed to engage trainee teachers in:

- co-operative planning, teaching and reflective practice;
- maintaining a reflective journal;
- teaching regularly across curriculum areas;
- attending and presenting at curriculum committees and seminars;
- interacting with the wider school community;
- seminars with school staff and liaison lecturers;
- a 6,000 word report on a topic;
- computer conferencing with other participants;
- compiling a professional employment portfolio.

(Standards Council of the Teaching Profession 1995)

The course was premised on notions of 'collegiate relationships' between participants, 'negotiated curriculum' in terms of activities in schools, and 'research about practice' (problem-solving, evaluations) (Cairns et al, 1995). Trainee teachers (n=26) maintained regular contact with one primary school throughout the year. Part time 'liaison lecturers' provided guidance and support to trainee teachers and classroom teachers. Since schools had no useful hardware, the university provided computers, modems, printers and telephone connections in each school, installed the communications software (First Class), and provided training in its use for all participants. No requirements about the nature and extent of usage of the network were imposed on participants.

3. NETWORK USE BY TRAINEE TEACHERS

Figure 1 shows the nature and extent of network use by trainee teachers. Trainee teachers accounted for 85% (n=1256) of loggias to the network, 82% (n=721) of private messages created, and 68% (n=130) of messages placed in conferences. Figure 1 reveals that trainee teachers used the network extensively for private messages but only to a limited extent for conferencing.

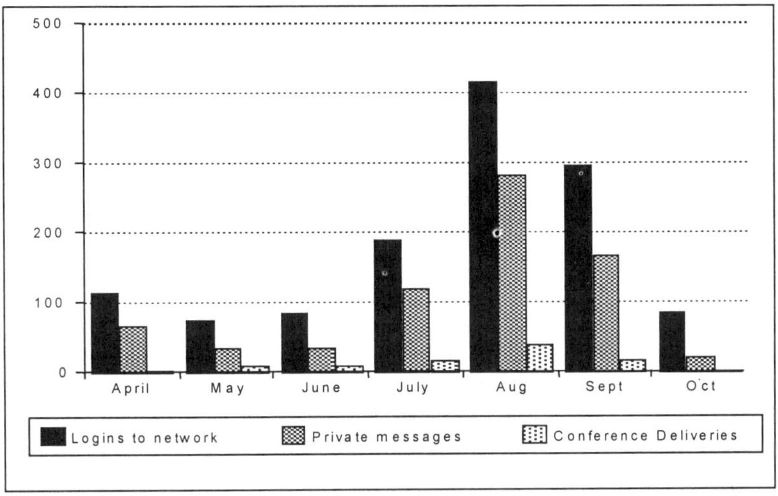

Figure 1. Network use by trainee teachers

Data from questionnaires revealed that few difficulties were experienced using the First Class communications software, which was considered to be 'easy' (90%) and 'fun' (77%) to use. Only 14% thought they were at a 'basic level' when using the software, the remaining 86% considered they were at 'higher' or 'advanced' levels. Strongly positive responses were received about the value of the network; electronic communication was considered to be very useful for 'receiving information' (91%), 'social contacts' (95%), 'teaching projects' (86%), 'discussing educational ideas' (81%), 'dealing with personal and professional problems' (71%) and 'developing a sense of community' amongst participants (81%).

These are interesting and useful findings, indicating that there is scope to incorporate electronic networking in initial teacher education courses and that trainee teachers consider that there are benefits in doing so. However, a more detailed examination of the messages contributed to conferences indicates that only three conferences – Stafford (67 messages), Course Comments (57 messages) and Projects (36 messages) – had relatively high message counts. Other conferences (n=11), set up at the request of trainee teachers to discuss curriculum issues, were poorly supported (0-15 messages). Conferences other than Course Comments were noticeboards, with messages publicising forthcoming meetings or social events, rather than forums for comments about teaching practices, curriculum issues or educational ideas. To investigate why this occurred, interviews were completed with trainee teachers (n=21) at the end of the year.

4. FACTORS INFLUENCING PARTICIPATION BY TRAINEE TEACHERS

While concerns about features of the 'school-based' programme (such as workload and assessment) impacted on participation on the network at various times, the focus here is on concerns directly related to the use of the electronic network for discussion purposes.

4.1 The public nature of communication

'Negotiating' a relationship with the electronic network and, in particular, the conferencing facility proved to be a particularly difficult task for many trainee teachers (TTs). They found that nothing in their teacher education course had prepared them to put forward ideas in the 'public' way required in conferencing. In previous years, they had been passive listeners rather than active contributors in university classes.

> Looking back over the three years you could count on your fingers the number of times you actually had to get up in front of everybody and do something. And then you're stuck on this thing where everything you do is in front of everyone else. So it's a big change. [TT12]

It might also be anticipated that teaching practice in previous years may have developed confidence about public presentations. However, trainee teachers were unable to transfer the skills and confidence gained during face-to-face interaction (with children, as well as adults) to the electronic medium.

> Teaching children isn't as intimidating as presenting your own ideas to people your own age or older. Even though you might be quite confident in front of 30 or so kids, when it comes to actually participating in conversations relating to class work or whatever it's just dramatically different. [TT13]

4.2 Envisaging the audience

Another problem for trainee teachers thinking about contributions to conferences was envisaging the audience. In assignments in other subjects, trainee teachers had written what they perceived the lecturer wanted:

> In most of our Uni life we've gotten to know the lecturers in the classes we've been in and you'll tend to write what you think the lecturer wants

> from you. You know what particular lecturers look for. I don't think you necessarily write the same way for all lecturers. [TT13]

However, on the network they were uncertain about how to compose messages which would be read by an audience which comprised other trainee teachers, classroom teachers and university staff.

> You're thinking: 'Who am I actually writing to? How do I write this?' You've got a whole range of people reading what I'm writing [on the network]. You've got lecturers, other teachers. You've got fellow students. What sort of stuff do I put in it? [TT13]

The content of messages was not the only problem. Without previous experience of 'network genre', trainee teachers were uncertain about how to write.

> I've got to write in a non-relaxed form for me when I'm on the network. I feel like I've got to write in a formal way and that puts me off. [TT3]

The difficulty of making decisions about writing 'style' is also reflected in the following passage from another trainee teacher.

> You have to adjust to it. You can't just write exactly what you mean when you're typing it. You have to really explain yourself a lot. When you're having a chat with someone they can fill in the gaps really easily. [TT5]

'Time' was another problem. In some cases, this referred to the competing demands of other components of the 'school-based' programme, but in other cases the concern with 'time' related to 'reflective writing'.

> It takes me a long time to think about what I'm going to write and edit it. I edit and edit all the time to try and make the point that I want to make so that its not ambiguous. So, I'm constantly editing and that's time consuming. And sometimes I've felt under pressure with time on the network and I've sent something and thought afterwards that I could have done better. [TT20]

4.3 Cues

Another difficulty for some trainee teachers was the loss of visual and verbal cues associated with face-to-face conversations when communication was mediated via an electronic network.

> It's hard typing something on the computer because, when you are talking to someone, you know with the tone what they're meaning. If they're being sarcastic you know, but on the computer you don't. [TT1]

Another trainee teacher made the following comments:

> If you're there you can read what a person's body language says and you can see if they're understanding what you mean and you can communicate more effectively face-to-face or over the telephone because you can listen to what they're saying in response to what you're saying and you can modify your message so that they understand what you mean. [TT16]

In the 'school-based' programme, the electronic network had been introduced to facilitate *communication* between course participants. But for trainee teachers, computer-mediated communication was about *writing*, since active participation in computer conferencing involved composing written messages. Their fundamental concern was the written nature of communication, evident in the language they used in interviews when talking about the network; sending messages was described as 'writing on the computer'; messages were referred to as 'letters'; and replies involved 'writing back'. Only a few trainee teachers talked about the network as a place to share ideas, to become familiar with other points of view or to justify their own ideas about concepts and issues to do with teaching.

4.4 Criticism

Since computer conferencing was about writing, rather than communication, it is not surprising that the major concern of trainee teachers – mentioned in almost every interview – was fear of criticism from others about what they had written. An incident early in the year reinforced their worst fears.

It was a response to one project outline (contributed by a trainee teacher) which heightened anxiety about the vulnerability of written communication. This response, by a university staff member (US), was designed to foster discussion and provide helpful information, but this was not the way it was perceived by the trainee teacher who had proposed the project. According to another university staff member:

> [She came] tearing into my office after school one day saying, 'Who *is* this?', and she used a very short word for him. And then she gave me a half hour diatribe on why she thought he had no right to have any opinion on what she did. And she was deeply offended. There was no

idea of the contribution of a colleague or why he wrote it. It just offended her utterly. [US2]

The same university staff member made another contribution a few days later clarifying the meaning of 'hypothesis' and the way a hypothesis was framed. Again, the message was designed to assist trainee teachers to design their projects in schools, but the 'academic' language used was construed as intimidating. Not surprisingly, trainee teachers decided to avoid written contributions to conferences which could expose their own inadequacies. As one trainee teacher commented: Better to remain silent and be thought a fool than to open your mouth and remove all doubt. [TT10]

These comments by trainee teachers reveal some of the problems they experienced negotiating the conferencing facility on the network. The fear of criticism about what they wrote was a particular problem which most failed to resolve. Hence, public messages addressed to conferences usually took the form of notices about professional development courses or social activities, 'safe' because these messages simply conveyed information and nothing about their own views which might be open to 'criticism'.

5. PARTICIPATING ANONYMOUSLY – THE MARY SMITH ACCOUNT

The suggestion for a Course Comments conference, and an anonymous account which could be used to contribute messages, arose at a campus meeting three months after the 'school based' course commenced. Course Comments (often called the Mary Smith conference) was the most successful of the conferences on the network – message counts were relatively high (n=57), and message content revealed a high level of interaction (comments on issues raised in other messages) amongst participants.

The Mary Smith account enabled many trainee teachers to handle problems associated with using their own accounts. As anonymous participants, it did not matter what, or how they wrote. One trainee teacher, who had made no contributions to conferences except Course Comments using the anonymous account, considered that:

It wasn't personalised. No-one knew who it was so they couldn't attach a name to it. So the criticism wasn't taken to heart. [TT12]

Another trainee teacher thought that the anonymous account was a good idea because:

> You don't feel so bad about coming back as Mary Smith and giving feedback. It's not friends or people you know. You don't want to step on peoples' toes. You can actually give feedback whether its critical or positive. [TT18]

Mary Smith was also a way to contribute ideas with 'no strings attached':

> I wrote it under Mary Smith because I couldn't be bothered getting back all the garbage that would come if I wrote it under my own name. I'd be getting personal comments back to my [mail]box and on to me personally and I didn't want that. [TT14]

6. ANONYMITY AND NETWORK PARTICIPATION

The use of an anonymous account was an interesting innovation which is perceived to have increased participation in one conference. In view of this outcome, the literature was reviewed to locate previous research which might present insights about anonymity and network participation.

Some electronic networks have provided opportunities for participants to use pseudonyms, although the justification for this decision, and an explanation for its effects, has not always been provided (Kimmel et al, 1988). In another reported application in a first year elementary teacher education course, the instructor in the course did not participate in discussions and all students did so anonymously 'to encourage non-dominated dialogue' (Harrington and Quinn-Leering, 1995). However, the impact of these decisions on participation was not discussed.

Two case studies located in the literature did provide some justifications for decisions taken and effects observed. At San Diego State University, computer conferencing was used to supplement face-to-face lectures and class discussions in one subject. The 'majority' of students in the class were 'adult Hispanic women' who were reported to have become 'very assertive' by the end of the course. In this case, the use of 'pen names' was considered to be important in initiating discussion, but not necessarily in sustaining it:

When students met in class, they did not engage in heated debate, nor was any attempt made to criticise the ideas and comments of anyone in the class. Although the class began with no one knowing anyone else's identity, the students soon began to share their pen names with friends. Within the first two weeks, either through direct revelation or second-hand gossip, all identities became known. Consequently, the use of anonymous identities was a valuable pedagogical resource for initiating the discussion, but it was the anonymity provided by the medium that sustained it and promoted the strong assertive remarks (Bellman 1992:60).

The 'anonymity provided by the medium' was not fully explained but presumably referred to network discussions in which 'women are able to express themselves much more easily and fully without being interrupted or ignored' (Bellman 1992) by other (male?) participants. If the 'characteristics of the medium' sustain discussion, anonymity may only be important in the *initial* stages of network interaction.

The impact of anonymity in the initial stages of network use has also been identified in a case study of the TeleNex (Hong Kong) network for non-native speaking English teachers. After four months, teachers reported that it was 'very threatening to have their names appearing in the messages, and even more threatening to have their school names appearing as well' (Tsui 1995). These teachers were concerned about perceptions of their personal competence with English, their knowledge about teaching English as a second language and, as a result, the reputation of their schools which might be held by others.

Modifications were made to the software so that public messages to conferences could be:

> anonymous, using personal name only, using school name alone, or using both... Subsequently, it was felt that signing off a message as anonymous has an undesirable effect on secrecy and this option was changed to 'An English Teacher'. (Tsui 1995)

Data on usage patterns with these options were not presented but Tsui (1995) noted that:

> The implementation of this modification ['An English Teacher'] for two months shows that most new users preferred to use 'An English Teacher' whereas the old users, especially panel chairs, used the default option of having their personal and school names appearing.

Hence, it would appear that 'pen names' may be useful in the initial stages of network use. As participants develop confidence in writing messages, and gain familiarity with the ways other users respond to messages, the use of actual names may be generally adopted.

7. CONCLUDING COMMENTS

Lurking occurs frequently in electronic discussions, but the reasons for this phenomenon have not been widely researched. The findings presented from this case study involving trainee teachers revealed special reasons for this behaviour, which may help to focus further research on the difficulties experienced by some users. The impact of an anonymous account on the participation by trainee teachers has also been outlined, but the opportunity to fully investigate the effects of network participation and message contributions was not realised by the author while the research was in progress. However, the effects observed with novice users of communications software in this case study, and the available reports of other evaluations of electronic networking, would appear to indicate that anonymity may increase participation particularly in the early stages of network use. The benefits of asynchronous communication (equal opportunities to participate, no interruptions by assertive members) cannot always be realised when users lack confidence in using the medium as the trainee teachers in this case study demonstrated. Further research on the effects of anonymity on network participation might result in earlier and more confident participation by novice users without the need to resort to sanctions (such as specifying the nature and extent of contributions) as is often the case.

REFERENCES

Bellman, B. L. (1992) Computer communications and learning. *New Directions for Teaching and Learning* 51, 55-63.

Cairns, L., Southcott, J., Osborn, M., and Clingan, R. (1995). The Monash primary school-based teacher education programme. Paper presented at the 25th Annual Conference of the Australian Teacher Education Association, Sydney. [URL: ftp://info.mq.edu.au/pub/edu/lcairns.doc]

Harrington, H. L. and Quinn-Leering, K. (1995) *Fostering moral discourse with technology*. Paper presented at the Annual Meeting of the American Educational Research Association under the title 'Using technology to prepare effective and responsible educators'. San Francisco, April.

Kimmel, H., Kerr, E. B., and O'Shea, M. (1988). Computer conferencing as a resource for in-service teacher education. *Science Education*, 72 (4) 467-473.

Standards Council of the Teaching Profession (SCTP) (1995) *Partnerships in teacher education*. Melbourne: SCTP.

Tsui, A. B. M. (1995) Social factors in the implementation of a computer network for English language teachers. *Journal of Information Technology for Teacher Education*. 4 (2) 149-164.

BIOGRAPHY

John Pearson is Senior Lecturer in the Faculty of Education, Monash University, Victoria, Australia. He has taught for many years in initial and continuing teacher education courses. His current research interests focus on the ways in which communities of practice can be fostered through the use of computer conferencing in professional education and training.

Computer-mediated communication in adult education

Kate Denning and Mike Davis
Centre for Adult and Higher Education, University of Manchester, Oxford Road, Manchester, M139PL, UK. kate.f.denning@man.ac.uk

Keywords: equality, facilitation, lurking, moderator, pedagogy

Abstract: In this paper we consider one asynchronous computer conference and begin to define, within this context, some of the issues which set the virtual classroom apart from the traditional classroom. The repercussions of using a text-based medium are profound. We have focused on the ways that silence is experienced; the equality which occurs when all participants are dependent on the written word; and the added importance attributed to tutor comments as a result of being written. We have also considered a broader definition of the role of the conference moderator after Berge (1995) in order to continue the process of enquiry into the possibilities of the role.

1. INTRODUCTION

One of the teaching strategies possible in Information and Communications Technology (ICT) is the use of the asynchronous conference in which students contribute to ongoing discussions unrestrained by the need to be in the same time and space. In an asynchronous learning network (ALN) students and tutors respond to the conference as and when they are able. Entering the conference is a consciously solitary event. Some conferees have previously prepared statements, questions and comments which they upload once they are connected to the conference. This highly conscious and reflective discussion-based learning medium is perhaps unique to ALNs and a valuable educational tool.

The course on which this research is based is called Reflective Technologies in Work-based Learning and is offered at Masters/ taught

Doctoral level by the University of Manchester, UK and the University of Georgia, USA. The aims of the course are to encourage students a) to become tolerant of ambiguity, b) to develop interpersonal skills, particularly within a cross-cultural context, c) to develop intervention skills, and d) to make use of action science in dealing with work-based problems. The course is experiential and has five phases:

- *Phase 1* - pre-reading and writing
- *Phase 2* - T-group laboratory
- *Phase 3* - Action Science laboratory
- *Phase 4* - Computer-mediated communication, based on action science case study groups
- *Phase 5* - revision and examination.

The focus of this paper is on Phase 4, the online phase. Previous papers have dealt with issues related to teaching and learning (Davis Watkins and Milton 1998a), cross-cultural matters (Davis, Watkins and Milton 1998b) and levels of participation (Davis and Denning, 1998).

During the face-to-face (f2f) and online phases of action science, the students worked in three groups of five. They took it in turns to present and have interrogated, an action science case (Brooks and Watkins 1994). Analysis of the transcripts of the conferences revealed significant differences between the three groups. For the purpose of this paper these differences could be categorised in terms of output, that is the quantity of data produced; the atmosphere of the three virtual communities and the extent to which each group relied on the tutor.

As a result of the experience of attending these virtual conferences and analysing the data we feel able to draw some early conclusions about online small group work.

2. THE EFFECT OF ICT ON THE CLASSROOM

Anyone who has experience of using a computer conferencing package to enhance student learning will be aware that it alters the dynamics of the classroom in certain specific ways. In our research we have found the following areas to be of significance:

- silence/lurking;
- CMC as a text-based medium;
- equality within CMC;
- the tutors' presence.

2.1 Silence or 'lurking'

Silence in CMC can be attributed to many causes: an individual might be unavailable for a few days, unable to think of a response, offended by a previous message, or they could have lost interest in the discussion. It is also likely that some silent conference members are lurking. Lurking is a term used to describe less active participation in a computer-mediated activity: in other words, reading but not writing. It has traditionally been viewed in a negative way conjuring up images of voyeurism more than uncertainty or shyness. The issue of lurking in cyberspace was a controversial one for two of the groups we studied and they dealt with it in different ways. One of the groups decided to create a 'lurk room' within their conference where they could indicate their 'presence' without making comments on the ongoing discussion. The other group talked about creating a lurk room but did not do so. All appeared to agree, however, that lurking should not be viewed as non-participation.

In the course evaluation students commented favourably on the opportunity to enter a conference, read and then leave, only to return afterwards with their more reflective observations. The tutors always presented an unbiased attitude towards lurking which was noted by a member of Group One.

> *Martha:* Mike Davis referred to this aspect of online group work, too. Here is a suggestion. We could have a "lurk room" like we have a "chat room" now and, if and when we get on the site and "listen" but do not "speak," we could just put the date and time there, so that others would know of our presence. What do you all think?

The part that the tutors can play in viewing the lurking persona as arguably the most reflective one is important, and by modelling tolerance towards different styles they can affect the views of the other participants. Indeed, it is not only the students who can and do lurk but also the tutors. Both tutors visited Group Three more than Group One and both report that they were bothered at the time by the lack of activity in Group Three. These frequent visits may have given the tutors an impression of active involvement which was not borne out by the printed texts. This is a potentially dangerous area and facilitators need to be aware that whilst they may feel involved when they are lurking, there is no evidence for the rest of the community.

2.2 CMC as a written medium

The repercussions of working within a purely written medium are substantial. Holt, Kleiber and Swenson (1995) wrote:

> To engage in the electronic debate one's voice becomes literate, written and bound in text. Without traditional non-verbal cues, inflection, tone, etc, participants must make the most of words.... The discussion is ... text bound and context poor. (Holt, Kleiber and Swenson, 1995:8)

It is easy to be aware of the restraining effect of communicating through script when struggling, not only to find the right words but also to be concise. Less apparent, at first, is the effect of operating without the benefit of non-verbal communication, so much of which we take for granted, that its loss is not always accurately calculated. Because e-discourse is a written form of communication, all activity, particularly any originating from the tutor, is powerful. Comments can be read many times over and interpretations changed and flippant remarks can take on a more weighty aspect than intended. Our analysis suggests that for some of the students the heightened sensitivity and weight of the medium, in combination with traditional power issues, meant that each intervention by the tutors may have been seen as overly significant.

One of the advantages of asynchronous, written communication is that there is time to compose a well-crafted response. This is a facility which tutors can use to great effect if they make a conscious note of the norms they see operating within the groups they are tutoring. Asynchronicity then provides them with the opportunity to take the time to make interventions which take these norms into account: an opportunity which is not possible in the clamour of the face-to-face seminar.

2.3 Equality within CMC

Research has shown that people who are reticent in a face-to-face situation are likely to contribute more in a computer-mediated setting (see for example Holt, Kleiber and Swenson, 1995). In a face-to-face environment where non-verbal cues can be overwhelming, voices are not heard equally. It could be argued that there is an unprecedented equality to CMC. In a computer-mediated setting the context, content and cues are all written. Learner styles can be transformed by the medium. Hesitancy, volume and bravado are less striking than in a face-to-face situation. There is a democracy to the medium which allows the reader an autonomy they do not have in the conventional classroom. This autonomy can be experienced by scrolling through long or irrelevant postings, skipping entries by certain people and by focusing for extended examination on particular postings.

An examination of the transcripts created by the course 'Reflective Technologies in Work-based Learning' revealed that some of the students who had been reticent in the face-to-face component on the course were indeed active online group members. Students appeared to develop an online persona which was unique and in many cases impressively reflective and critically aware.

2.4 The tutors' presence

Wizer and Beck (1996) found that the roles of faculty and students were altered in the online setting so that courses become more learner driven and students more proactive. Wild and Winniford (1993) add:

> The fact that roles may change so that discussions are more open and learner driven indicates that students are engaged in the learning process in a different fashion than traditional classes. Students apparently are able to take the lead in asking and answering questions in this electronic environment. (1993:10)

We found that Group One demonstrated this proactive engagement in the learning process. As a result of the majority of their time being conducted without the tutors being 'present' they became increasingly autonomous. Not only did they ask and answer questions but they took active and territorial control of 'their' discussion, with, on one occasion, four out of the five group members lining themselves up in opposition to an observation made by one of the tutors.

Group Two appeared to be reliant on tutor interventions to guide and focus their discussions and as such resembled a face-to face tutorial in the first four weeks. However the following intervention by one of the tutors led them to re-examine the way they had been working.

> *Karen (tutor)* ...I am suggesting that it would be helpful for you to be explicit about what you think is going on ... and then inquire whether or not you are accurate. This exposes your thinking and reasoning... and thereby allows Charlotte to see exactly what you are driving at....
>
> *Kurt* Got you Karen. Thanks. This is a good intervention on your part.

In the final week the group had a thoughtful, open exchange in which four of them challenged their tendency to "*let details of the case get in the way of looking at feelings*." (*Dana*) and realised that it had held them back. It may well be that if these five students engaged in further online learning they would be able to gain far more as a result of the collaborative analysis which they carried out.

The experiences of these three groups might suggest that for many learners it takes time to adjust to being part of an ALN. The group which made the most rapid progress consisted of highly motivated learners who both acknowledged and tackled the challenges of the medium to make it work for them. Whilst the lack of the physical presence of the tutor might have given some students an excuse not to participate, it equally well liberated others to move into the exciting arena of interdependence.

3. AN EVOLVING PEDAGOGY

Berge (1995) explores how the teacher-learner dynamic is altered through a movement of focal position so that instead of the tutor being at the centre of the teaching-learning process it becomes the students. He describes the online tutor as a moderator whose role can be seen to be made up of four distinct functions.

3.1 Pedagogical

This encompasses writing and disseminating course materials and the guidance given by tutors drawing on their extensive knowledge of the subject. In a discussion-based course tutors can model such behaviours as challenging, probing, giving a personal opinion and seeking clarification. This role is similar in a face-to-face environment. However students will not always receive an immediate response to a specific enquiry from their tutor and there is room in the virtual environment for students to respond to each other by pointing out useful URLs, journals or books and making collective answers drawing on personal experience.

3.2 Managerial

In an administrative and organisational sense this includes such aspects as dissemination of information about the course and awarding body requirements. But more than that is the management of the discussion. In an asynchronous conference the moderator cannot keep the conversation flowing in the same way as face-to-face because they are not always 'present'. So responsibility for keeping the conference moving and for encouraging each other has to be taken up, in part by the students.

3.3 Social

The social moderator has to find online ways of fulfilling peoples' desires to hear a voice, to feel connected because this can be overwhelming. The moderator has to fulfil a supportive and consultative function and show an awareness of group dynamics. Time lag is a key element in the unfolding of unhealthy dynamics. New users in particular expect immediate and personal responses and are disappointed when they do not receive them. Some students may need to be encouraged in the early stages with the disorienting nature of cybertime. The handling of the first few days of a new computer conference is perhaps critical to its success. Tutors who are sensitive to the desire to receive a written response in the early part of a conference can monitor whether or not participation is occurring without their intervention and react accordingly.

3.4 Technical

This role is vastly different from any experienced by a face-to-face tutor and needn't actually be fulfilled by the person responsible for academic content. It covers such aspects as technological backup, and training to enable the course to run smoothly. Clearly it helps if the tutor can act in the role of technical moderator and have the necessary skills to troubleshoot. Proctor (1998) acknowledges that having help with the technical aspect of CMC may be a luxury which will soon disappear.

4. TUTOR INTERVENTIONS

Table 1 gives a summary of the four moderator functions suggested by Berge (1995). In the bottom half of the table we have listed the codings we used in analysing the data produced by the course under discussion. These codings were based initially on the typology designed by Harasim (1987) with such additions and alterations as an interrogation of the data necessitated. It can be seen that some codings could be placed in more than one category as they fulfil more than one function. For example, the students created the facility to check in and out as a way of managing the discussion but it in fact also fulfilled a social function of providing information on who was present and was seen as a courtesy to the week's leader.

In order to find out what effect the tutors were having we used the software package NUD*IST (Non-numerical Unstructured Data Indexing, Searching, and Theorising; Richards and Richards, 1994) and made a qualitative analysis of tutor interventions. Table 2 shows the distribution of tutor interventions according to the data codings used. Just as a coding can be placed in more than one of Berge's four categories we have chosen on occasions to code an intervention in more than one way.

Table 1. The four moderator functions after Berge (1995)

Pedagogical	Managerial	Social	Technical
Writing course materials Providing educational 'leadership' through an awareness of group dynamics.	Dissemination of information about course and awarding bodies. Providing course materials.	Supportive and consultative function fulfilled through an awareness of group dynamics.	Technological backup and input of course material into groupware
Ongoing guidance given by the tutor.	Management of the discussion		Training conference users
Data codings			
coaching *asking question* *giving opinion* *thinking aloud* *exploring* *focusing* *challenging* *seeking clarification* *clarifying* *probing*	*new direction* *talk about cmc* *checking in and out* *integrating* *focusing* *seeking clarification*	*chat* *affirming* *checking in and out* *talk about cmc*	*process commenting* *technology*

We have highlighted the types of intervention which may be of greatest significance. Tutors did more coaching in groups Two and Three which implies they needed to engage in specific teaching of concepts or strategies. In contrast they made more attempts at encouraging members of Group One to dig deeper (probing) implying that the knowledge and structures were already there but further insights would be helpful. It may be significant that the tutors engaged in more chat with Group One, the group which chatted the most. The tutors also affirmed Group One the most and they were arguably least in need of external approval. We would suggest that it was precisely because Group One engaged with each other on a social level that the tutors, affected by this norm, acted similarly. Moreover the evidence would suggest that far from being irrelevant chat the social aspect was vital to building a sense of community and contributed to the immediate and continued success of Group One.

Table 2. Tutor interventions by category

Category	Group 1	Group 2	Group 3
Affirming	6	2	4
Exploring	-	-	2
Process commenting	1	2	1
Coaching	**3**	**5**	**5**
Probing	**6**	**2**	**1**
Focusing	3	1	4
Giving opinion	3	-	3
Thinking aloud	2	1	3
Integrating	-	-	-
Challenging	-	1	-
Seeking clarification	1	2	1
Clarifying	3	2	2
Checking in or out	2	3	-
Chat	**5**	**3**	**2**
Technology	-	2	1
New direction	1	-	1
Asking question	4	1	3

5. CONCLUSION

In this environment, as in face-to-face, some students benefit and flourish and others find it alienating or unhelpful. Asynchronous computer conferencing with adult learners encourages students to rely on one another because the tutor is not always present. Harasim et al. note:

> Teachers, trainers, and professors with years of experience in classrooms report that computer networking encourages the high-quality interaction and sharing that is at the heart of education. (Harasim et al. 1995:173)

Computer conferencing can engage learners and foster collaborative learning but more research is needed into the different types of learner-experiences of computer conferencing. Berge (1995) suggests a re-evaluation of the role of the conference moderator to incorporate an awareness not only of pedagogical issues but also, managerial, technological and social. Consideration of these different roles, and how aspects of them can be taken on by motivated learners, are important steps in improved conference facilitation.

REFERENCES

Berge, Z. (1995) Facilitating Computer Conferencing: Recommendations from the Field. *Educational Technology* 35(1) 22-30.

Brooks, A. and Watkins, K. (eds.) (1994) *The Emerging Power of Action Inquiry Technologies.* San Francisco: Jossey-Bass.

Davis, M. and Denning, K. (1998) Learning in Virtual Space: Potential and Pitfalls in Electronic Communication. *Proceedings of the SCUTREA 28th Annual Conference*, Exeter, UK.

Davis, M., Watkins, K., and Milton, J. (1998a) Reflective Technologies: An Analysis of Teaching/Learning Practices in Computer Mediated Communication. *Proceedings of Networked Lifelong Learning: Innovative Approaches to Education and Training Through the Internet*, Sheffield, UK.

Davis, M., Watkins, K., and Milton, J. (1998b) Reflective Technologies: An Analysis of Cross-cultural Issues in Computer Mediated Communication. *Proceedings of IFTDO Conference,* Dublin, Ireland.

Harasim, L., Hiltz, S. R., Teles, L., and Turoff, M. (1995) *Learning Networks: A Field Guide to Teaching and Learning Online*, USA: MIT.

Harasim, L. (1987) Teaching and Learning Online: Issues in Computer-Mediated Graduate Course. *Canadian Journal of Educational Communication* 16(2) 117-135.

Holt, M. E., Kleiber, P. B., and Swenson, J. D. (1995) The Changing Face of Evaluation in Distance Education. Paper presented at the *American Evaluation Association* November 1-5 1995, Vancouver, Canada.

Procter, P. M. (1998) The Tutorial: Combining Asynchronous and Synchronous Learning. *Proceedings of Networked Lifelong Learning: Innovative Approaches to Education and Training Through the Internet*, Sheffield, UK.

Wild, R. and Winniford, M. (1993) Remote collaboration among students using email. *Computers in Education* 21(3) 193-203.

Wizer, D. R. and Beck, S. S. (1996) Studying diversity issues in teacher education using online discussions. *Journal of Computing in Teacher Education*, 13(1) 6-11.

BIOGRAPHIES

Kate Denning is a researcher at the University of Manchester with interests in online group dynamics and teaching and learning in virtual space. She teaches on the Masters level courses. Before working in adult education she taught in primary schools specialising in Music and Drama.

Mike Davis is a lecturer in Adult Education at the University of Manchester, teaching on learning and organisational change. His research interests include virtual learning communities and situated cognition. Before working as a researcher in curriculum development projects, he taught English and Drama in urban secondary schools.

Projects in networked learning: European experiences

Reports from panel sessions

1. INTRODUCTION

In the last 5 years 'networked education' has come to refer not only to computer networks in education but to co-operative networks of educators working together to research, address issues and define good practice in the use of ICTs in education. At the ComNEd99 conference, European colleagues from a number of these co-operative projects presented panel sessions where they shared their work, the issues and findings arising out of their work. Each of these panel sessions was attended by rapporteurs who have written the following accounts of the sessions and projects. Where possible World Wide Web addresses have been provided to allow the reader to seek out more information about each of the projects. The paper ends with a number of reports of Finnish projects. These projects highlight good practice in networked education taking place in Finland, the host country of ComNEd99.

2. TRAINING EDUCATORS THROUGH NETWORKS AND DISTRIBUTED SYSTEMS (TRENDS)

Chair: Raymond Morel, CH
Presenter: Chryssa Koutra, GR
Rapporteur: Jan Wibe, NO
Detailed information about the project at: www.lrf.gr/english/trends/trendshome.html

TRENDS started in 1996 and ended in September, 1998. The following countries were involved: France, Greece, Italy, Portugal, Spain and United Kingdom. The Lambrakis Research Foundation in Greece was the project leader. In each country the main partners involved were ICT training centres, schools with school-leaders, and national telecommunications companies.

The project had the following objectives:

- Training in the use of ICT in teaching and learning;
- Development of a school-based (on-the-job), open-distance learning (ODL)/ICT-based training model for in-service teachers;
- Development of a teacher training network;
- Validation/Evaluation in the national and European environment.

The following points were the main focus of the presentation and discussion.

2.1 Training centres

The training centres played a crucial role in the project. In addition to training, they were also suppliers of educational resources. It was said that the centres had no or very little contact with schools before the project and that the project established such contacts. In the beginning they could not offer all of the services needed, but this improved through the project period. In many training centres, they have now established so-called 'Virtual Training Centres' with a broad scope of services for teachers.

2.2 Selection of schools

The only criteria for selecting schools to take part was that they should be equipped with computers. This lead to some difficulties in the project because there were significant differences in the various schools' experience and expertise and also in what they wanted to do in collaboration with other schools. It is perhaps unfair to look back to 1996 from the perspective of 1999, but the outcome of the project could have been better if there had been other criteria for taking part in the project. For example, choosing teachers with common interests and more experience with ICT may have proved beneficial. Particular subject areas could also have been selected for international co-operation.

2.3 The schools

The role of the school leaders was an important feature of the project. While not experts, generally they were familiar with ICT, and were close to the daily life of the schools. They acted as an interface between the schools and the training centres and acted as both facilitators and brokers. Generally, the project seemed to be a success within the schools, due in part to the effective role of these leaders. At times, overload for school leaders caused tension in the schools.

2.4 National and international activity

An important aim of the project was to create an European network of teachers. At the start of the project, international co-operation was at the forefront. But over time the various elements of the projects became more focused at the national level and finally, in some projects, at the international level. There were many reasons for this, some of which were cultural differences. Generally, the teachers were well supported within their own schools but lacked the motivation to go beyond their school. Self learning by the teachers was seen as more valid than collaborative learning. The teachers did not see the wider national or international network as a space for collaboration.

The international aspect of the project was clearly the weakest part of it. Common elements were not stressed enough. International discussions did not appeal to the teachers and there was not enough stimulus from the moderators. This may have been different if, at the beginning of the project, there had been clear criteria for participation; carefully selected schools based on such criteria as school profiles and leaders' profiles; and clearly defined aims that all participants were expected to work towards.

2.5 Accreditation

The teachers taking part in the project wanted official recognition and accreditation for the work they did and the expertise they built up during the project. For example, a certificate recognising the learner activities would have been appropriate. The teachers also saw the project as part of their personal career development. The school leader's role was crucial within the project yet they were also not rewarded through official recognition and accreditation. This created tension in the schools. The project administration now recognise the importance of this aspect for future projects. There must be clear motivation and recognition for teachers who take part in such projects.

3. FORMATION DES ENSEIGNANTS AUX TECHNOLOGIES DE L'INFORMATION ET DE LA COMMUNICATION: CHANGEMENTS ET EVOLUTIONS (FETICHE)

Chair: Bernard Cornu, FR
Presenters: Patricia Marzin, FR, Mario Maia and Cecilia Monteiro, PT, Deryn Watson and Barry Blakely, UK, Raymond Morel, CH, Bernard Cornu, FR, Leena Vainio and Tuija Karppanen, FI
Rapporteur: Don Passey, UK
Detailed information about the project at:www.grenoble.iufm.fr/tic/ fetiche.htm, French language only

The project FETICHE was an open-distance learning (ODL) European project run as part of the SOCRATES Programme in 1995-97. The project involved 6 partner institutions from 5 European countries: Institut Universitaire de Formation des Maîtres (IUFM) of Grenoble, France; University of Helsinki, Finland; King's College, London, United Kingdom; Escola Superior de Educacao de Lisboa, Portugal; CNRS-CEGELY, Lyon, France; CIP and TECFA, Geneva, Switzerland.

The stated objectives of the project were to predict the nature of a future teaching profession when teachers use information and communication technologies (ICT). It aimed to identify pedagogic competencies required, and to develop teacher and teacher trainer competencies through the use of ODL, as well as to facilitate co-operation between teacher training institutions in Europe, and to be reflective of those training practices undertaken. The outcomes of the project included state-of-the-art integration of aspects of ICT use into teacher training education in the partner institutions, reports about the experiments carried out in each partner country, and the production of two written documents that offered recommendations for users and policy makers.

The session offered an overview of the project and its outcomes, as well as more specific details of the experiments carried out in four of the partner groups. The session overview indicated that the major project results had been used to inform the production of two overview documents. The 'Users' Needs' document indicated that teacher training education in the future should be underpinned by having the use, role and concepts of ICT integrated into the curricula of schools and teacher training institutions. It indicated that teacher education should have full access, full infrastructure and availability to global networking as essential elements for all schools.

The project showed that there is a merging of pre-service and in-service teacher education into a single lifelong professional development process, and that all schools and teacher education institutions should have a proactive policy to address this aspect. The 'Guidelines for European Education Decision Makers' indicates that outcomes show that a necessary starting point for developing appropriate future needs for teacher training should be from a position of having a policy in place, which should tackle the needs of developing practice where conceptual shifts involve the taking of steps to a 'new' cultural position. The project showed the need for developing integrated tasks and activities to exemplify curriculum practice, but that each teacher or student teacher will need to experience open learning methods for themselves. The project recommends that networks are used to bring classrooms and institutions together, and that certain levels of equipment and human resources will be necessary to enable particular levels of progress in these forms of ongoing development.

3.1 Escola Superior de Educacao de Lisboa, Portugal

Two experiments were undertaken by this partner institution. The first experiment involved only pre-service teacher education, and was concerned with developing pedagogical practice. The outcomes of this experiment showed that Internet use can result in benefits and gains in pedagogic terms, but that it is necessary to engage teachers and teacher trainers at a subject level to consider more carefully the potential uses of the Internet in teaching and learning. The second experiment involved the continuum from the pre-service to the in-service sectors, and was concerned with the training of teacher trainers. This experiment involved the design and development of a training programme for teacher trainers and teachers in schools. The training programme considered pedagogical practice in schools, and involved seminars with teacher trainers, school teachers, and student teachers in schools, as well as discussion forums. The outcomes of this project indicated the need for teachers to have more time to integrate use into their practice, and the need to be alerted to the advantages of using the practice in daily work. The project had ultimate impact at an institutional level.

3.2 King's College London, United Kingdom

The experiment in this partner institution involved the introduction and use of the World Wide Web (WWW) as a common interface for a forum to enable discussion and communication between researchers, teacher trainers and teachers in a PGCE course. The experiment involved three subject areas (modern foreign languages, religious education, and science), with three university teacher trainers and six school teacher co-tutors. A number of problems were highlighted at the time of the project, including the fact that the ICT equipment present in each of the schools was different and different to that within the teacher training institution, that the schools had limited communications equipment and access to such equipment, and that setting up the systems took a great deal longer than expected. The access provided ultimately was Web-based, and schools were given modems and remote access accounts on the teacher training institution's email system. Support was provided for those involved, and was reported as becoming a significant part of the experiment. Teacher trainers were given one-to-one training, while school teachers were offered support through visits from research staff and a specifically designed help sheet.

The Web-based discussion areas covered six topics. However, contribution levels were much lower than anticipated, the majority of discussion being in the 'Meeting Point' area, with conversations being generally linear, and mostly about non-professional matters. Issues identified by the experiment were that access for teachers and teacher trainers must be simple, that the technology used must be able to support access and reaction adequately, that the imposition of structure on the access might not be helpful, that joint interest must be aroused before use is stimulated, that wide access through the World Wide Web was considered by participants to be useful, and that the archiving facility of the Forum aided the research activity.

Fundamental outcomes identified were that technology and infrastructure are not necessarily critical to outcomes, and that having a physical ICT presence does not in itself ensure communication results. However, the average technical infrastructure in schools at that time did not encourage use. To support use, the experiment outcomes suggested that developing levels of conversation or discussion requires an appropriate stimulus, that there needs to be a level of commonality across users, and that users need to have concern for the pedagogy of the subject rather than the pedagogy of teacher education itself.

3.3 Institut Universitaire de Formation des Maîtres (IUFM) of Grenoble, France

The experiment in this partner institution involved the development of co-operative work for student teachers, tutors and trainers through the use of video-conferencing and email. A system was developed to train student teachers to work collaboratively through class to class communication, to offer distance class observations for teacher trainers, and virtual visits to classrooms. Eleven primary schools were equipped with ICT systems, as was the IUFM at Grenoble. In all, twelve teacher trainers, twenty-three primary school student teachers and their tutors in schools were involved. Daily video-sessions were used to develop collaborative practices, as well as the use of chat meetings, and teacher observation of student teachers through video-conferencing techniques in geography and art lessons.

The main outcomes of the project were the realisation that different ways of working with student teachers, and different pedagogical styles had developed and were recognised by those involved. The techniques used enhanced critical practice and reflection by enabling regular contact and comment. It was found that some student teachers experienced difficulties in school integrating ICT into practice, however, and while the tools available were used for communicating externally from school, there was no evidence that internal communication could be provided through this medium. The experiment showed that training was a requirement for those in the future, and the IUFM developed a considered plan as a consequence.

3.4 University of Helsinki, Finland

The experiment in this partner institution was integrated with the five-year national plan produced in 1995 by the Ministry of Education, which involved the linking of schools and educational establishments to an information network. This plan considered also the development of initial teacher training education, and the organisation of continuing education. The experiment involved the development and use of a teacher training course that would be run over 5 study weeks, involving initially 1 or 2 teachers from each participating school. The course focused on pedagogic concerns, the development and integration of ICT in subjects and on school-wide developments as a whole, with teachers developing plans and implementing them by involving other teachers. The course was delivered through two face-to-face sessions of two days duration, and one session of a single day's duration. Sessions run at a distance were also involved, as well as email contact, a discussion list, World Wide Web pages, video-conferencing and audio-lectures, project work and tutoring at an individual level.

Aims of the research for the experiment were identified and stated in advance. Of 234 teachers who were initially approached, 91 responses were received (considered to be a representative group across schools as a whole), but all schools were located in the area around Helsinki and the southern district of Finland. Features and background factors of respondents were considered in terms of whether they related to particular levels or types of ICT use. It was found that most respondents were female (65%), that most (about 80%) of the respondents were between 25 and 45 years of age, that some 90% had a university degree, and that many (some 41%) were subject teachers. When teacher skills, attitudes and views were identified, these indicated that there was a need to consider how to motivate other teachers, how to implement appropriate use of tools, how to tutor distance learning, and to share 'new' ideas. The experiment had effects at a national level: the outcomes indicated that training should perhaps involve 2 to 4 members of a school rather than one or two, that teachers should be made aware of how to develop possible ICT strategies in school and be offered examples of 'good' practice.

3.5 Discussion points

Each project was uniquely different, and the ways in which outcomes were utilised were specific to their contexts, and to the context of the stage reached by respective national developments at that time. The four presentations generated a range of issues, and a range of comments arose from those present in the audience. Results suggested that when developing innovative teacher uses, attendance of two or more participants from a school is necessary, and that conceptions of technology use should be developed fully within any teacher training activity. Strong mentoring systems may be needed to support teacher development, but teachers may listen to other teachers more than they do to others. Those willing to undertake innovative practice are not necessarily age related, but are more likely to be related to risk-taking willingness. Stages of learning, levels of uncertainty, risk-taking willingness, boredom levels, assessment needs, and perceived time availability are all factors that influence innovative practice and outcomes. Women teachers may take longer to engage in innovation, but then can become highly enthusiastic users. Pre-service teachers are often asked to learn a large number of things in a limited period of time.

Clearly the outcomes of this project relate to results from those of other innovative projects, and these results help to confirm elements of the wider picture of our understanding of the innovative constructive demands for developing innovative practice and implementation effectively.

4. LINGU@NET-EUROPA

Chair: Raymond Morel, CH
Presenters: Clare Power, UK, Pierre Dunand, CH, Aino Korhonen, FI
Reporter: Gail Marshall, US
Detailed information about the project at: www.linganet.org.uk.

Lingu@net-Europa is a multilingual virtual resource centre designed to support the teaching of foreign languages. The three papers in this panel session addressed the history, goals, content, programme structure and features as well as issues related to management and evaluation of the Lingu@net-Europa materials, resources, and interface.

4.1 History and goals of the project

The first third of the panel presentation addressed Lingu@net-Europa's history, goals and content. The website, funded by the European Commission (DGXXII), Lingu@net-Europa provided information links to quality-assured online resources in Dutch, English, French and German to eleven European countries and Canada during the first pilot year. In the next two years it is planned that Italian and Spanish language materials and resources and then Eastern European-based materials and resources will be added to the metadata core.

The project's goal is to support the mobility of citizens and business, enhance lifelong learning, motivate teachers, trainers and researchers, and promote the sharing of expertise, experience and resources. Lingu@net-Europa has been designed as a one-stop shop with many different source and target languages. It can be accessed from any computer with an Internet connection and enhances collaboration across borders and linguistic communities. The quality assurance process, designed to ensure that materials and resources contained in the metadata core are of high standard, was explained as well as the procedures used in the construction and modifications of the entire website. The core programme's management procedures, featuring dynamic processing of records, were illustrated.

4.2 Content and processes of Lingu@net-Europa

The second part of the presentation featured a demonstration of access to the materials, professional development resources and research reports. Sample records of foreign language materials were accessed via the World Wide Web and procedures for selecting both source and target materials were also demonstrated.

4.3 Evaluation of the materials and procedures

The third part of the presentation described evaluation strategies at four levels: data from workshops designed to present Lingu@net-Europa, data from focused user groups who completed online questionnaires, data from larger groups invited to provide evaluative comments and data from the large group of users who have accessed the materials and resources since the inception of the project. Both quantitative and qualitative data have been collected and a variety of data summaries, all showing a high level of user satisfaction, were displayed and analysed.

Members of the audience commented that the project's resources are needed by the educational community and they also asked if the project assisted educators in establishing partnerships with classrooms and individual students around the world. Project personnel reiterated the fact that the principal goal of the project was to provide web-based materials and resources for education and professional development and was not designed to serve as a clearinghouse for partnerships designed to facilitate person-to-person or classroom-to-classroom communication exchanges.

The fact that Lingu@net-Europa provides resources and materials at no cost to users was viewed as a valuable aspect of the project, and plans to eventually expand both the number of source and target language materials and the access to those materials to a wider geographical range was viewed favourably by the audience.

5. THE TELEMATICS FOR TEACHER TRAINING PROJECT (T3)

Chair: Ian Lam, NL
Presenters: Niki. Davis, UK, Jyrki Pulkkinen FI, Donatella Persico, IT, Andrée Klein, FR, Ditte Lockhorst, NL
Rapporteur: Hubert Christiaen, BE
Detailed information about the project at: http://telematics.ex.ac.uk/T3/

5.1 The T3 project and questions it raised

The Telematics for Teacher Training project was a project where seven European partners worked together to develop online courses in the areas of mathematics, languages, science and technology. Also courses for teacher trainers, for primary teachers and librarians were developed. It was a project in the framework of the Telematics Application programme of the European Commission. The project started in 1996, when online courses on the World Wide Web were still rare. Nevertheless it was decided from the beginning to use the Web. Although the project finished at the end of 1998, the results are still available at the above website.

While the project was quite successful, Niki Davis from the University of Exeter, the first presenter via a video-conference link, warned against too rosy picture being painted. Projects such as these need a lot of collaboration and very explicit guidelines about how partners are to collaborate. The project developed new insights on aspects of pedagogy, networking and collaboration and management of change. At the end of the presentation the question was asked what had been the most difficult thing to do. Niki Davis answered creating a common meaning for terms. Niki Davis also argued that experts should also use the technology in a way which fits with the beliefs and the traditional way of acting of teachers.

The second presenter was Andrée Klein from the Institut Universitaire de Formation des Maîtres (IUFM), Grenoble, France. Her topic was New Roles of Learners and Teachers. From her experiences in the project she formulated some risks and needs of the autonomous learner. The main risks were isolation and 'the long distance runner syndrome'. To avoid this one should take care of:

- permanent technical support;
- pedagogical support: careful planning, reflection on collaborative knowledge;
- communicative support: the learners should describe to others what they do, confront their ideas with others and reconstruct their understanding about what they are studying.

Andrée left the audience with the following question: Should or could computers and conferencing software replace the social context of learning?

The third presenter was Donatella Persico from the Istituto Tecnologie Didaticche at Genoa, Italy, speaking on Social Structures for Virtual Learning Communities. From her experiences in running distance education courses she saw different structures arise between the participants and the tutors.

The first is the **dissemination model**. It is the closest to the face-to-face situation and characterised by a few students trained by tutors who are also the domain experts. The dominant communication is between the tutors and the trainees. The website is mainly an external resource of training material.

The second model is the **peer-tutoring model**. In this model tutors are not the experts in the domain. The website here had a more important role containing all the information on the course (goals, agenda, resources) Students work individually or in small groups following the activities of another student or group. This accounts for a domination of peer to peer communication. It allows a small group of tutors and experts to handle a relatively large group of trainees.

The third model is the **two-level model**. Here students are grouped locally, one of them acting as the local tutor. The participants are required to develop a project and have discussions with the other participants on methodological aspects. The website contains both learning material and dynamic course information. Remote tutors check and monitor the progress of the groups, providing them with learning material and encouraging discussions between the groups. Experts on the technical matters of the CMC environment assist in technical problems. Experts in the content domain could be consulted through the CMC system.

In this configuration communication took place both locally within each group and between groups at a distance. The existence of local groups allowed for the translation of course instructions and some material in the local language and to the adaptation of some guidelines to the local style of the students, which was felt of great importance for the success of some groups. This two-level model facilitated the communication between groups because the other groups and the remote tutors saw the groups as a single entity. It allowed for handling a high remote tutor/student ratio.

The question Donatella Persico asked at the end of her presentation was: what kind of virtual communities have you experienced and what comments do you have towards the advantages and drawbacks of different social structures?

The fourth presenter was Jyrki Pulkkinen, research manager at the University of Oulu, Finland. He spoke about the cultural context of web-based learning. In developing learning environments, mostly attention is given to learning theories and technology. The latter is usually considered as a neutral element although it influences the learning process and should rather be considered as an active component. The choice of technology to be used (e.g. chat versus email) will influence the learning process.

A third component, which should be considered, is the cultural dimension. Considering this component is really important for the adaptation of the learning situation to real life. In an international context there are many differences between participants, everybody bringing something of their own culture. In these circumstances, half a year is relatively short for forming a real learning community. There is a need for a common language, not only at the linguistic level but also at the semantic level. A better mastering of the common language (mostly English) may favour some participants and make them dominant in the exchanges. At the semantic level there is a need for having all participants giving the same meaning to terms.

The last presenter was Ditte Lockhorst from the IVLOS/Institute for Education, Utrecht University, the Netherlands. She put the four previous presentations in the perspective of one of the main evaluation research questions of the project: is there a European market for online teacher training? At the beginning of the project it was thought that this should be possible, but at the end there was much doubt about this. There are tremendous differences between the different countries. The are differences in national curricula, cultural differences, differences in pedagogical approaches, and technological thresholds. The international dimension of teacher training is still underdeveloped and in most places the initial teacher training is state owned. A commercial teacher training service would have to compete with subsidised organisations.

5.2 Issues from the discussion

The following issues were raised during the discussion: virtual communities and differing social structures; feedback from the trainees; computers and conferencing software and the social context of learning; and appropriate technologies for different cultures. Each is discussed in turn below.

Different nationalities react quite differently to a situation. When looking at a video of classroom activities, some participants found everything normal but people from other countries were horrified. Students from certain countries are accustomed to a non-directive style and start working immediately, while others started a discussion and needed some more detailed instructions to start working. The second run of some courses worked better after trainers had added extra instructions to address these differences.

Jyrki Pulkkinen mentioned a lot of technical problems, but most participants remained motivated and liked the way they could work autonomously and individually. In the beginning of one project a high dropout was noticed, but the participants who continued were very enthusiastic. But do we know how many drop out in the traditional setting? Evaluation of the courses was based on web-based questionnaires, interviews and the products delivered by the participants.

The impression was that the environments are not completely satisfactory and that new techniques or software is needed. There is a need in the group to feel like a community by the exchanges they have. The question was asked why we talk of 'web-based learning' but not of 'book-based learning'. A better term should be 'collaborative learning'.

There are different feelings about computers in different cultural contexts. For example, in developing countries teachers don't like a heavy use of computers. On the other hand most academics have rather a culture of writing and don't like video-conferencing.

Finally the remark was made that a lot of different technologies have been used in education, but that only the technologies which have had a commercial underpinning have survived. Education can not maintain technologies with constant subsidising unless they are technologies already in existence and use in other sectors in society.

6. EE-NET

Chair: Raymond Morel, CH
Presenters: Helmut Stemmer, AT, Vittorio Midoro, IT, Ella Kiesi, FI
Rapporteur: Pieter Hogenbirk, NL
Detailed information about the project at: www.ecmc.de/eenet/nav.html

EE-net stands for European Experts' Network for Educational Technology. It consists of individual members of 13 European countries. Its mission is to spread knowledge about multimedia and ICT use in education in order to promote individual growth and European co-operation, and develop competitiveness. EE-net produces a series of reports that aim to:
- highlight main issues of ICT policy and its implementation;
- disseminate effective implementation strategies and show barriers to progress;
- provide a critical overview of the challenges and implications confronting the development of ICT in education within Europe;
- where there is evidence, show the effects of introducing new digital technologies into education on learning and its organisation.

The first report of EE-net covers ICT in education policy. It is an analysis of policies and actions designed to implement new technologies in education systems, mainly at school level, in countries across Europe. The report is available on the web: http://www.becta.org.uk/Eenet. In the panel session the 9 recommendations in this report were presented and discussed.

6.1 A holistic approach to policy development

"A holistic model for policy development for ICT in schools, should be considered by policy makers. Future innovation needs to involve all players in the education system, including the public and private sector." It was clarified that this recommendation involves producers of hardware, software, teacher trainers, curriculum developers, schools, teachers, local communities and the government. Also the relationship between all these sectors should be addressed. If you start, as many countries do, only with the supply of hardware, it does not work. Also the holistic approach should apply to schools. It was recognised however that every sector has its own responsibility, so the governments should aim at commitment from the different sectors, rather than prescribing things to one of them, for example, the schools.

6.2 A bottom-up / top-down convergence

"For teachers to take ownership and implementation ICT strategies effectively, policy makers should listen and respond to successful and appropriate ICT developments which start at the school level, when developing large-scale policies." It was agreed that the school level is very important. In examples of successful practices you should very carefully analyse which underlying conditions were favourable for this success. That could help to define the elements of the top-down measures, leaving the core of the process with the schools. There was a support for the idea not to develop in depth with model schools, but directly going for a broad approach. One other idea is to give grants for those schools which want to implement ICT, in exchange for sharing their ideas with others.

6.3 Sustainability

"Policies and strategies for implementation should be designed to achieve the sustainable and generalisable use of ICT in education. It should be borne in mind that sustainability can only be achieved through a synthesis of economic and human measures." Governments and local authorities should provide initial money for ICT in schools. But even more importantly, they should provide structural funds for maintenance and replacement. In that way ICT can be considered as a normal financial element of the school budgets.

6.4 The curriculum

"Ideally, comprehensive plans for implementing ICTs should start with learning targets related to the curriculum. Linked to this, examination and assessment systems should be reviewed to ensure that they are appropriate to the digital age." To integrate ICT into the learning targets would be a start, but at the same time it is important to improve the quality of education, didactics and pedagogy itself by ICT. In order to force teachers to really cover the ICT learning targets, the examination system should indeed be changed.

6.5 Teacher training

"Specific measures need to be taken to ensure that ICT use is covered in all pre-service training courses and that all serving teachers have access to appropriate in-service training that responds to their individual needs." Especially for the in-service training this is a real bottle-neck, because teachers are often themselves responsible for their training. Schools and government can only influence these matters by giving credits or incentives.

Also it was mentioned that in-service and pre-service training should be have much the same goals and training aspects.

6.6 A wider concept of learning

"Policies and implementation actions need to recognise the wider concept of learning that generalised ICT use will bring and should reflect the consequential empowerment of the learner that is likely to take place. This empowerment will demand new and more subtle skills from teachers as they are less able to rely upon the formal didactic aspects of their role." Some people were favouring the wider concept of learning as the key element of teacher training. This has to do with the 'new' role of the teacher, however there was a preference to speak about an 'extended', or better, 'redefined' role. There was an agreement to link this recommendation strongly to the previous recommendation.

6.7 The importance of research

"Decision makers at all levels must take more account of existing educational research, within Europe and beyond, when formulating their educational policies and actions. Research on new topics with relevance for this area should also be initiated. Consideration should also be given to the literature on innovation and change at organisational level." This was agreed upon, with the suggestion to combine ICT research with other educational research.

6.8 Content and national languages

"Most countries need to address the issue of the shortage of Multimedia and Web-based content for educational use in national languages. It may in some cases require government pump-priming to stimulate market activity and it is sensible to encourage commercial developers to use teachers and others as advisors or to help at the trialling stage." It was mentioned that financing the development of software by the government often leads to experimental products, which are not commonly used. Two suggestions were given: solve the problem of copyright on materials which could be used in educational settings and stimulate software developers to invest in translation of foreign software.

6.9 Evaluation

"Central ministries and regional authorities should co-operate in gathering, analysing and disseminating data, not only on inputs into the system such as pupil/computer ratios, but also on process variables such as development and pupil/teacher access times and actual outcomes." There was a full agreement on this recommendation. EE-net wants to continue the job (which was supported by the audience). There will be more emphasis on certain themes. Furthermore EE-net wants to design and fill a database with the aspects and figures of all the nations involved.

7. THE NORDIC EXPERIENCE

Chair: Mike Aston, UK
Presenters: Peter Bollerslev, DK, Matti Sinko FI, Anna Kristiandottir, IS, Sindre Røsvik, NO, Kersti Hjertquist, SE, Ulf Vastrom, DK,
Rapporteur: Erling Schmidt, DK

The chair, Mike Aston, opened the session by noting that the Nordic countries have an unique tradition for working together and co-operating on matters of culture and education. One of the areas for such collaboration is ICT in schools where a special unit has been formed under Nordic Council of Ministers. The Nordic Countries also have an especially good background for sharing ideas and inspiration on ICT in schools as the education systems in the different countries share common structures and traditions.

7.1 Denmark (Peter Bollerslev)

ICT is now integrated cross curriculum and on all levels in schools. The latest action plan for ICT in schools is a 'rolling plan' covering year 1998 - 2003 to be revised in 2000. The plan deals with five central areas – each with its own goals and actions:

- Students and ICT;
- Teachers and ICT;
- Subject and ICT;
- Equal and flexible access to lifelong education;
- Co-ordination of ICT-based research and education.

Peter Bollerslev also drew attention to the fact, that what goes on in schools reflects the general development in society, and he presented some intriguing statistical background for this:

- 3% of IT investment in Denmark is connected with education;
- 52% of homes have a PC;
- 31% have access to the Internet;
- the use of PC's and Internet in homes rises with level of education.

7.2 Finland (Matti Sinko)

All the Nordic countries are relatively small and have thereby been forced to co-operate. But at the same time there has been a brotherly competition which also has stimulated development. Nordic countries have been able to share and learn from one another. The use of ICT itself has also structured co-operation moving from traditional conferences to sharing experiences continuously through networking. The collaboration has especially been successful in opening a door to developing a design for learning environments with ICT and also sharing programmes between the Nordic countries on the basis of 'give 4 and receive 16'.

There have been two major problems emerging from the Nordic Council of Ministers educational ICT initiatives. What has been done by the Nordic task force has been superb and unique, but the level of resources available for joint efforts has been so minimal that the impacts inevitably have been crucial for the educational ICT development in Nordic countries. This has been mainly due to lack of co-ordination and continuity on a national level in each of the countries.

7.3 Iceland (Anna Kristiansdottir)

Many activities with ICT in schools started earlier but were co-ordinated with a government plan for 1996-1999. Iceland is in a remarkable position in that 69% of all homes have a PC and 61% have access to Internet. The Icelandic Schoolnet started in 1991 through the private initiatives of a teacher, but was taken over by Iceland University of Education in 1996. The government is supporting integration of ICT into the whole community by providing special grants for the years 1999-2004.

7.4 Norway (Sindre Røsvik)

Norway has also integrated ICT in all plans for schools. It is considered important that all teachers and students become effective users of ICT, but it is also recognised that this has to happen with some economic constraints. Students should learn to use ICT to extend their learning both on subject matters and on methods of working. The main challenges for further development will be to support the teachers and activities in schools. It also calls for better administrative and political planning on all levels of education.

7.5 Sweden (Kersti Hjertquist)

Since 1983 the Swedish government has funded large national initiatives on ICT in schools. In 1995 a foundation was established to promote

'Knowledge and Competence' on ICT in the whole school system. Through the years there has been a systematic effort to update the school system with teacher training, computer hardware and infrastructure. And yet today, the traditional pattern of 'one teacher using one book in one lesson in one class' still persists. The governmental initiative continues and now 60.000 teachers (1/3 of all teachers in Sweden) are participating in an in-service training programme which includes providing each teacher with a PC at home. The project deals with cross curriculum work using ICT in the classroom and is supported by facilitators coming to the schools. For basic computer skills, each school has to teach their own teachers. A major outcome of these initiatives is for all students to take responsibility for their own learning and to develop a passion for lifelong learning.

7.6 Nordic Council of Ministers (Ulf Vasstrom)

The collaboration between the Nordic countries has been supported by a formal organisation for more than 15 years. Since 1995 it has been the IDUN project: Nordic Co-operation on Information Technology and Didactics in Education which from 1999 shall be continued as IDUN II. The proposal for the IDUN II programme focuses on four key areas: innovative school environments, IT in teacher education, the education and training of adults and flexible learning. It is considered important that IT collaboration in education be an integral part of the general Nordic co-operation in education. With its focus on three sub-projects clearly linked to educational levels in the organisation of educational co-operation, the proposed structure does not mean that inter-sectorial collaboration and its potential for synergies will be lost. The three sub-projects will therefore have to be organised to ensure optimal interplay within the framework of the activities of IDUN II.

7.7 Discussion

Erik Dam, Denmark: With networks on all levels – local, national, Nordic, European and worldwide I am confronted with a problem where to put my ideas and take part in discussions. What is being done to connect such levels of information sharing? Ulf Vasstrom: It is most important that the national network is working and is connected to others' networks. Jiqing Wang, China: The Nordic collaboration is a nice project but would it continue without special funding? Ulf Vasstrom: I think so. Our budget is low – only 500.000 USD. Sindre Rosvik: Much is depending on national funding, which in fact is available. Jiqing Wang, China: How many courses are available? Ulf Vasstrom: We are sponsoring about 25 courses per year.

Mike Aston: And the good thing is, that practitioners are participating – not politicians!

8. FINNISH PROJECTS

In their presentation Matti Sinko and Ella Kiesi provided a background and a framework for the presentation of a number of Finnish projects in ComNEd. The core problem of ICT in Finnish education as in any country is scaling up individual innovative practices. The projects presented should be understood as examples of such emerging good practices identified.

8.1 Matilda-Telematic Literature

Chair: Liisa Huovinen, FI
Presenter: Minttu Ollila, FI
Rapporteur: Lisbeth Appelberg, SE

Matilda is a Finnish online project for young book-lovers. The name of the group comes from Roald Dahl's book *Matilda.* A selected group of primary school children study literature in virtual study groups. They read two books a month and they discuss the books and exchange ideas by using the Matilda website (http://www.edu.espoo.fi/~matilda/) and email. Every school which takes part in Matilda has a teacher who works as a tutor. Teachers work with a home group of 8 students from 3–4 different schools. The Matilda website contains information about the reading programme and the assignments. Books are divided into eight categories according to their contents.

Everybody reads the'Book of the Month' chosen by the students. In addition to that, each student chooses one optional book from the same category. The students keep journals while reading the books. The idea is to reflect one`s ideas and feelings in the journal and then share the impressions with the group by exchanging email. After reading a book the students send their assignment to the home group and tutor. Every student gets personal feedback from the tutor. The students are encouraged to comment on each others' ideas in order to have true interaction within the home group. In 1997-1998 there were 32 Matilda students from 6 different schools. This year there are more than 80 students from 11 schools and next year there will be even more students and schools taking part in the project.

In the presentation of the project Minttu Ollila pointed out some interesting outcomes of the project. These were that the students had really become interested in reading a broad variety of books and they also became ardent readers. In the beginning there were mainly girls taking part in the project but after a while the boys also became interested and some of them thought they had found a new world. Today the teachers have started other projects for 'booklovers'. They are *Literature happenings* and *Literature theme days.* For example, students dress up as characters from 'Alice in Wonderland' and go out in the forest and build up the story very much like the adventures happening in the story. Another example is 'Chamber of Horrors'. These are all planned by the students and many things are presented to the students in the lower grades. Minttu Ollila also mentioned that the face-to-face meetings for the virtual home groups 4–6 times per year had been of great importance.

Jaana Ikkala, Iiramaria Ojanen and Le The Cam Van, three students who had been in the project were in the panel to answer questions from the audience. All three of them thought that the project had been of great benefit and that the timetable concerning their work had been well organised. The teachers were very positive as well and the project is now growing faster than ever before. There are currently 20 schools involved from all over Finland.

8.2 The teacher's changing role in Kaukajärvi Lower Secondary School

Chair: Martti Piipari, FI
Presenter: Jari Ikola, FI
Rapporteur: Lisbeth Appelberg, SE

Kaukajärvi School has been engaged in a distance learning project from 1995 to 1998. This school has been working with distance learning, telecommunications applications and producing teaching material. Partners during the project were Digital Media Institute of Tampere University of Technology, Nokia Research Centre, Sonera, the Teacher Training School of the University of Tampere and hardware manufacturers. The aims of the project include increasing interaction, creating new learning environments, improving civic skills, developing multimedia material and utilising telecommunication applications.

The technical applications that have been used are video-conferencing via ATM, video-conferencing via ISDN, and video on demand.

The co-operation with the universities has been seen as very important as there was a need for scientific research. The advantages of networking included: it was easy to use, it increased international contacts, it increased contact with parents, and it increased co-operation with the surrounding community. It has also been a channel for advertising and has had an effect on the school's role and function.

8.2.1 Elementary course in Russian between Kaukajärvi School and the Teacher Training School of the University of Tampere

This project involved a distance-learning elementary course in Russian between Kaukajärvi School and the Teacher Training School of the University of Tampere. The on-site class with the teacher was at the teacher training school. The remote class with six students was at Kaukajärvi School. As the students were not familiar with the equipment there was a technical assistant from Tampere University of Technology responsible for the computers and the video camera. The assistant also monitored and supported the group activities. The electronic learning material was mainly transmitted by using NetMeeting since email turned out to be too complicated. Russian was certainly not the easiest subject as a first trial in distance learning. To learn the Cyrillic alphabet and the pronunciation was not an easy task but the students did quite well considering the circumstances. This project helped to diminish prejudices against distance learning and encouraged teachers in other subjects to work in distance courses.

8.2.2 Distance learning of mathematics

One of the courses where they have used modern information technology to deliver distance learning at Kaukajärvi Lower Secondary School is mathematics. The project concentrated on the organisation of the course, the learning processes used for distance learning, the learning outcomes in Mathematics and ICT, the learner's motivation and the role of the teacher. Key aims of the project were to test the net and the suitability of different support programmes in studying mathematics as well as to revise and deepen the students' mathematical skills. The course content includes classroom studies and work at home. During six classroom lessons, the students were introduced to and worked with the programmes that they would use at home on their own computers. After this, there were 12 lessons delivered in distance learning mode. During the whole period there were two double lessons per week. In the beginning of the distance learning period the students were in contact with the teacher via Netmeeting. The teacher also sent exercises to the students via this mode. The students used the mathematical programme Ahjo to solve the problems. They were able to check their answers and if they had any problems they contacted the teacher via Netmeeting or the Ahjo-window. Using the Ahjo-window the teacher could see what the students had done and could give advice on how to proceed.

As there was not much material available the teacher had to prepare a lot of new material. The teacher also had to take in consideration the different level of the students and give them suitable exercises. There were some technical problems during the course but these were discussed and solved. The presenter told the audience that the students have been satisfied with the courses and it has been a challenge to the teacher as well. The students and the teachers have been solving problems together which illustrates a different way of teaching and learning. As a result of the project the school has changed the curriculum.

8.3 FLE-tools: A World Wide Web-based application for collaborative learning

Chair: Liisa Huovinen, FI
Presenter: Teemu Leinonen, FI
Rapporteur: Anna Kristiansdottir, IS

The Future Learning Environment (FLE) is an ambitious research and development project initiated by the Media Lab at the University of Art and Design in Helsinki (UADH). Research partners are from the Research Group of Applied Cognitive Science, Department of Psychology and also the Media Education Centre of the Department of Teacher Education, both at the University of Helsinki. The project has received financial support from the government as well as industry.

The aim of FLE is to explore the use of new media within learning, by generating a rich innovative learning environment and methods based on recent cognitive research and study of learning. The three research partners are focusing differently according to their particular research interest and educational activities. Some of the students who are trying out the FLE are working towards a Ph.D. or already University teachers, others are in their Masters studies. Having such a high quality of students the project is based on self-reliance, the students interact in a variety of ways with their teachers, tutors and each other.

Theoretically the FLE project refers to and makes use of the Inquiry Learning Process (Muukkonen, 1998) thereby supporting collaborative problem-solving, collaborative evaluation and development of metacognitive skills. The first Internet version, an inside prototype, was published in the beginning of 1999 including what is called FLE-tools which contain the following modules:

- **Webtop**, personal desktop in the web.
- **Discussion** for collaborate problem solving, knowledge construction and knowledge sharing.
- **Jam Session** for collaborative construction of artefacts. Creating and changing the model takes place here.

- **Library** intended for publishing and browsing multimedia learning materials. Every participant can add links to the library.
- **Administration** which includes tools for administers users and groups.

FLE has a web-site. The URL is: http://mlab.uiah.fi/fle/ Further information about the public admission will be found on this site as the project runs into further stages.

8.4 Creating and developing a centre for distance education

Chair: Leena Vainio, FI
Presenters: Erkki Pitkanen and Paivio Peltokorpi, FI
Rapporteur: Anna Kristiansdottir, IS

The Centre for Distance Education is placed at the University of Jyväskylä and runs a service to teachers in the surrounding area and for students there in upper secondary schools and primary schools. There is a co-operation with the Finnish National Board of Education which is the primary financial supporter of the project. This project is running in accordance with the programme for an information society developed by the Ministry of Education and the National Board of Education.

It can be said that this project takes pride in using what is already available and possible and to allow teachers and students around the University of Jyväskylä to benefit from the equipment, wealth of resource found on the University computer and human expertise at the university. By this project the following was thus considered of great importance:

- Multivariate learning environment, accessible even by means of a modem and a basic PC.
- Distance learning should be possible without video conferencing.
- An easy way should be offered, versatile resources and computer technology expertise of the centre to remote users.
- It should be inexpensive to become a user.
- No special skills in computer technology should be needed, everyday applications offered for use.
- The centre should be a pedagogically functioning entity.

Courses available from the centre include philosophy, French, history and mathematics. Furthermore one student who moved to USA could through the service of the centre continue studying with his Finnish classmates. The centre has made it possible to open up for new optional subjects for primary school students in the areas, made interaction with distant classmates virtually real and helped students to increase social skills, initiativeness, responsibility and communication. The students have been enthusiastic and made many new contacts. There have been some technical drawbacks with weak sound quality and time consuming explanations and instruction. This is being looked into to develop the work further. The centre has a website whose URL is: http://www.norssi.jyu.fi

8.5 NetD@ys in Finland

Chair:Martti Pipari, FI
Presenter: Riitta Karvinen, FI
Rapporteur: Lisbeth Appelberg, SE

NetD@ys started in Silicon Valley in 1996 as a project to have schools working on the Internet in a friendly learning network. NetD@ys Europe 1998 was presumed to be the largest educational technology event in Europe. Approximately 35 000 schools participated in the project and organised various activities. According to the analysis approximately 77% of the projects focused on facilitating awareness of the pedagogical possibilities offered by ICT and the Internet. Many of the projects focused on facilitating the acquisition of subject-matter knowledge. Others represented initial attempts at starting to use ICT in some specific educational environments. Students who took part in the project found the use of ICT very motivating . It is now important not only to focus on improving students' and teachers' technical skills but also to guide them to use ICT as a tool for teaching and learning.

NetD@ys 99 will be held from 13–21 November 1999. The opening events will be arranged in Helsinki on the 12 November and it will be possible to follow on the Web, radio and TV. There will be a great number of projects from many countries. These include Mediterranean cooking, The circus is in town!, Europe goes opera, Internet del Arte, This is no normal museum, Learning science is fun, Space fun, and Where was my town three centuries ago? More information on these events can be obtained from the NetD@ys Europe 99 site: www.netdays99.org

8.6 Flexible learning over the high speed Internet Web University

Chair: Matti Sinko, FI
Presenter: Riita Rinta-Filppula, FI
Rapporteur: Anna Kristiansdottir, IS

Web University (WU) started in 1996 as an international co-operative pilot project between CERN (European Laboratory Particle Physics) and Finnish universities. Since 1997 a collaboration has taken place with the Finnish Distance Learning in Multimedia Network project (ETÄKAMU). The project has on its agenda to trial out high technology for work of researchers, teaching and learning in an international networked environment. It has since 1996 extended its transmissions to Holland, Italy and Slovak.

WU has developed and explored working, teaching and learning methods in an international network environment. Students have been able to select spesialised seminars agreed by the local professors to be a part of their studies and researchers have had opportunity for distance work and collaboration as well as tailored in-service courses. Transmissions are real-time and selected seminars and lectures are available as videos on demand. These are provided by the Wrtp project developed at the IT/CS Group.

Among the pedagogically important conclusions are the importance of preparing sessions well in advance; distributing presentation material before sessions via WWW, giving learners time to adapt go the new learning situation, having credits as a motivation for undergraduate students and the latest research results for the post graduates. Among areas to give future attention are content production and development and adaptation of group work methods to new high speed network tools. Further information: Riitta.Rinta-Filppula@cern.ch

PART 3

MODELS AND ISSUES IN NETWORKED LEARNING

A model for the study and design of teaching situations with ICT

Steve Kennewell, Howard Tanner and John Parkinson
Department of Education, University of Wales Swansea, Swansea SA2 7NB, UK.
s.e.kennewell@swansea.ac.uk

Keywords: learning theory, affordance, pedagogy, evaluation

Abstract: Any situation in which activity takes place provides *affordances* for the activity. We use this idea first to characterise learning, and then to discuss the way in which the educational environment is manipulated by the effective teacher in order to foster learning. ICT provides some particular affordances which successful teachers exploit in their classroom practice, and the use of an affordance model helps us to analyse the pedagogy involved. We provide a number of practical illustrations and draw general conclusions concerning the effective use of ICT in teaching and learning.

1. INTRODUCTION

During the first 20 years of microcomputers in education, much has been achieved by enthusiastic teachers who have recognised the power of the medium of ICT in their teaching. As the medium becomes as pervasive in schools as it is in other walks of life, we expect its features to be harnessed by all teachers in order to help promote learning.

Mere exposure to a medium is not, however, any guarantee that learning will occur. Saloman (1997), while examining how various media influence the representation of information, points out that children perceive TV as a medium to be fun, simple, and useless. Consequently they learn nothing from it, unless they are told that learning is expected of them. This is in contrast to the early days of TV, when it was perceived as a serious medium, and much learning took place.

As ICT becomes a natural feature of children's lives, we can observe that ICT, too, is seen as simple and fun. There are already signs (Robertson 1997) that ICT may have a similarly impoverished relationship to learning at the start of the 21st century that TV has had towards the end of the 20th. Teachers must therefore manage the use instructional use of ICT carefully if it is to fulfil our current expectations.

The importance of pedagogy in the study of ICT and learning has been highlighted in research (Somekh and Davies 1991; Kennewell 1997) and in UK government policy (TTA 1998). However, our ability to characterise the teacher's contribution to the ICT learning situation has been hampered by the lack of an adequate framework for analysis. Traditional models of instructional design and evaluation for ICT are based on rationalist assumptions about educational objectives and teacher planning, together with positivist ideas about the relationship between instructional material and individual cognition. Squires and MacDougall (1994) have highlighted the inadequacies of traditional models, and have developed instead the Perspectives Interaction Paradigm for evaluating educational software. Crook (1991) argues for the application of cultural psychology if we are to evaluate computer-based interventions effectively:

> To be valuable, an evaluation must be sufficiently open-ended to unravel *what* is being learned and *where* the learning is located. (1991:82)

We have refined these interpretivist ideas to create a framework which takes into account the whole of the environment in which the learner and the computer are situated – the teacher, the other resources, the other learners, and the cultural context, as well as the knowledge that the individual brings to the classroom.

We first explain some of the terminology and relationships that we have found useful, and then illustrate how they can be used to interpret some particular didactic situations.

2. ACTIVITY SITUATIONS, AFFORDANCES AND ABILITIES

An activity situation comprises a person, some activity involving the person, and the environment in which this activity takes place. When studying an educational activity situation, we can focus our analysis on the individual learner, on the situation as a whole, or on the *interaction* between the individual and the environment during an activity In this paper, we will take the interaction as the focus of analysis.

We will thus consider the relationship between:

- the individual learners – their cognitive and metacognitive skills, their concepts, their attitudes, and their goals;
- the environment in which the individual is situated – the location; the resources available; the other people involved such as the teacher and classmates.

Teachers are in a special position in the classroom, of course. They have some choice concerning what role to adopt, what the relative roles of pupils will be, what resources should be made available, and even the location. Other students, too, have an important influence over an individual's learning, but we will not be able to focus on this factor here.

We assume that the cognitive contribution which an individual brings to an activity is not fixed; it is dependent upon the particular features of the environment in which the activity is situated. Greeno (1994) uses Gibson's (1986) idea of *affordances* for the properties of the environment, and suggests the term *abilities* for the individual's potential to act within the environment. An activity will be completed satisfactorily if the individual's abilities are sufficient in combination with the affordances of the situation to enable the desired outcomes to be achieved.

We find it helpful to extend the idea of affordance to cover intentional support in social situations: thus we include the informal notions of help and guidance, and the more formal neo-Vygotskyan ideas of *scaffolding* (Bruner 1986); *assisted performance* (Tharp and Gallimore 1988); and *contingent support for learning* (Wood and Wood 1996). Abilities are also related to more familiar ideas: those of knowledge, skills and understanding. They should not be identified with an immutable 'intelligence', however.

3. LEARNING AND TEACHING

It is beyond the scope of this paper to consider abilities and how they develop in detail, but we do need to consider how to characterise *learning* in this perspective. We consider that learning has taken place *when an individual's abilities change in some way.* We cannot determine directly whether someone has learned anything in a particular situation, but we can characterise the changes observed in their future activity in situations with similar or reduced affordances. Clearly, then, we are adopting a *situative* view of learning (Greeno and Moore 1993).

It is quite possible, of course, for an activity (whether successful or unsuccessful) to result in no learning at all. In educational contexts, however, we presume that there is some expectation that learning *will* take place, and that teachers devise classroom situations with the intention of promoting learning. We will call these didactic situations.

Teachers typically plan, implicitly or explicitly, to manipulate the didactic situation so that:

1. the affordances are initially insufficient to enable the learners to be successful in their activity on the basis of their current abilities;
2. the affordances can then be increased by the teacher to enable the learners to succeed – an information sheet, a calculator, simpler language, a question, a demonstration, an analogy, a brainstorm, a discussion group, pairing with a more able student;
3. learners' abilities will change as a result of this experience.

Thus, when a didactic situation involves computer use, we need to consider: what the computer affords the learner in carrying out activities; how the computer's affordances relate to other affordances of the didactic situation; how the affordances may be manipulated by the teacher so as to promote learning.

In England, the Teacher Training Agency (TTA 1998) requires newly qualifying teachers to know:

> the features of ICT which can be used ... to support teaching and learning in subjects, including:
>
> – speed and automatic functions ...
> – capacity and range ...
> – provisionality ...
> – interactivity ... (1998:14-15)

In the following two sections, we shall examine some examples of didactic situations which we have recently observed. We consider:

- how the above features of ICT which afford certain aspects of activity in the typical classroom;
- how ICT relates to other affordances;
- how learning is promoted.

Our focus is on the teacher, students and computers in this analysis, although the school culture, the location, and other resources in the classroom all have some influence on the learning which takes place.

4. EXAMPLES OF ICT'S ROLE IN DIDACTIC SITUATIONS

4.1 Situation 1: Simulation

Students studying Roman life are using a multimedia simulation programme. They have to play the role of a Roman citizen, carrying out a trade in order to earn money, making decisions what to buy in order to provide for their families, and moving around the town to find the relevant shops and services they need. They achieve these simulated actions by clicking on appropriate screen images.

ICT affords cues and prompts for their decision making – options represented visually on screen, oral explanations of matters through headphones, graphics of money available and costs of products. It affords planning and evaluation of progress in the task, through structuring their environment, displaying quantities visually, and limiting their decisions if they attempt an action which the rules of the simulation do not allow.

4.2 Situation 2: Multimedia database

Pupils are using a multimedia CD-ROM on world religions to answer questions on a printed worksheet concerning Judaism and Islam. The questions are structured so that the first few require simple factual answers, the next ones require explanations, and the final ones require comparative discussion.

The computer affords selection of information for the factual questions through hierarchical searching or keyword searching with Boolean logic. These techniques require some abilities in search strategies from the students, and little success will be gained from trying to look at all the information haphazardly.

4.3 Situation 3: Desk top publishing

A group of students are working individually on a class of designing a logo for a business which they have selected for a marketing simulation. In the same class, another group is working on the same class with manual equipment.

The computer affords:

- the drawing of a number of pre-defined shapes, line styles, shadings;
- the writing of text in a variety of sizes and coherent, accurate type faces;
- the deletion, movement, and copying of any particular feature of the drawing;

– the reflection of part of the drawing in order to achieve symmetry.

It also affords the selection of these facilities by providing symbols on the screen and menu headings which just have to be clicked to implement a feature or to choose an operation. It affords errors, of course, but it also affords instant 'undoability'. Above all, then, it affords experimentation.

4.4 Situation 4: Arithmetic skills tutor

Some students with learning difficulties are using software designed to develop their arithmetic skills. They are presented with subtraction sums set out to be solved by a standard written algorithm.

The students are first provided with a calculation to work out. They type in an answer, and if it is considered correct by the software, they receive a reassuring message. More calculations are provided in a graded sequence which covers most common errors in the intended algorithm. When they go wrong, the computer prompts them to check whether their answers are reasonable and gives them a chance to correct their working. If they still go wrong, the computer increases the affordances for carrying out the algorithm correctly. It prompts to write their working figures in suitable places, and if they write in an incorrect figure, the computer displays a clear message about their mistake and prompts them to try again. When they do this correctly, the affordance is reduced again.

4.5 Situation 5: Word processing

A class learning German as a foreign language is producing tourist information, in the target language, concerning a particular town which they are using as a setting for role plays, comprehension exercises and narrative writing. Using ICT, the students work in pairs to type in their first thoughts on what to write and then they check that the language is correct: the computer affords continuous evaluation of the text by the authors.

This could be supplemented using a spelling and grammar checker, but the teacher has found that these tools afford acceptance of inappropriate suggestions. They often lead the students often to change a word which was spelt only slightly wrongly into a completely different word. Furthermore, the computer's comments on grammar are not helpful to students with only a limited range of constructions. So instead, the teacher checks all pupils' work at each stage of development so that he can provide carefully targeted affordances for correction.

The teacher is expecting students to use a wide range of vocabulary and grammatical construction because the text is provisional: the computer affords 'editability'. When the language is correct, the students design the layout, import pictures, adjust the font and size, and print their professional-looking brochure. The computer affords effective presentation.

5. LEARNING WITH ICT

In Situation 1, the students are encountering aspects of Roman life through their surrogate experience. The intention of the software author is that, in order to prosper in this virtual world, they should understand certain relationships between the Roman people and their environment. A successful route through the simulation may be devised through the trial and error involved in the initial exploration, but the intended learning is only likely to arise through strategic thinking and discussion. This is afforded in two ways which do not depend on the computer: first, students are required to work in pairs or threes, so that decisions have to be discussed and justified to others; secondly, the teacher intervenes to ask questions concerning what they have found out and what they plan to try. These questions can direct the learners very generally or quite specifically, depending on the minimum degree of affordance the teacher decides will stimulate learning.

In Situation 2, there are two aspects to the learning. The first one is the factual detail of the two religions, their similarities and differences, their origins and development. Basic facts are unlikely to be retained from the simple experience of retrieving them from the CD-ROM and writing them down: the affordance for access is too high. Comparison and explanation, on the other hand, may be afforded by the computer to students who would find such analysis impossible using traditional linear text.

The second aspect is the process of enquiry from a large database. The computer affords the narrowing down or expansion of a search by means of Boolean operations. The students are unlikely to learn this naturally, however, because they are already able to search visually through text. Since the computer affords this visual searching by displaying easily readable sections of text and providing a familiar navigation procedure, there is no need for them to expend the mental effort required to use the search features. The teacher, then, must provide initially the strategic thinking which affords effective use of search techniques.

In Situation 3, similarly, there are two aspects to the learning: design concepts and CAD software techniques. There is a complex interplay between the two. The design skills are learned more easily through the CAD software which provides much greater affordances for the drawing process than the manual techniques. But the CAD software is not trivial, and some drawing abilities are not easily developed merely by attempting to apply the software features to tasks. The teacher thus stops the students at carefully judged moments in order to demonstrate particular features and explains how to use them purposefully in design. This demonstration and explanation affords application of the features to subsequent tasks.

In Situation 4, the computer itself is programmed with a mechanism for adjusting affordances so as to set tasks just ahead of the student's abilities. Whilst this may aid the memorisation of specific arithmetic techniques, it is more difficult to explain how such a mechanism could handle conceptual development. This is a more complex matter for which the expert teacher has a rich, extensive repertoire of activities and affordances, well-tuned to the ways in which learners think.

In Situation 5, the students are learning a greater range of language because they do not feel limited to the words and constructions which they already know well. Their goals can be set at a higher level without leading to conspicuous failure, because the computer affords the editing of text and the teacher can talk in terms of developing their work rather than correcting their errors.

6. CONCLUSION

Our illustrations show how didactic decision making can be represented using the constructs of affordances and abilities. We have considered how ICT can afford aspects of student activity, and what affects this may have on learning. In order to promote effective learning, the teacher sets tasks which are beyond the students' current abilities, and uses affordances to narrow the gap to one which the students can bridge themselves with some 'mental effort' (Saloman 1997). The computer's value is in the range of affordances for *activity* it can provide; the teacher's role is to manipulate the activities and affordances in order to promote *learning*.

If the affordances which the computer provides are not carefully judged, they may actually restrict the development of the intended abilities. This happens in the following circumstances.

1. The computer makes the task trivial, so that no mental effort is required and no learning is likely to take place.
2. The students may not have the abilities required to operate the computer as intended. In this case, instead of support for an activity, we have the 'IT interference factor' (Birnbaum 1990), and again there may be little or no learning.
3. Learning does take place, but the abilities developed are dependent on access to the computer. If the aim is develop conceptual abilities which

can be utilised in non-computer contexts, then the teacher will need to design further didactic situations in which the computer is not used.

Our framework for analysis and planning of didactic situations is based on teachers' familiar practices – creating learning environments, designing and setting tasks, and interacting with students to manage their learning. The framework is sufficiently powerful to help describe and explain the processes we observe in the classroom, sufficiently general to incorporate the special role which ICT has in the learning process, and sufficiently practical to help teachers plan effective lessons.

REFERENCES

Bruner, J. (1986) *Actual minds, possible worlds.* Cambridge: Harvard University Press.

Crook, C. (1991) Computers in the zone of proximal development: Implication for evaluation. *Computers and Education* 17(1) 81-91.

Gibson, J. J. (1986) *The ecological approach to visual perception.* Hillsdale, NJ: Lawrence Erlbaum Associates.

Greeno, J. (1994) Gibson's affordances. *Psychological Review* 101(1) 336-342.

Greeno, J. and Moore, J. (1993) Situativity and symbols: Response to Vera & Simon. *Cognitive Science* 17, 49-59.

Kennewell, S. (1997). The integration of information technology into teachers' decision-making. In D. Passey and B. Samways (eds.) *Information technology: Supporting change through teacher education.* London: Chapman and Hall.

Robertson, J. (1998) Paradise lost: Children, multimedia and the myth of interactivity. *Journal of Computer Assisted Learning* 14(1) 31-39.

Saloman, G. (1997) Of mind and media. *Phi Delta Kappan* January 1997, 375-380.

Somekh, B. and Davies, R. (1991) Towards a pedagogy for information technology. *Curriculum Journal* 2(2) 153-168.

Squires, D. and MacDougall, A. (1994) *Choosing and using educational software.* London: Falmer Press.

Tharp, R. and Gallimore, R. (1988) *Rousing minds to life.* Cambridge: Cambridge University Press.

TTA (1998) *The use of ICT in subject teaching: Expected outcomes for teachers.* London: Teacher Training Agency.

Wood, D. and Wood, H. (1996) Contingency in teaching and learning. *Learning and Instruction* 6(4) 391-397.

BIOGRAPHIES

Steve Kennewell taught mathematics and computing in secondary schools, then worked as a specialist computing teacher and IT Advisory teacher. Since 1990, he has been at the University of Wales Swansea. He teaches initial teacher training courses in mathematics and in IT as a subject, and Masters' courses in teaching and learning. His research interests include the development of IT capability and IT in mathematics education. He is joint editor of the journal Computer Education.

John Parkinson taught chemistry in secondary schools in England and Wales for eight years before joining the Education Department at the University of Wales Swansea. He presently teaches on the Postgraduate Certificate in Education and Masters' degree courses and is responsible for supervising PhD students. His main areas of research include the study of pupils' attitudes towards science and ICT, and the development of ICT across the curriculum.

Howard Tanner taught Mathematics and IT in secondary schools for sixteen years before joining the Education Department in the University of Wales Swansea. He has been involved in several nationally funded research projects concerning the teaching and learning of mathematics and the development of IT capability. He is particularly interested in the impact of ICT on styles of teaching and learning.

Modelling online education

Vittorio Midoro
Istituto Tecnologie Didattiche, Consiglio Nazionale delle Ricerche, Via de Marini 6, 16149 Genova, Italy. midoro@itd.ge.cnr.it

Keywords: online education, modelling, virtual community, online courses, communication technology

Abstract: In this paper a model of an online education system is proposed. The proposed model involves three basic elements: a virtual community (composed of learners, tutors, technical support staff, experts and observers); a pool of learning materials, available on the web and sent via ordinary mail; and information and communication technologies used by the community to communicate, co-operate, and access and produce information. These elements and their relationships are described. The relations among the components become clear when developing and conducting online courses.

1. INTRODUCTION

Online education can be considered from different points of view (Harasim 1989; Kaye 1991). From the learner's point of view, it represents a new way of learning. In an online course the learner becomes a member of a virtual community composed of learners, tutors, technical support staff, experts and observers. In the context of this community they carry out individual and co-operative activities, which result in understanding a given topic and acquiring new skills. From the point of view of an instructional designer, online education is a learning system in which the learners interact with one another and with the tutors via computer network. Access and production of information in this system is strongly enhanced by information and communication technologies (ICT). From the point of view of an educational institution, online education is a new way of delivering distance courses in which tutors and learners interact with one another asynchronously via computer network. Finally, from the point of view of a researcher, it is a new social learning strategy in which knowledge is not only 'consumed' but also produced by learners, interacting at a distance.

This paper presents a model of online education that embraces all these points of view. It involves three basic elements and their relationships: a virtual community (Community) (Riel 1992), a pool of learning material (Material), a computer network and related services (ICT). See Figure 1.

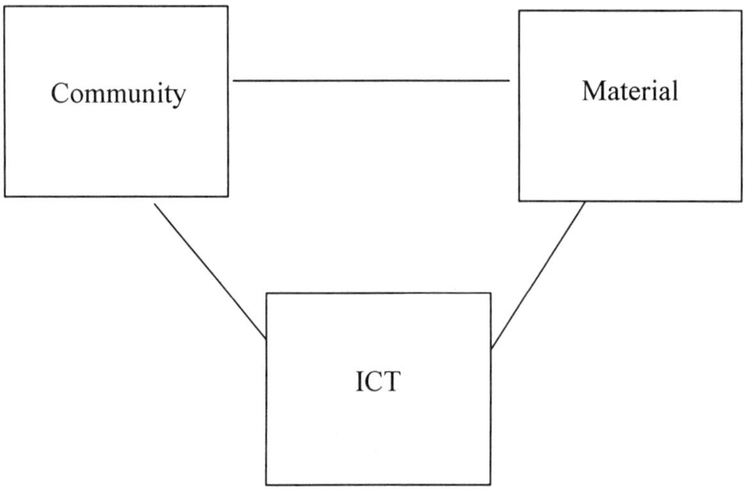

Figure 1. A model of an online course

Instructional designers and tutors create the Community and define the interaction among the community members and the ways to access the learning material. The Community uses ICT to communicate, co-operate and access the Material. Learners may receive and/or access Material (videocassette, books, learning kit, websites etc.) produced ad hoc for the course or access information sources pointed out by the tutors. In this paper each element will be discussed along with its relationships with other elements. These relations become explicit when designing and running online courses. The examples refer to online courses developed at Istituto Tecnologie Didattiche (ITD, Genova, Italy) in recent years.

2. THE COMMUNITY

The Community involves Learners, Tutors, Technical support staff, Experts and Observers.

2.1 Learners

Participants in an online course are either individual learners or groups of learners. In the case of individual learners, the interaction among the participants takes place mainly via the web. For instance, in the Polaris course (Trentin 97) addressed to online education designers, the participants are individual learners. In such courses, virtual groups can be formed to implement co-operative learning strategies. The interaction among members of these groups is based on First Class, a Computer-mediated Conferencing (CMC) system.

In the case of groups of learners, there are two levels of interaction and communication: inside the local group and among the virtual groups. The first takes place locally and is very dynamic, while the second is conducted via computer network and is rather low-key. Two examples of online courses addressed to groups of learners are MEDEA (Briano, Midoro and Trentin 1997) and EuMedea (Midoro et al. 1998), which deal with a methodological approach to environmental education in the classroom. The MEDEA groups, based in different Italian cities, are composed of teachers who belong to the same school and teach different subjects. The EuMedea groups are composed of teachers and student teachers, co-ordinated by a local tutor, spread throughout Europe. The local tutor is responsible for organising the work of the local group and co-operates with the remote tutors on all organisational problems.

There are also mixed cases, however, in which participants can be both individuals and local group members. This is the case in I Fiori Blu, an online course dealing with design methodologies for online education. This course not only addresses groups of practitioners operating in local environmental education labs but also individual researchers.

2.2 Tutors

The online tutor's role is quite different from that of a face-to-face tutor. Their work has two phases: course preparation and course management. In the first phase, online tutors may be responsible for designing the course, implementing the learning material, and setting the CMC system and course interface. In some cases, they are alumni of a previous run of the same course. In all cases, they are in charge of creating the Community, often by recruiting participants, contacting experts, accepting observers; making the Material available; and providing access to the CMC system.

In the second phase, the functions they perform include the following.

- *Socialisation.* They operate to create a friendly climate using several means. They may invite participants to introduce themselves online and sometimes organise face-to-face social gatherings to break the ice. Most of our online start with a kick-off meeting held either face-to-face or online, in real time, using video-conferencing. Thus participants get the chance to meet personally. In the first edition of EuMedea, a multipoint video-conference was organised, as the participants were unable to afford the travelling costs. Furthermore, tutors can propose or accept online ‘‘chats’ with participants in real time or send personal messages to individual learners. A good online tutor should be able to choose the most suitable initiatives and tools for creating motivation, group spirit and enthusiasm among the participants.

- *Stimulus.* Tutors propose activities and materials and help the participants reach the course objectives.
- *Online help.* Tutors help students in carrying out the activities. They intervene either when learners require help or when they think that the learners' activities are not converging towards meaningful results. They can either ask experts for help or invite learners to help their peers. With problems, they encourage and motivate the participants.
- *Response.* They respond to the learners' specific questions, dealing with areas like content, course management or the technology.
- *Feedback.* They give the learners feedback about the way they have carried out the proposed activities.
- *Explanation.* They can either explain unclear topics or suggest material that can help learners understand these topics.
- *Moderation.* They moderate discussions among the participants, discouraging aggressive or inappropriate behaviour and encouraging the conversation when it flags.
- *Planning.* They can modify the course plan, changing modules' starting or ending dates, or adding or deleting entire modules.
- *Evaluation.* They gather data to evaluate the results, both during and at the end of the course. The online tutor's role requires a commitment in the social interactions, interest in participants' learning progress, a capacity to cope with unforeseen situations, ability to negotiate, and savoir faire that puts participants at their ease. Most of these qualities can be acquired with experience, but some of them are part of the individual's personality.

2.3 Technical support staff

Technical support staff (TS) help participants who have problems with technicalities. In our courses TS provide the groups with technical support on the CMC system installation procedure; the CMC system functions and facilities; and technical problems that cannot be solved at local level with the support of the local tutor.

2.4 The experts

Experts are people with competence in one or more course topics who offer online help to both tutors and learners. Experts are not necessarily involved in the whole course, but rather in given modules. Their role is to explain unclear topics, help participants in solving problems, point out suitable material, correct misconceptions, give feedback on learners' activities, propose new activities, and so on. Tutors can ask experts to provide new stimuli for the participants, for example presenting interesting cases or open questions.

Some experts can be asked to conduct a module or part of one. For instance in the first edition of EuMedea, an expert was called upon to help groups design web pages that described their project. Often the same person can play the dual role of expert and tutor.

2.5 The observers

These are people who are interested in observing the course, but who are not allowed to intervene. Tutors can ask an observer for his/her opinion during the course or for informal evaluation at the end of it. An observer can act as a tutor's helper, but in some cases they may be an external course evaluator. A description of the EuMedea Community is at http://paradiso.itd.ge.cnr.it/english/projects/t3/eumedea/community.html.

3. THE MATERIAL

The learning material of an online course concerns organisation and management, the technology used, and the content domain.

3.1 Materials related to organisation and management

In all courses developed at ITD, participants receive a course guide with aims, contents, structure, schedule and available materials. In EuMedea, a publicly accessible website is available with the course guide, a description of the community, the links to the learning environment and other interesting sites, questionnaires for the participants and anything that may give a picture of the course and its state of progress.

3.2 Materials related to technology used

Almost all the courses developed at ITD use First Class (FC) as the CMC system. In these cases, participants receive the FC user manual and some notes on how to download the client from the web.

3.3 Materials related to content domain

These are materials the learners use either for individual study or for carrying out the suggested activities. For example, in EuMedea, these are printed material, a videocassette and links to relevant websites.

4. THE TECHNOLOGY

In online education, ICT is used to perform four main functions – communication, information sharing, information access, and co-operation.

4.1 Communication

In the first edition of MEDEA, members of the community used email. This has several drawbacks. In electronic mail, all messages end up in a single mailbox: personal messages, those regarding the course, various exchanges from other mailing-lists, etc. In these conditions, contributions that are sent in after the deadline fixed for the various module activities get mixed up with messages dealing with the current discussion topic, creating 'noise' in overall exchange. Such problems can be solved using computer conferencing systems; these are far more reliable in that the user in a sense 'hands over' the message, i.e. has to log on to the conferencing server in order to deliver/pick up the mail, in exactly the same way as they would post or remove a message from a notice board. At ITD, the CMC system First Class is used to deliver online courses.

First Class is much more suitable than email for running online courses since CMC systems offer the following advantages.

- They clearly reflect any ongoing changes in the structure of online courses.
- It is easy to understand which module the activities belong to.
- Overlap on the timing of one module and another does not lead to confusion, as happens using email.
- Tutors keep control of the course more easily, since messages are written directly on the server in conference areas they can manipulate. For

example tutors can intervene at any time to redirect messages the participants have sent to the wrong area.

The latest release of FC allows the creation of a closed community (Intranet) that can be observed by Internet users on a read-only basis; in other words, these observers are unable to intervene. The client that the tutors provide to the participants can also be used by those without Internet access. However in some courses, such as MEDEA and EuMedea, Internet navigation facilities are required to access the learning material.

The user-system interface plays a key role in an online course, since an effective interface allows the participants to understand where they are at any given moment and to focus on the contents, without being distracted by the interaction with the system. Thus choosing a suitable metaphor is very important. For instance, in EuMedea, a school metaphor is used, with several classrooms, a lab, a library and a café.

4.2 Sharing information

The information shared by the community is stored in documents produced or chosen by the course designers. These are available as texts, printed material, video, etc., mailed to participants or available on the web. Some online courses like MEDEA and EuMedea point to learning material available in several websites. In our courses, a virtual library is created, containing both the documents for accomplishing the activities and those produced by the participants. In EuMedea an ad hoc site has been developed containing all the information the community may need, and this is also a course showroom for Internet users.

4.3 Accessing information

In some courses information stored in existing websites is required. In this case, learners have to be able to access Internet using a web browser such as Netscape or Explorer.

4.4 Co-operating

Participants can co-operate with other remote learners or, in the local groups, with local group members. Local groups usually work together face to face. However, in EuMedea, the Exeter group worked both locally and at a distance to overcome space and time problems. In our online courses, participants co-operate through the CMC system. In some cases, however, video-conferencing or other groupware systems can also be used. Co-operation is often aimed at developing a product (an essay, a project). In EuMedea, the participants developed several websites describing the environmental projects they had designed for their school pupils. In this case an HTML editor and a net browser were required.

5. DESIGNING AND RUNNING ONLINE COURSES

The relationships between Community, Material and ICT become evident in designing and holding online courses. In the following, the relationships between Community-Material, Community-ICT and Material-ICT are discussed. The life cycle of an online course is similar to that of any Open Distance Learning (ODL) course and comprises the following phases.

- Definition of requisites – the educational needs are identified and aims and content are defined.
- Definition of specifications – the subject matter structure is defined.
- Design – the subject matter structure is divided into modules, and microdesign, in which the individual modules are designed.
- Implementation – where the individual modules are implemented and the user-system interface is defined.
- Course management – in which the course is run.
- Validation – in which the quality of the course is assessed.
- Maintenance – in which the course is updated.

The definition of requisites and specification is the same as in all ODL courses. In the other phases, instead, the three fundamental elements of online education and their relationships should be taken into account. The community has to be created, the materials have to be developed and made available, the technology has to be chosen and configured and learning activities have to be identified. In the following, the relationships between the fundamental elements are discussed.

5.1 Community-material relationship

The community uses material to increase the level of shared knowledge. In practice, the course designers define an initial body of material. During the course, tutors point out when and how participants should use this to accomplish the suggested activities. This pool will be enriched with new material produced by the participants as they carry out their activities. For example in EuMedea, the participants produced web pages describing their own project; in I Fiori Blu, the student designers produced text documents describing their own environmental education project; and in Polaris, learners produced text documents summarising some proposed papers.

These new products are discussed by the general community. In this way a dynamic self-generative process is triggered which reinforces the community's shared knowledge and sense of identity. In addition the material produced can be reused in a later edition of the same course.

5.2 Community-ICT relationship

ICT is used by the community to access information, to share knowledge and to create new common understanding through co-operation. More precisely, ICT is used to send and receive written messages from the Community members (Feenberg 1989; Mason 1993) in an environment of computer-mediated communication (CMC); in our courses we use First Class. As far as access to information is concerned, WWW plays a key role in making available a wealth of material for use in the participants' activities.

5.3 Material-ICT relationship

In online education, ICT is used to produce, access and work on Materials. Most of these materials are available in the CMC system or at websites. In some of our courses, however, a package of learning material is sent to the participants via ordinary mail.

6. CONCLUSIONS

Models describe the fundamental elements of systems and their relationships. The model of online education presented in this paper features three basic elements: a Community (comprising learners, tutors, experts and observers), a pool of Material (available on the net or sent by post) and ICT (CMC system and Internet). The Community uses ICT to interact (communication and co-operation) and to access and produce information. Online courses have proved extremely effective in collaborative learning, where the experience and knowledge of each participant represents a learning resource for the whole community. In addition, co-operation within the course community results in the production of new knowledge and materials and in this way the social nature of learning becomes clear.

REFERENCES

Briano, R, Midoro, V and Trentin, G. (1997) Computer mediated communication and online teacher training in environmental education. *Journal of Information Technology for Teacher Education* 6(2) 127-145.

Feenberg, A. (1989) The written world: On the theory and practice of computer conferencing. In R.D. Mason and A.R. Kaye (eds.) *Mindweave: Communication, computers and distance education.* Oxford: Pergamon Press.

Harasim, L.M. (1989) Online education: A new domain. In R.D. Mason and A.R. Kaye (eds.) *Mindweave: Communication, computers and distance education.* Oxford: Pergamon Press.

Kaye, A. R. (1991) Learning together apart. In A.R. Kaye (ed.) *Proceedings of the NATO Advanced Research Workshop on Collaborative Learning and Computer Conferencing*, Series F: Computer and System Sciences, 90, Berlin: Springer-Verlag.

Mason, R. (1993) Written interactions. In R.D. Mason (ed.) *Computer conferencing: The last word.* Victoria, BC: Beach Holme Publishers.

Midoro, V., Briano, Persico, D., Sarti, L., and Trentin, G, (1998) EuMedea: A European online course to train European teachers in environmental education. In G. Davies (ed.) *Proceedings of XV IFIP World Congress, Teleteaching'98* 31st August-4th September, Vienna-Budapest, 1998.

Riel, M. (1992) A functional analysis of educational telecomputing: A case study of learning circles. *Interactive Learning Environments* 2(1) 15-29.

Trentin, G. (1997) Telematics and online teacher training: The Polaris Project, *Journal of Computer Assisted Learning* 13(4) 261-269.

BIOGRAPHY

Vittorio Midoro, a researcher fellow at Istituto Tecnologie Didattiche, CNR, has been responsible for research projects dealing with both methodological issues, (definition of methodologies, prototypes and tools for courseware production), and theoretical issues (applications of Pask's conversation theory to instructional processes). The project manager of LABNET, a developing network of environmental education laboratories, his present activity embraces on line education, co-operative learning and use of telematics in environmental education.

Online university degree programmes

Terence R. Cannings and Sue G. Talley
Pepperdine University, 400 Corporate Pointe, 90230 Culver City, CA, USA.
cannings@pepperdine.edu

Keywords: online learning, communities of practice, reflective practice, problem-based learning, action research

Abstract: Pepperdine University introduced three degree programmes over the last four years that incorporate the use of online technology: a Doctor of Educational Technology degree and two Master of Arts degrees with an emphasis on educational technology. During the implementation of these degree programmes more has been learned about the critical need to incorporate into online learning the concepts of communities of practice, reflective practice, problem-based learning, and action research. In addition, an increased understanding of the role of face-to-face meetings has developed. As technologies mature and understanding of the underlying learning theory increases, additional technology use is being explored.

1. INTRODUCTION

For an online degree programme to be successful a fundamental shift must occur in the teaching and learning strategies typically found at universities where students regularly meet face-to-face. Our experiences at Pepperdine University over the last four years have led us to incorporate a new set of teaching and learning strategies in our online courses, strategies that have produced in students deeper understanding of concepts and demonstrated ability to apply these concepts to the problems they encounter in their own educational settings. In fact, the affordances of online encourage a degree of community of practice and a level of reflection well beyond that found in students who participate in graduate school by attending weekly face-to-face classes. We believe this is because of the continuation of the dialogue in between any official synchronous online classes or occasional face-to-face meetings. This is a sort of 24/7 (twenty four hours a day, seven days a week) type of presence that has not existed in education before.

2. BACKGROUND

Rheingold (1988) wrote in an article foretelling the growth of online communities, 'If computer-mediated communication (CMC) has potential it is in the way people in so many parts of the net fiercely defend the use of the term 'community' to describe the relationships we have built online.' This sort of community has come to fruition in the online programmes at Pepperdine. Hiltz and Wellman (1997) summarise the current understanding of virtual communities and CMC as follows.

- The limited bandwidth of CMC can reduce 'social presence' and 'social cues'.
- CMC seems good for giving and receiving information, opinions, and suggestions; it is less suited for communicating agreement and disagreement; and it is worst for social-emotional tasks involving conflict and negotiation, such as showing tension or tension release or showing strong emotions.
- There is no 'turn-taking', so all participants can key in entries whenever they like.
- There is more equality of participation in CMC than in face-to-face group interaction.
- Asynchronicity makes interaction more convenient but raises new co-ordination problems, such as information overload. (1997:45)

These findings have definitely held true in our work with the online graduate programmes. However, there are some additional elements we have identified beyond those of Hiltz and Wellman.

3. NEWLY IDENTIFIED ELEMENTS

Our experience with the use of online tools for technology degree programmes leads us to the belief that certain key elements must be present for an online course to succeed. First, students must establish an identity face to face. This identity can then be carried into their online work. In their online work they must be encouraged to work as a community. In addition, they must be encouraged to continually reflect on their individual thinking as well as the work of the community. To assess their learning we encourage participation in collaborative work groups and we also require that students complete an action research project. These elements are discussed in more detail below.

3.1 Importance of identity

In each of the Pepperdine online degree programmes, students are admitted as a cohort and continue to move together through their coursework. This sense of community is important to the building of a fundamental language used by this group. This language reduces the potential for misunderstanding in online settings where the contextual cues are reduced. As Wenger (1998) proposes:

> ...an identity must incorporate a past and a future. Learning communities will become places of identity to the extent they make trajectories possible—that is, to the extent they offer a past and a future that can be experienced as a personal trajectory (1998:215).

To better ensure that this identity is created for each cohort, we require students to attend 'VirtCamp' before their online sessions begin. VirtCamp was conceived first as a place where students learned the technical skills required for online learning, i.e. use of chat rooms and threaded discussions. However, these sessions are even more important as a vehicle for creating this identity and common language for each learning community. Thus it appears that face-to-face plays an important role in online learning. Without this ability to initially establish identity, the learning community is much more likely to experience discord in its dialogue because of semantic and cultural differences in the language used by the students and the instructors. This sense of the learning community as a culture is important. Many of the initial efforts in a programme are focused on moving students from thinking of learning as an individual enterprise to recognising it as a community enterprise.

3.2 Membership in a community of practice

Once the course moves from a face-to-face environment to an online environment, the online technology tools are used to enable the learners to engage in dialogue that is facilitated by the instructors. The content of the course is typically presented via artefacts such as books or other web pages that students read in advance of the discussions. Over time, Pepperdine instructors in the online programmes have developed two different formats for online dialogue:

1. chat rooms in the form of a multi-user object-oriented environment (MOO), and

2. threaded discussions in the form of newsgroups.

The chat room, in this case a specialised MOO, is provided by Tapped In (1998), a non-profit organisation funded by the National Science Foundation. Tapped In provides both a graphical and a text interface to the chat environment. Pepperdine University maintains a virtual campus facility as part of Tapped In where both students and faculty may create their own offices. Virtual classrooms are also provided with 'whiteboards' where notes may be posted to guide students in their synchronous chats.

These synchronous chats have evolved the most over the four years of our experience with online. At first we attempted to meet with an entire class at one time (typically 25 students). However, we learned that this is chaotic in an online environment where the text is scanning by rapidly and where it is difficult to recognise when it might be appropriate to call on students for input since there are no visual cues available. Now we either divide the class into small sections (6-8 people) to accommodate time zones or we divide the class into smaller virtual meeting rooms. The instructor 'moves' from room to room to listen in on the discussion and facilitate as needed, just as they might with smaller groups in a face-to-face classroom. When the discussion is complete the students post key ideas from the session to a threaded discussion for further asynchronous reflection and discussion.

This synchronous time is not an opportunity to deeply consider topics. Rather it appears to be a time for idea sharing and initial brainstorming about the concepts in the materials that students have read. Just as McGrath (1994) indicates in his circumplex model of group tasks, synchronous chat rooms are best used for creativity or intellective tasks such as generating ideas or plans, discussing issues with no right answers, or sharing points of view. As Hiltz and Wellman suggest, it is more difficult to use synchronous time to resolve differences of opinion or to finalise a project. However, the sense of intimacy generated by the immediate contact of a synchronous discussion does lead to a further sense of community and a more developing sense of common language.

3.3 Reflection on practice

One of the most surprising discoveries of our online work has been the degree to which the depth of student reflection is enhanced by the use of asynchronous discussion tools. Schon (1987) proposes that by encouraging education apprentices to reflect on their practice in a way that encourages reflection, mentors can improve the apprentices' practice and their appreciation for the 'art' of the practice. Schon's concepts of reflection-in-action and reflection-on-action are now a major portion of our online graduate programmes throughout the threaded discussions. Our use of threaded discussions now extends to our graduate programmes that meet in a more traditional face-to-face manner.

Spitzer, Wedding, and DiMauro (1994) report that their experiences with LabNet indicate a need for a moderator to foster reflective dialogue. The moderator must specifically engage members in doing activities and in thinking. DiMauro and Gal (1994) indicate that the following technological design factors contribute to reflection.

- Protecting workspace for reflection;
- Communicating asynchronously;
- Maintaining a chronological record of dialogue.

At Pepperdine we have found that the threaded discussion tool provided by Netscape's newsgroups is an adequate tool for this purpose. The biggest problems are the inability of students to accurately maintain threads and the sheer number of posted messages generated as students become facile with this tool. Spitzer, Wedding, and DiMauro also note that there are several contributing social factors.

- Dialogue needs to have an organising principle;
- Reflective dialogues need to be linked with action;
- The right questions need to be asked to blend structure and openness;
- Participants need to be personally committed to the network;
- An extended timeframe is needed for reflection.

Our experience corroborates that of Spitzer, Wedding, and DiMauro. In particular, instructors must develop good guiding questions for the newsgroup dialogue and appropriate guidance in the discussion of key concepts. Socratic questioning style has become fundamental.

3.4 Problem-based learning

We are often asked how we assess students in an online environment. We find that final projects, requiring students or groups of students to construct a product reflecting their learning, especially one applicable in their individual educational setting, provides best evidence of their learning and their understanding. This product construction is typically done by creating a website to reflect the students' knowledge of the area as well as their understanding of other resources available on the Web.

This use of problem-based learning has a dual benefit. Bruckman (1996), in her use of the Moose MOO, indicates that not only does community support construction activities, but construction activities also enhance community. 'A community is a group of people brought together for a purpose . . . A particularly felicitous type of community often emerges when people are brought together to construct things.' In those courses that have a face-to-face session at the end of each course, the students present their work to their peers as well as the instructor in a final face-to-face session. In the primarily online programme, students construct a portfolio of their work that is exhibited to peers, instructors, and outside evaluators in the final week of the programme.

3.5 Action research

The culminating element for all programmes is an action research activity. In this research the students actually try to implement changes in their practice based on the theories they now understand. As they implement these changes they reflect on what is happening and document the process. In some instances, they also mentor other teachers in the process and reflect on the entire change process that does (or does not) occur. The students are guided in their efforts primarily by the work of McNiff, Lomax, and Whitehead (1996). By doing action research, students are not only learning from their own practice but they are applying their practice in a very localised way. In this culminating activity, students begin to 'think globally but act locally.'

3.6 Video Case studies: the future

In a recent study, Talley (1998) found that video case studies are a highly desirable element for online learning. Out of 17 highly desirable elements in Table 1 that experts identified for an online learning environment for teachers, video case studies was rated the most desirable. (Note: Table 1 reflects a set of interwoven characteristics for a suggested online resource that combines elements found today in separate online tools: a website with embedded links, a chat room, a threaded discussion area, and features such as those found on Amazon.com where regular users of the site are guided to items of special interest to them.)

For this reason, Pepperdine is exploring the use of new software and technology that will allow for more desktop video-conferencing between students and instructors. While we have not yet had experience in this area, we believe, based on the work of Buxton (1992) and others, that the ability to share workspace and products will be more important than being able to view isolated faces. The use of video focused on faces provides access to cues such as non-verbal expression that are otherwise missing from the online environment but it appears that the more important element is context.

Table 1. Desirable Characteristics of an Online Learning Environment

Information Source	Format for Providing Feedback	Expert Help	Scaffolding Help	Technical Functionality
Online video demonstrations of best practices	Both asynchronous + synchronous discussions	Mentors who understand the practice and can provide expert help	Modelling of reflective practice Modelling of mentoring	Authentication of the expertise of the mentor
Links to related work and resources	Asynchronous discussion	Instructors		Amazon.com like list of interests
Collaborative units of study	Both asynchronous + synchronous discussions			All must contribute; no lurking allowed
Action research	Both asynchronous + synchronous discussions	University researcher(s)		

4. CONCLUSION AND RECOMMENDATIONS

Our experiences with online programmes have led us to understand the importance of several key elements in online learning for educators. Identity, community, and reflection are among the most important. Currently, identity is best established in the context of face-to-face meetings. Community, on the other hand, is well-supported organised and facilitated synchronous online sessions. The use of asynchronous threaded discussion to expand dialogue between limited synchronous meetings and to increase the depth of the reflection is most key. Many current online courses are web-based, click-through tutorials. We would recommend that more attention be paid to the effect of adding the concept of community of practice to these tutorials.

More research needs to be done about the differences between student learning that occurs in online courses and student learning that occurs in traditional face-to-face courses. Currently, most information is anecdotal. Finally, further design work needs to be done on the most appropriate form for the online environment.

REFERENCES

Bruckman, A. (1996) *Constructionist Culture.* Unpublished Thesis, MIT, USA. URL: ftp://ftp.media.mit.edu/pub/asb/papers/thesis [12.11.1997]

Buxton, W. (1992) Telepresence: Integrating shared task and person spaces. *Proceedings of Graphics Interface 92,* 123-129.

DiMauro, V. and Gal, S. (1994) The use of telecommunications for reflective discourse of science teacher leaders. *Journal of Science Education and Technology*, June URL: http://hub.terc.edu/terc/LabNet/Articles/Reflective/reflective.html

Guzdial, M., Hmelo, C., Hubscher, R., Nagel, K., Newstetter, W., Puntembakar, S., Shabo, A., Turns, J., and Kolodner, J. L. (1997) *Integrating and guiding collaboration: Lessons learned in computer-supported collaborative learning research at Georgia Tech.* URL: http://guzdial.cc.gatech.edu/papers/lessons [12.11.1997]

Hiltz, S. R. and Wellman, B. (1997) Asynchronous learning networks as a virtual classroom. *Communications of the ACM* 40(3) 44-55.

McGrath, J. E., and Hollingshead, A. B. (1994) *Groups Interacting with Technology.* Thousand Oaks, CA: Sage Publications.

McNiff, J., Lomax, P., and Whitehead, J. (1996) *You and Your Action Research.* New York, NY: Routledge.

Rheingold, H. (1988) *A slice of life in my virtual community.* Whole Earth Review. June 1992. URL: gopher:gopher.well.sf.ca.us/OO/Community/virtual_communities92

Schlager, M., Fusco, J., and Schank, P. (1998). Cornerstones of an Online Community of Education Professionals. IEEE Technology and Society, 17(4) 15-21 URL: http://www.tappedin.sri.com [15.10.1998]

Schon, D. A. (1987) *Educating the Reflective Practitioner.* San Francisco, CA: Jossey-Bass Publishers.

Spitzer, W., Wedding, K., and DiMauro, V. (1994) *Fostering reflective dialogues for teacher professional development.*

URL: http://hub.terc.edu/terc/LabNet/Guid/Fostering_REfl_Dialogues.html [8.11.1994]

Talley, S. (1998). *The use of online technology tools and teacher professional development.* Unpublished doctoral thesis, Pepperdine University, Culver City, CA.

Wenger, E. (1998) *Communities of Practice.* New York, NY: Cambridge University Press.

BIOGRAPHIES

Terence C. Cannings, Associate Dean of Education at Pepperdine University, California, has been a teacher, school principal, member of the State Department of Education, researcher, and Professor of education.. He is currently the Programme Director for the Doctorate in Educational Technology, a 60/40, face-to-face/online nationally recognised degree.

Sue G. Talley, Visiting Professor of Education at Pepperdine University, California, has been involved with educational technology as teacher, provider of teacher professional development, executive for Apple Computer, executive director of a non-profit foundation, and professor of education. Currently, her research is focused on the use of online technology for teacher professional development.

The teacher as a mediator in a networked society

Andrée Klein and Hélène Godinet
Institut Universitaire de Formation des Maîtres, 30 avenue M. Berthelot, 38100, Grenoble, France. andrée.klein@grenoble.iufm.fr

Keywords: teacher's role, multimediated learning, networking, language learning, mediation

Abstract: As an increasing number of schools are being connected to the Internet and equipped with telematics tools, there is a growing fear among teachers who do not know how to make effective use of the machines. In this paper, we are concerned to pinpoint through our day to day practice as teacher trainers, and our involvement in European projects, the competencies that emerged from our activities with our students. The paper defines the essential role of the teacher regarding ICT, examines the changing role of the teacher in an ICT-based school environment and a networked society, and calls for vigilance in the use and integration of ICT in education and teacher training.

1. INTRODUCTION

Today, there is a widespread belief that, with the advent of ICT, networks and hypermedia, the role of the teachers will change, and that the teacher will no longer be the only one to convey knowledge. These glib and typically superficial ideas provoke as many fears as enthusiastic reactions among the teaching profession. Some fear that computerised teaching gradually take over or distance learning will supersede face-to-face teaching. Others are enthusiastic because they support the notion of a radically new and improved educational paradigm and wish to infuse into the profession an innovative spirit.

It is clear that when new technologies are incorporated, they are no doubt important when they serve to overcome material and technical obstacles to teaching and learning. But there is no clear evidence, on a larger scale, that ICT, networks and hypermedia in themselves are sufficient as tools aimed at adding value to the educational process, or at improving the quality of education and its output. Nevertheless, from our day to day practice as teacher trainers, we have a body of experience and now have reasons to believe that this particular combination of pedagogies and technologies is likely not to revolutionise educational practice, but rather to bring about some noticeable changes, especially in the role of the teachers.

Firstly, we will present these changes in terms of the competencies needed to grapple with ICT and the roles that must be held by teachers. Secondly, we will try to re-position the use of ICT and reflect on it in a more general context, to gain a better understanding of where we stand and assess the credibility of some routes in initial teacher training.

2. DEFINING A PROGRESSIVE EVOLUTION IN TEACHING COMPETENCES

Starting from our specific framework of language learning and teaching, we have been experimenting for some years with our student-teachers some practical ways of integrating ICT. We believe that through a set of key functionalities of interactivity, multimodality, and evolutivity, hypermedia have contributed to that ICT integration is possible and can transform the teaching and learning environment.

Over the years, we have tested different software and CD-ROMs, organised online tutoring via email and video-conferencing, participated in online virtual workshops, shared good practice via video-conferences, used and designed online resources. We have worked with European partners, in Socrates projects like APPLAUD and T3 (telematics for teacher training; a telematics application programme for education and training supported by the European Commission DG XIII). From these various observations and experiments we have identified three types of competencies to be developed in teacher training. They are technical, pedagogical and communicative abilities.

2.1 Technical ability

Competent teachers can use a wide range of appropriate telematic resources, such as browsing and/or creating networked resources, email, video-conferencing, to enhance personal and professional efficiency, and to update skills in the light of new developments.

2.2 Pedagogical ability

Competent teachers can plan and implement lessons with telematics taking into account the needs, experiences and abilities of individual students. They can organise resources effectively, to ensure differentiation and progression, monitor and evaluate the progress of students and the use of telematics and the outcomes. They can manage the classroom appropriately according to their teaching objectives when using telematics.

2.3 Communicative ability

Competent teachers can optimise the interaction between medium and message in order to adjust to the mode of communication. To use hypermedia and networks, teachers need to understand that information and resources are open, virtual, distant, multimodal. Networking opens schools to other contexts, other communities and other cultures. Telematics tools introduce opportunities to 'pick up' non-verbal communication cues such as gesture, body language, facial expression and human behaviour in general.

Learning and teaching a language involves studying another culture and accepting the 'otherness' in it. Learning and teaching a language includes cultural and factual knowledge, e.g. of history and current events. It is not only learning texts but more increasingly understanding sound, hearing, interpreting pictures and video. And finally, teachers have to plan and deliver hypertextual rhetoric, and evaluate and assess their students' learning in dealing with non linear networked information. The competencies identified here, though not exhaustive, imply a re-organisation of the roles of the teacher.

3. DEFINING THE CHANGING ROLES OF THE TEACHER IN A NETWORKED SOCIETY

Reflecting on social and human artefacts and activities, we are struck by the fact that they all are the results of a mediation. For example, there is no science, no religion without mediation. Education falls into the same category and an important message to deliver is that there is no education without mediation. Therefore, the role of the teacher is above all that of a mediator i.e. the one who verbalises experience and knowledge to ensure successful acquisition.

This fundamental role has some very practical implications when it comes to integrating ICT and can be seen as a core feature to be broken up into several parts.

- The teacher as a designer;
- The teacher as an expert;

- The teacher as a tutor;
- The teacher as an evaluator.

3.1 The teacher as a designer

The teacher as a designer is a mediator between the students and the environment. Authentic learning environments are ones which allow participants to gather information from multimedia data bases, and to communicate with others via multimedia technology. In term of resources, the web or ICT based packages form a universal library.

In terms of collaborative work, with teachers and students or students and experts outside the classroom, real-life communication can be established with peers in other countries, by email or video-conferencing. Project work can be shaped around sharing and negotiating. It may involve a reorganisation of pedagogical time and places, reshuffling teaching hours, and rethinking classroom management. The teacher can turn their classroom into an open, international space, thus adding to it a virtual dimension.

3.2 The teacher as an expert

The teacher as an expert is a mediator between the students and knowledge. The teacher's traditional task is to organise and structure information. It is even more so with ICT because they have to turn the vast collection of information, sometimes uncontrolled, into knowledge. The teacher decides whether a site meets their educational objectives; tailors the materials to suit them; helps students to discriminate between information and the processing of relevant information; and stimulates the students to use online resources in a shrewd, cautious manner to form a critical community of users.

3.3 The teacher as a tutor

The teacher as at tutor is a mediator between the students and their learning styles. Electronic online tutoring enables the teacher to have frequent feedback and therefore an acute idea of his students' learning and cognitive styles. Edward (1997) relying, on Anglo-Saxon sources on cognitive psychology, showed how hypermedia enable the interaction between contents, methods and learning.

This will enhance the traditional moral support given by teachers. They can tutor not only the students' products but the process of learning. The computer provides the students with a learning programme, the tutor organises the content according a progressive approach adjusted to the individual needs of the student. The student needs to receive, in real time, a feedback which is more than a computer-calculated result. The role of the teacher is to structure their pedagogical online material and create hyperlinks in the provided resources. In this way users get an appropriate feedback, when browsing and re-structuring information, which may, when necessary, have been pre-selected by the teachers.

3.4 The teacher as an evaluator

The teacher as an evaluator is a mediator between the students and their productions. The teacher provides their students with clear insights into their progression, storing files of their work, defining their weak and stronger points to help them come to terms with their learning and cognitive styles.

After engaging in these experiments that have led us identify and define competencies and roles, we must acknowledge the fact that teaching with ICT is an uphill task. The teacher has to reflect on their practice and on the learning processes and procedures even more than in a traditional learning environment. They have to become – which may be quite new with teachers – a professional.

4. THE TEACHER IN A NETWORKED SOCIETY : A WATCHFUL MEDIATOR

The teacher has not only to reflect on their practice but much more on the interaction between school and society. They have to reflect on the pedagogical relevance of ICT. A reflective attitude is possible only if at some point the teacher can take up a critical attitude. To keep distance from the 'wired-up' society, to ponder on the forceful hype around ICT (pros and cons alike) is the best way to escape unscathed. A cautious approach, as suggested Wolton (1997), supported by a strong sense of discrimination and relativity, must be taken to escape the 'cycle of deception' promoted by manufacturers and some researchers in order to give credible answers to the call for evidence coming from our colleagues.

Where do we, teachers and educators stand in the 'information society'? How can we find our way through the 'webby' maze and find suitable strategies to integrate ICT and train student teachers? Here again, the teacher is a mediator between what is going on in both society and school. Information and communication technologies are, so it seems, vested with an intrinsic ability to solve social and cultural problems. We actually cannot demonstrate that a rich authentic ICT-based learning environment will solve them. If the mediation is effective in the classroom and at school, it also has to be effective in society. Actually, about ICT, the teacher has to be able to distinguish between different levels and services.

4.1 Between different levels

The three fields, that is of innovation (discovery), of application (industrial implications) and of service (usage) overlap, and there is nothing worse than confusing them. Economists and manufacturers are inflicting the effects of the raging battle waged to occupy the unchartered lands of the ICT market on us. The consequences are that they tend to impose their rhythm, their pace of change, and their vision of the future, shaping it with the improbable concept of information society. We must clearly state that we are playing in a different field.

4.2 Between services

The use of ICT in services varies considerably. While they may be useful in entertainment and tourism, it is an altogether different story with education, health and work. Oversimplification and generalisation are to be avoided in these matters. Transferability from one to the others is not that easy! The more sophisticated the activities, such as learning and teaching, the more difficult it is to *standardise* them.

The main question is what is access to information for? There is no relation between the increasing volume of information available and its effective use. The greater the flow of information, the greater becomes the need to acquire conceptual tools to decipher complex systems. Cultural inequalities to access and use of information will grow when going from services like tourism, entertainment to those related to teleworking, telecommuting, telematics in education. In other words, it is necessary to discriminate between the widespread availability of data and the competencies needed to process, use, and integrate them.

We have to demystify common and superficial assertions related to two notions often associated with ICT : time and autonomy. The technological literature abounds in terms of 'real time', 'speed', 'faster', 'instant access' as if all of a sudden time like space was abolished and turned into instantaneous data. Compressed time like space seems to be the new panacea that will save the world of education. As teacher trainers we have to defend and even reintroduce the term 'learning time', and state clearly that the unavoidable ingredient in the learning process is *time*.

Most of the time, in papers or speeches, educational multimedia software and autonomy (self-training) are synonymous. Since this new form of packaging changes the how, when and where of the teaching/learning approach, it tends to be presented as an incredible opportunity to move away from the traditional constraining learning environment, as something deceptively simple, almost magical, the ultimate in terms of individualised learning. This inordinate trend to see the individual as the nucleus of everything tends to deprive us of what is the most needed in our western societies, i.e. the social link or social context of learning. The social fabric is the locus of social interactions at school.

5. CONCLUSION

We wanted to stress the necessity to train our students not only to become capable and critical ICT users, but also and above all to become aware of the underlying concepts and the social and economic implications attached to it. We are in a transitory period, in which schools rely on tested tools and methodology. Talking about the ICT revolution does not solve most of the difficulties our societies encounter, it simply 'technisices' them. Our role as teacher trainers is to make future teachers' competencies evolve towards a progressive integration of ICT in a networked society, if such a thing exists or will ever exist. If ICT instrumentalises the mediation, it neither changes its nature nor questions its necessity.

REFERENCES

Authier, M. and Serres, M. (sous la direction de.) (1998) *Le monde de l'education hors série: Apprendre à distance.*

Davis, N. and Teartle, P. (1998) A core curriculum for telematics in teacher training. In G. Davies (ed.) *Proceedings of IFIP World Congress, Teleteaching'98* 31st August-4th September 1998.

Dieuzeide, H. (1994) *Les nouvelles technologies, outils d'enseignement.* Paris: Nathan .

Durpaire, J. L. (1997) *Internet à l'école en france: Guide d'usages pédagogiques.* Collection l'ingénierie educative. Poitiers: Centre Regional de Documentation Pedagogique for CNDP.

Edward, N. (1997) Development of a cost effective computer assisted learning package to facilitate conceptual understanding. In *Proceedings of Cal 97,* April, Exeter, UK.

Linard, M. (1998) La nécessaire médiation humaine. *Les cahiers pédagogiques: A l'heure d'internet.* 362.

Tardif, J. (1998) *Intégrer les nti. Quel cadre pédagogique?* Paris: Edition Scientifique Francaise.

Wolton, D. (1997) *Penser la communication.* Paris: Flammarion

BIOGRAPHIES

Andrée Klein, teacher trainer at the Institut Universitaire de Formation des Maîtres, teaches English as a foreign language, foreign language methodology and pedagogy. She is an expert on integrating ICT, especially multimedia and web resources, in foreign language learning and teaching for secondary student-teachers. She is involved in different European ICT projects, and co-responsible of the T3 project.

Hélène Godinet, teacher trainer at the Institut Universitaire de Formation des Maîtres, teaches sciences of language, integrating CAL and ICT in writing and reading. She is an expert on networking and hypertext producing and has published different papers on this subject in educational journals. She is involved in different European ICT projects, and co-responsible of the T3 project.

Social interactions and the construction of knowledge in computer-mediated environments

Carolyn Dowling
Australian Catholic University, 412 Mt Alexander Rd, Ascot Vale, Victoria, 3032, Australia.
c.dowling@mercy.acu.edu.au

Key words: social/cultural issues, social construction of knowledge, Internet, computer-mediated communication, electronic learning environments

Abstract: A growing body of research suggests that the interpersonal relationships and interactions that mediate learning online may differ in a number of respects from those pertaining within face-to-face educational environments. Even people whom we 'know' in other circumstances may not interact with us in the same way within computer-mediated contexts. Furthermore, electronic learning spaces often encompass a greater range of participants than is customary within traditional classrooms, in some cases including personified and 'intelligent' software and interfaces. This paper explores some theoretical perspectives that support recognition of the importance of these factors in designing online educational experiences for students.

1. INTRODUCTION

While the social dimensions of learning in face-to-face contexts are well recognised and researched, in relation to computer-mediated educational environments they are less well understood. A considerable body of research, much of it taking place outside the specific domain of education but of great relevance to it, suggests that computer-mediated interpersonal interactions have particular qualities which differentiate them significantly from their face-to-face equivalents. Even people whom we 'know' in other circumstances may relate differently to us within electronic contexts. Furthermore, within these notional social spaces, students are increasingly being required to interact with a far broader range of people than in the traditional classroom.

Other potential participants in the social interactions which mediate learning may include significantly personified interfaces and software 'agents'. At a conscious level both we and our students are well aware of the difference between a fellow human being and a computer. Nevertheless certain aspects of the way we talk and think about this technology, combined with factors such as the part played by language in the majority of interfaces, encourages us to frequently respond to computers much as we do to people. Where personification is a deliberate part of the design of an interface, this tendency is almost irresistible. A further dimension of personification exists in the form of programmes, in particular those now known as 'agents', designed specifically for the purpose of interacting with users in a manner indistinguishable from that of a human being. Yet another ground for making a distinction between the social aspects of computer-mediated and traditional educational environments is the belief held by a number of theorists that our own self representation through electronic text may encompass qualities and attitudes not characteristic of our face-to-face 'selves'. The result is an educational milieu encompassing a more complex social scenario than that to which we are accustomed in the traditional classroom. If we are to seriously accept the concept of knowledge as being socially constructed, then a close examination of the special qualities of the interactions which take place within these new educational environments is imperative.

2. REPRESENTING OURSELVES WITHIN ELECTRONIC ENVIRONMENTS

In the physical world we represent ourselves through a range of behaviours, signs and symbols which together constitute a complex and multi-faceted impression of who we are. These include aspects of our appearance, our voices, our facial expressions, our clothes and other possessions, our chosen companions and so on. In the traditional classroom both teachers and students quickly become 'known' through such characteristics of their physical presence, both as individuals and as elements of the social dynamic of the class. Where the 'self' is revealed solely through electronically mediated text, this richness of information is obviously not available.

It has long been established that even word processing, the most apparently straightforward of all computer based writing environments, can involve subtle but significant changes to the way in which we constitute ourselves through language. Theorists such as Heim would go so far as to suggest that, " … the word processor creates a new relationship to symbols, to language, and, by extension, to reality" (Heim 1993), including the reality of the 'self' as manifested through these symbols. As Poster writes, "... electronically mediated communication upsets the relation of the subject to the symbols it emits or receives and reconstitutes this relation in drastically new shapes" (Poster 1990). It seems possible that the apparently infinite malleability of computer based text may itself militate against the realisation of a coherent and integrated personality through this medium. If there is no limit to the changes I can make to my textual representation, is there actually a 'real' me? At a more practical level, even factors such as lack of expertise at keyboarding can have a marked effect on choice of words and structure of sentences, giving an 'impression' of the writer which might be significantly at odds with that obtained during a face-to-face conversation.

Not everyone perceives this as cause for concern. While most of take comfort from the concept of at the very least some stable 'core' to our selves, we readily accept the fact that we often behave, speak or dress differently in different contexts, according to what we believe to be appropriate. This may be in part involuntary and in part deliberate – a mix which most likely pertains to electronic environments as well, though not necessarily in the same proportions.

Apart from the involuntary differences which might exist between our physical and our online selves, electronically mediated environments provide a wealth of opportunities for the deliberate creation of alternative manifestations of ourselves which are welcomed by many computer users and theorists. The exploration of dimensions of our personalities which are denied expression within the traditional ideal of the integrated persona is not necessarily detrimental to our well-being. Turkle, for instance, suggests that the creation of multiple online personae is very much in keeping with many contemporary theoretical positions in which flexibility, multiplicity and openness to change are increasingly considered to be valuable and appropriate qualities. As she puts it, " ... the many manifestations of multiplicity in our culture including the adoption of online personae, are contributing to a general reconsideration of traditional, unitary theories of identity" (Turkle 1995). She also aligns these developments more specifically with strands of thinking within established psychoanalytic theory which encompass the possibility that, "You can have a sense of self without being one self" (Turkle 1995). Examples and discussion of flexible self representation within electronic environments, including the often contentious area of gender identity, are documented by a growing body of literature (Dery 1994; Jones 1995; Spender 1995; Cherny and Weise 1996; Mitchell 1996).

Beyond the creation of identity through text alone, networked contexts already exist within which users are also able to represent themselves graphically, with increasing sophistication. While fewer people as yet have access to the modelling capabilities of three dimensional virtual reality environments, these will certainly offer increased opportunities for personal choice and creativity in determining how we represent our electronically mediated selves to others.

The fact that our 'telepresence' may differ in certain respects from our physical presence lends an unprecedented degree of uncertainty to the extent to which we 'know' our fellow participants in online learning environments. While not necessarily a 'problem', it is certainly a feature which distinguishes such educational contexts from more traditional settings, and one which has the capacity to impinge on our usual understandings of the way in which the interpersonal relationships between the participants will mediate the learning which takes place.

3. INTERACTING WITH OTHERS WITHIN ELECTRONIC ENVIRONMENTS

The special qualities of interactions taking place through the medium of screen based text have been recognised since the earliest use of electronic mailing systems. Reports of the implementation of the Minitel electronic mail system in France in the 1980s, for instance, feature heartfelt complaints of the disruption afforded to a hitherto rigid social system by the new-found capacity for communication across different strata of society (de Lacy 1987). At around the same time, research undertaken within large organisations which were early adopters of this technology suggests that in some cases the processes of corporate decision making are altered by those qualities of electronically mediated communication which blur the usual hierarchical distinctions between participants. More recently, reports have abounded of extreme levels of verbal abuse or 'flaming' recounted regularly and often gleefully by the popular press, of normally quiet and retiring individuals pouring out their hearts online to relative strangers, or of people deliberately adopting personalities far removed from their usual identities and expressing themselves accordingly. It should be noted that instances of unwelcome interactions are well balanced by accounts of the many groups and individuals who describe, with great eloquence, supportive relationships and a new-found experience of community (Rheingold 1994; Turkle 1995; Spender 1995; Jones 1995; Preece 1998).

An interesting aspect of the descriptions of both positive and negative social experiences online is the degree to which they are given the same emotional status as a face-to-face encounter. For the participants, the feelings and reactions evoked are as strong and as 'real' as those pertaining to interactions in the physical world. The old adage that "sticks and stones can break your bones, but names can never hurt you" may not hold as true in electronic realities where sticks and stones are absent, and 'names' are everything. The effects of both positive and negative remarks on students might well be magnified under these circumstances.

In face-to-face situations, a multitude of cues and constraints determine the manner in which we speak to one another. These may include the nature of the space in which the interaction takes place, the perceived status or role of the each participant relative to one another, physical appearance including age and gender, and so on. Within electronic environments, few of these indicators apply. Such liberation, while intrinsically democratising, is also well removed from the ethos of many classrooms.

The role and relative status of each participant within the face-to-face classroom is generally clearly defined and understood, whether explicitly or implicitly. While the traditional scenario within which the teacher has the knowledge and the authority and the student is there to learn, primarily from the teacher, has long been under challenge, the potential for undermining its fundamental assumptions is greatly magnified within most online environments. These contexts incorporate the capacity for a range of styles of interpersonal interaction, all of which need to be fully explored and evaluated in terms of their efficacy in promoting learning. For example, within real time interactive educational environments of the Multi-User Dimension (MUD) type, should the persona adopted by the teacher incorporate 'wizard-like' capacities for control, commensurate to an extent with the advantages enjoyed by teachers in physical learning spaces, or should all participants be of equal capability and status? Where the teacher adopts the role of facilitator rather than instructor, a scenario currently favoured in many existing learning contexts where constructivist principles apply, will other, perhaps unanticipated configurations and hierarchies of inter-relationships arise, and will these necessarily be conducive to learning? It is through consideration of questions such as these that we can determine whether online learning environments will simply replicate the social organisations which exist in face-to-face settings, or will provide the possibility for new types of interaction through which knowledge may be socially constructed.

A frequently cited benefit of electronic classrooms is their capacity to extend beyond regional or national boundaries. This raises a whole range of issues to be considered. It is well recognised that different cultures vary in the types of interactions between teacher and student that are considered acceptable. From a young age, students are inculcated with a range of protocols and expectations in regard to matters such as who speaks first under different circumstances, the type of language which is acceptable in particular situations or when addressing certain people, the various means of showing degrees of acknowledgement of and respect for the opinions of others, an appreciation of the rights of others to be 'heard', a common understanding in relation to the 'ownership' of work and so on. Many of these understandings differ across cultures. More generally, there may be different cultural expectations governing interpersonal interactions for instance between young and old, or between novice and expert. A lack of awareness of and sensitivity to such differences can cause misunderstandings, particularly in online situations where, for instance, a consequence of keyboarding rather than speaking may be the use of short sentences which could convey an unintended impression of being peremptory or simply rude.

4. INTERACTING WITH ELECTRONIC 'LIFE FORMS'

In addition to interacting with electronic manifestations of other human beings, students in online environments are increasingly likely to encounter software 'entities' in some cases so thoroughly personified as to be indistinguishable from real people.

Indeed there is a sense in which the computer itself may be regarded in this light. Whether or not the interface through which the computer's 'self' is manifested is deliberately personified, a degree of personification is conferred automatically and inevitably through our widespread acceptance of the 'intelligence', albeit 'artificial', of computers, allied to the use of language as a significant component of most interfaces. Intelligence and language use are, after all, traditional distinguishing attributes of human beings. As Shirk puts it:

> Although there is some dispute among software critics concerning the advisability of having 'personalities' in computer programmes, their presence seems unavoidable. Any time there is communication between a computer and a human, the information presented by the computer has a certain style, diction, and tone of voice which impact upon the human's attitude and response toward the software. (Shirk 1988:320)

While some theorists, perhaps most notably Shneiderman (1992), play down the importance of personification in favour of the advantages of 'direct manipulation', a term which has become a focus for that style of interaction most familiar to us in the form of graphical user interfaces, other researchers and software developers see it as conferring some important advantages. Laurel, for instance, suggests that deliberately personified computers, whether portrayed as companions, servants, pets or whatever, are helpful in mobilising our existing understandings of social interactions in mediating "... a relationship between the labyrinthine precision of computers and the fuzzy complexity of man" (Laurel 1990). Andersen, on the other hand, warns that some users are threatened by the potential for 'interpersonal intimacy' implied by a heavily personified interface (Andersen 1990). This relates to the concern of a number of theorists and software designers for appropriateness and consistency of rhetorical 'tone' throughout any one interface.

The tone of the interface is particularly important in defining the status of the computer within the social milieu of the classroom. Many students perceive computers as possessing an aura of expertise, indeed of infallibility, which may not sit well within a constructivist environment. Indeed the 'authority' of the computer might often appear to surpass that of the teacher. While it can certainly be argued that such considerations are less important in online learning environments than in traditional computer assisted learning, the reality is that many students use computers in a variety of modes, often including segments that are effectively CAL applications. Even accessing the Internet involves interaction with particular styles of interface.

Attempts to design to design interfaces imbued with 'character', capable of interacting in varying degrees with the user, have so far met with mixed success. Many of us are familiar with various versions of Apple Computer's 'Phil', an entity realised in different graphical formats, and having some capacity for 'conversation' with the user. Microsoft's 'Bob', a later attempt at an anthropomorphic interface, has been abandoned in its present form, although Microsoft has not rejected the overall concept in relation to future interface developments. In their representation and behaviour, both of these interfaces relate to Laurel's original conception of an 'agent', as "A character enacted by the computer, who acts on behalf of the user in a virtual environment" (Laurel 1990).

With the expansion of the Internet, 'agency' has become a flourishing area of research and development. In addition to interface agents of the type described above, a range of software 'knowbots', 'spiders', and the like already scurry around the Net in the service of increasingly sophisticated search engines, while software 'personalities' interact, often undetected, with human participants in MUDs and Object Orientated MUDs (MOO). The work of Pattie Maes and her team at the Massachusetts Institute of Technology (MIT) is particularly interesting in relation to the connections which have been made between the idea of agency and research into 'artificial life'. This approach encourages a high degree of autonomy in software agents, which raises many questions of a psychological, philosophical and ethical nature concerning the nature and definition of our own 'personhood' and the many implications of interacting with artificially constructed 'persons'. The role of software agents within electronically mediated educational contexts is rapidly becoming a focus for discussion at educational computing conferences (Chan et al. 1998).

It certainly seems likely that, in the near future, students in online environments may be required to interact with software interfaces and entities which are far more deliberately and deeply anthropomorphised than is the case today. Will they be able to distinguish between these artificial 'personalities' and real human beings? Will it matter? In what sense will such entities be able to participate actively in the social construction of knowledge within computer-mediated educational environments? What sort of intellectual collaborator is a piece of software? The answers to these and other such questions might well change over time, as agents grow in complexity and sophistication.

5. CONCLUSION

Within electronic environments, the dimensions of the social interactions which mediate learning are undoubtedly increasing in complexity. In addition to a degree of unavoidable 'social' engagement with the computer itself, within the vast social space constituted by the Internet there is the potential for a huge variety of other participants, both human and digital, to be involved in those social and cognitive relationships and interactions through which students learn.

What this will eventually mean for student learning, only time will tell. The move from the tightly structured, enclosed environment of the traditional classroom in which relationships and information are strongly mediated by the teacher, to a world which is in some senses more open and diverse even than that of the student's own environment outside the school grounds, is without precedent. Perhaps one of the skills which will grow in importance as a consequence of the unregulated nature of the social aspects of knowledge construction within these new contexts is the capacity to be 'people smart'. This might involve students being more conscious and aware of the subtleties of interpersonal interactions and using these understandings in order to better comprehend and evaluate the rich and complex information sources and exchanges which are becoming available to them.

There are considerable challenges here for researchers, for teachers and for students themselves. The one thing that is certain is that there is no going back!

REFERENCES

Andersen, P. B. (1990) *A theory of computer semiotics.* Cambridge, UK: Cambridge University Press.

Chan, T.-W., Collins, A., and Lin, J. (eds.) (1998) Global education on the net. *Proceedings of ICCE '98*. Beijing: China Higher Education Press and Springer-Verlag.

Cherny, L. and Weise, R. (eds.) (1996) *Wired women: Gender and new realities in cyberspace*. Washington, USA: Seal Press.

De Lacy, J. (1987), The sexy computer. *Atlantic Monthly*, July 1987, 19–26.

Dery, M. (ed.) (1994) *Flame wars: The discourse of cyberspace*. Durham: Duke University Press.

Heim, M. (1993) *The metaphysics of virtual reality*. New York: Oxford University Press.

Jones, S. G. (ed.) (1995) *Cybersociety: Computer mediated communication and community*. California: Sage Publications.

Laurel, B. (1990) Interface agents: Metaphors with character. In B. Laurel (ed.) *The arts of human-computer interface design*. Reading, Massachusetts: Addison-Wesley.

Mitchell, W. J. (1996) *City of bits: Space, place, and the infobahn* Cambridge, Massachusetts: MIT Press.

Poster, M. (1990) *The mode of information: Poststructuralism and social context*. Cambridge, UK: Polity Press.

Preece, J. (1998) Empathic communities: Reaching out across the web. *Interactions* March/April 1998, 32–43.

Rheingold, H. (1994) *The virtual community: Finding connection in a computerised world*. London: Secker and Warburg.

Shirk, H. N. (1988) Technical writers as computer scientists: The challenges of online documentation. In Barrett, E. (ed.) *Text, context and hypertext: Writing with and for the computer*. Cambridge, Massachusetts: MIT Press.

Shneiderman, B. (1992) *Designing the user interface: Strategies for effective human-computer interaction*. 2nd edn. Reading, Massachusetts, Addison-Wesley.

Spender, D. (1995) *Nattering on the net: Women, power and cyberspace*. Melbourne, Australia: Spinifex Press.

Turkle, S. (1995) *Life on the screen: Identity in the Age of the Internet*. New York: Simon and Schuster.

BIOGRAPHY

Carolyn Dowling is an Associate Professor and Head of the School of Arts and Sciences (Victoria) at the Australian Catholic University. Prior to becoming a university academic in the area of computing and information technology she worked as a high school teacher of English Literature, French and Mathematics, then for a number of years as a freelance writer. Her teaching and research interests focus on a range of HCI issues, social and ethical aspects of computing, computer-mediated writing and aspects of Internet use.

ICT as a tool for learning to learn

Paola Forcheri and Maria Teresa Molfino
Istituto per la Matematica Applicata, Consiglio Nazionale delle Ricerche, Via de Marini 6, 16149 Genova, Italy. forcheri@ima.ge.cnr.it

Keywords: autonomous learning, information communication technology, lifelong learning, education systems

Abstract: The paper discusses the potential of ICT (Information Communication Technology) as a tool for autonomous learning, and suggests approaches to follow that will allow the education system to exploit this potential. In particular, we will analyse the key factors at the basis of autonomous learning, and will discuss the difficulties which prevent the education system from helping people learn to learn. We will then analyse the effects of ICT on learning from two points of view, the changes in the education system and the motivational effects. The educational potential of ICT will then be discussed according to the key elements of autonomous learning's education factors, and examples of applications will be shown, relating ICT based activities to these elements. The analysis of the role which should be played by educator to render these activities effective from an autonomous learning point of view will complete the discussion.

1. INTRODUCTION

Present trends in the job market require people to adapt their knowledge and skills to changes in the workplace, thus making it crucial to have access to lifelong autonomous learning (European Commission 1995a). Notwithstanding this situation, neither the scholastic nor the training system, at least in Italy, includes education for autonomous learning among its objectives. Several factors underlie this problem: the lack of a widespread culture of autonomous learning; the difference between the instructional model usually implemented by the education system and the self-learning model; the difficulty for motivating people for self-learning, especially in the case of topics requiring time and effort; and the difficulty of creating, within an educational structure, an effective context to support autonomous learning.

The increasing importance of lifelong learning, however, gives impulse to projects regarding the design and testing of new learning models for the development of skills and essential knowledge to support autonomous learning (European Commission 1995b). The experience gained through these and other projects gives numerous indications about the potential of Information Communication Technology (ICT) as a tool for autonomous learning, and suggests approaches to follow that will allow the education system to exploit this potential.

In this paper we will discuss some of these aspects, beginning with a brief analysis of the keys factors at the basis of autonomous learning. We will then go on to discuss the difficulties which prevent the education system, embracing both schooling and training, from helping people learn to learn. We will then analyse the effects of ICT on learning from two points of view, the changes in the education system and the motivational effect. The educational potential of ICT will then be discussed according to the key elements of autonomous learning's education factors, and examples of applications will be shown.

2. AUTONOMOUS LEARNING

Autonomous learning requires a positive attitude towards learning and a number of capabilities.

Among the key factors of a positive attitude we include motivation, self-confidence and sense of responsibility. Among the capabilities, we include evaluation of personal difficulties and learning strategies, awareness of the gap between the knowledge already acquired and that to be acquired, construction of new knowledge starting from the existing one, identification of reasonable objectives and of the time needed to reach them, use of a methodological approach to learning, recognition and use of learning sources tailored to needs.

Time, organisational and institutional problems inherent in the educational setting often make it difficult to acquire the necessary positive attitude and capability. However, an education system can be designed to help people acquire these capabilities, at least to some extent. ICT constitutes a valuable support in this direction, as it introduces changes in the educational setting and increases motivation.

2.1 Changes in the educational setting

ICT suggests both new approaches to learning and new forms of interaction, thus modifying relationships in the classroom (Balacheff 1993).

As to learning, a typical example is the possibility of getting learners to handle real problems using simulation systems to analyse situations that are difficult, costly or too dangerous to handle in practice Hampel et al. 1998). As to interaction, we note that lab activity, which constitutes a central aspect of the use of technology, creates favourable conditions that help educators and learners create a climate of collaborative knowledge construction, thus modifying their traditional roles (Bottino et al. 1999).

To make the change in the educational setting effective, however, educators have to be trained on how effectively to use new technologies in their work (Bottino et al. 1998). Training must overcome the view of technology simply as a commodity useful for solving given practical problems. It must also be pointed out that computational environments can be useful tools in the educational process, but learning to use them takes time, and may involve specific pedagogical and epistemological decisions (Noss 1995). In the school context, moreover, teachers should be helped to establish links with the industrial world to understand operatively real technology applications (Kommers et al. 1996; Blandow and Dyrenfurth 1994).

Finally, educators themselves should experiment with the new possibilities offered by ICT. For example, technology can be used as a means to help teachers to carry out autonomous in-service training, individually or collaboratively. In this respect, we recall a recent project of the Italian Ministry of Education, for the design and production of a multimedia system for the self-training of mathematics teachers. The system analyses the conceptual difficulties involved in several mathematical topics, proposes keys for interpreting them and suggests questions that should be examined in designing activities to overcome them. The problem of comparing the different interpretations, answering the questions, and relating the activities to classroom teaching is left to the teacher. The system was tested with about 40 teachers of the different Italian regions: the results were encouraging in that teachers demonstrated interest in tools aimed at stimulating autonomous reflection on teaching rather than in receiving teaching models (Arezzo et al. 1998).

2.2 Motivations

In the first years of life, babies have considerable capacity for autonomous learning, as they are highly motivated by the immediate advantage thus gained. The same does not apply to schools, nor to training on the job.

School students usually do not see a concrete link between schooling and the outside world. Moreover, it is difficult to help them find motivations for learning, as these strongly depend on individual feelings, and 'objective' factors (such as the idea that learning is an investment for the future) are not always sufficient. However, we note that, generally, ICT stimulates students' curiosity and creativity, poses problems they usually find challenging, and represents a link between the school and the outside world, thus constituting a motivating tool (Rekkedal 1998).

Given these considerations, we seek to familiarise students with autonomous learning through activities centred on the learning of ICT. For example, companies can organise summer work experience courses devoted to helping students get to know the outside world and employ the knowledge acquired in school to the creation of an effective product. Such experiences are uncommon in Italy, but last year we carried out one at IMA in Genova: two seventeen year old students spent a month at the Institute working on the design and creation of part of the IMA web presentation (http://www.ima.ge.cnr.it/PROGETTI/ADAPT/adapt-bis.html). The kind of activity and the context helped these students develop sense of responsibility, the capability to evaluate the gap between their knowledge and that to be acquired, and the ability to evaluate the time needed to reach a given objective.

3. TWO APPROACHES TO AUTONOMOUS LEARNING THROUGH ICT

From an educational point of view, ICT can be used in accordance with both the individual and social views of learning, two perspectives which must be integrated to develop the abilities that form the basis for autonomous learning (see Table 1).

Table 1. Approaches to learning and autonomous learning capabilities

Individual learning	Social Learning
Looking inwards	*Looking outwards*
Reflection on learning strategies	Learning from each other
Discovery of personal objective	Comparison of experiences
Awareness of personal potentiality	Discovery of external sources of learning
Use of personal resources	Awareness of knowledge
Self-evaluation	Use of the personal to reach a common objective
	Learning to be rated by others
	Integration of individual views
	Sense of responsibility
	Time and objective evaluation

The individual approach helps people reflect about themselves, thus helping to develop independence and personal initiative. On the other hand, the social approach fosters a strategic approach to problem solving and flexibility in handling a task. In several cases, the flexibility of ICT permits both the approaches: for example, multimedia systems can be employed in both individual and collaborative learning. In the following, for sake of simplicity, we suggest uses of each kind of technology considered according the approach to learning that it is best suited to (see Table 2).

Table 2. Technology and educational uses

	Learners' activities	Technology
Individual learning	Individualised self-learning Analysis of different material Search	Multimedia tools Simulation environments Web browsing
Social learning	Role-play activities Assignments Articulated projects Problem solving Management	Teleconferencing systems Email Discussion lists Chat Application environments Computer lab equipment

Finally, we have to note that the teachers' use of ICT to co-ordinate the classroom work helps them to assume the role needed to encourage students to acquire autonomous learning capabilities (see Table 3). To this aim, in fact, teachers have to act as facilitators and providers of stimuli, rather than driving the educational process. In our opinion, psychological reasons and habits make it difficult to act in this way when working in a classroom. Communication technology makes it possible to maintain contact between teacher and students but, at the same time, the physical distance naturally gives students more independence from the teacher.

3.1 Learning as an individual activity

Individualised self-learning. Multimedia self-learning systems can be fruitfully used to encourage people to acquire initiative and to autonomously build active knowledge (Kommers et al. 1996) One example is Looking for Work, a self-learning tool aimed at orienting people in the activity of job-hunting: this activity requires autonomous learning capabilities such as personal initiative, setting objectives, deciding strategies, looking for useful information, etc. To encourage users to acquire these capabilities, the tool assists them in building a job-hunting strategy tailored to their personal needs and attitudes. Experimental uses of the tool have produced very interesting results: when asking for further help from those in the work orientation sector, users are submitting to them plans on how to move and are aware of their needs. In view of its success, the tool can now be consulted in numerous public institutions in our region and is to be adopted at national level (Forcheri ct al. 1997).

Table 3. Activities, role of the educator and educator's use of ICT

Learners' activities	Educator's role	Educator's use of ICT
Individualised self-learning	Indicate the tool Monitor the activity	Private email Analysis of student's history Chat
Analysis of different material	Suggest a range of tools Monitor the activity	Analysis of student's history Use of a shared data-base Private email
Search	Engage a discussion, based on the learner' previous experience	Discussion list Email
Role-play	Assign the activity Solicit any work involved	Mailing lists Discussion lists Electronic repository
Teaching	Monitor the activity Give help on demand	Discussion lists Frequently asked questions Private email
Articulated projects	Suggest a theme, based on the learners' interests Ask learners to organise the work and take over the management of the whole project Take part in the project (without management responsibility) Ask learners to choose the programme to use, from those available Give help on-demand	Electronic repository Shared data base Shared mailing list
Problem solving	Set the assignment Guide the learners' work by means of explanations, further material, etc..	Private and public mail Electronic repository
Management	Set the task Monitor the learners' work Take the control of the lab Give help on-demand	Email Chat Video-conferencing

Analysis of different material. Learners can avail themselves of different material (multimedia packages, simulation systems, etc.), so that difficulties can be graded with respect to personal needs, and learners work according to their personal attitude and learning interest. For example, the educator can propose different material on the same topic, and got the learners to choose what material to analyse, in what order, etc., in order to reach a given objective; this may be solution of a problem, analysis of a situation, or preparation of a report, within a fixed time. This kind of activity can help learners acquire meta-cognitive capabilities, such as that of evaluating difficulties and reasoning about their own learning strategies.

In this respect, it should be noted that the same kind of work cannot be easily carried out using another kind of material such as books, as the stimulus for the activity mainly lies in the kind of material proposed.

Search activities. Search activities are fundamental in learning to recognise and find sources of information, critically analyse and compare them, and choose those that are relevant to the objectives. This kind of activity is encouraged by the availability of the web for seeking material that can be re-used by the students. One very interesting topic to work on in this way is geography. For example, learners can be asked to plan a trip on the basis of a number of constraints: the number of days to spend, the budget, trip's historical value, museums, sight-seeing possibilities, etc. Using the web, learners can tackle the search, restrict the possibilities on which to focus, go back to the web to analyse further the options selected, then integrate the information with tourist guides and interviews with a travel agency.

3.2 Learning as a social activity

Role-play activities. ICT is a helpful tool for conducting collaborative activities where learners take on different roles and responsibilities. A number of activities should be planned so that all learners can try their hand at all roles, thus acquiring a sense of responsibility, the capability to recognise and find learning sources (such as other people), reaching self-confidence, self-rating capabilities, and flexibility in adapting themselves to a given situation. One example, drawn from our experience in the EU Adapt project Teleconferencing, regards the introduction of teleconferencing to a group of managers of small and medium enterprises (Forcheri et al. 1999). A first experiment consists in the use of the BSCW teleconferencing system (Bentley et al. 1997) to carry out project work in which each participant takes a different role. To make managers acquire autonomous learning capabilities in this area, we get them to use BSCW with different roles and responsibilities. At present, the work is centred on a questionnaire to enterprises; the activities include deciding the enterprises to be interviewed, managing the list of the interviews, analysing the results, preparing the report, etc. Each manager involved in the project takes responsibility for an activity; all of them have to inform the others of the state of play in the activity, ask for suggestions, and give their ideas on the other activities. The co-ordination of the whole activity is entrusted to us. Although still in progress, this work has already produced satisfactory results, in terms of both the awareness of the potential of teleconferencing systems and the understanding of the kind of autonomous learning activities required for useful introduction of such systems in enterprises.

Teaching. Giving learners the responsibility of teaching is a very useful assignment for making them aware of the knowledge already possessed, understanding the gap between what is already known and what should be known, understanding the level reached in the mastering of a topic. Asking them to handle this task at the distance using a written form enhances these aspects, and makes it worthwhile to set activities of this kind. An example can be made from our experience within the Qualification 2000 project of the EU Adapt initiative: this is a course designed for working people which aims to give them office automation knowledge and the capability to adapt autonomously to changes in software. The course combined face-to face and distance learning, and we set the trainees distant activities to be done in pair. This was organised so that one of the two had to propose a fixed task for the other, follow up his/her work, and answer requests for explanation. This work yielded very good results in terms of both the learning of the topic and the awareness of the difficulties underlying such learning (Forcheri et al. 1998).

Articulated projects. Working on an articulated project helps people integrate individual work, develop a sense of responsibility, acquire the capability to evaluate time and objectives, and follow a methodological approach in handling a given task. Widely used electronic tools such as word processors, spread-sheets, and automatic presentation systems help the educator to design projects of this kind, in which the final outcome is a product. An interesting example in the school world, is the production of a school magazine, carried out in various Italian secondary schools with very interesting results (AA.VV. 1998). This activity requires participants to work in a well co-ordinated team and to carry out a variety of well defined tasks (writing the editorial and other articles, running a letters page and guest correspondent column, preparing questionnaires for readers, designing layout, writing and choosing comic strips, making up the showcase page, organising news reports, deciding on and preparing pictures). This kind of activity is greatly facilitated by the use of communication and information technology. Students have a number of tasks to perform, especially when the activity is completely entrusted to them, having to decide the kind of software to use, running it, learning how to use a scanner, or a printer, or how to minimise the costs, and so on.

Problem solving activities. As is well known, problem solving is fundamental for acquiring the capabilities of abstracting from examples, setting up autonomous strategies, understanding the need to adopt a methodological approach to a given task. Widely used electronic systems can be used successfully to handle these kinds of activities. For example, in secondary-school mathematics education, algebraic activities can be organised using both electronic spread-sheets and symbolic computation systems, the aim being to give students the capability to adopt workable views of problems in light of the objectives, make conjectures and verify them, and compare tools. This kind of work seems to be particularly useful for students who have difficulties in mathematics problem solving (Dettori et al. 1998).

Management activities. Being entrusted with responsibilities is usually fulfilling, and helps to acquire self-confidence and the capability to design strategies for accomplishing a task. Referring to the school setting, a possible proposal in this direction is to give groups of students, in turn, some responsibility in the management of the computer lab, according to a practice usually followed at university level.

As to on-the-job trainees, a possible proposal we tested was to give them responsibility for the collection and editing of the training course notes, or in the distribution of the course written material.

4. CONCLUDING REMARKS

ICT, as shown by numerous research in the field (Liao 1995), has the potential to innovate education, but the exploitation of this potential strongly depends on the use. EU and national projects, in our experience, constitute a valuable impulse in this direction, as they help to realise research projects oriented not only to give new insights into the teaching-learning process but also to design methods to transform these new insights into educational practice.

REFERENCES

AA.VV. (1998) LeoVinci. *Giornalino Liceo Scientifica Leonardo da Vinci.* (1) 1-4.

Arezzo, D., Forcheri, P., and Lemut, E. (1998) *Multimedia tools for in-service self-training of mathematics teachers.* Techical. Report. 7/98, Genova, Italy: CNR-IMA.

Bentley, R., Appelt, W., Busbach, U., Hinrichs, E., Kerr, D., Sikkel, K., Trevor J., and Woetzel G. (1997) Basic support for co-operative work on the World Wide Web. *International Journal of Human-Computer Studies.* 46(6) 827-846.

Bottino, R. M., Chiappini, G., Forcheri, P., Lemut, E., and Molfino, M. T. (1999) Design and reporting on research projects based on information and communication technology. *Education and Information Technologies.* in press.

Balacheff, N. (1993) Artificial intelligence and real teaching. In C. Keitel and K. Ruthven (eds.) *Learning from computers: Mathematics education and technology.* Berlin: Springer-Verlag.

Blandow, D. and Dyrenfurth, M.J. (eds.) (1994) Technology education in school and industry. *Advanced technology self-learning tools*, NATO ASI Series, Berlin: Springer-Verlag.

Bottino, R. M., Forcheri, P., and Molfino, M. T. (1998) Technology transfer in schools: from research to innovation. *British Journal of Education and Technology* 29(2) 163-172.

European Commission (1995a) *The green paper on innovation,* December 1995.

European Commission (1995b) *White paper on education and training,* November 1995.

Dettori, G., Garuti, R., and Lemut, E. (1998) From arithmetic to algebraic thinking by using a spread-sheet. In R. Sutherland (ed.) *Algebraic processes and structure.* Dortrecht: Kluwer.

Forcheri, P., Molfino, M. T., and Riccio, F. (1997) Combining hypermedia and network technology to support active vocational guidance, *Computer Information Technology* 5(1) 51-61.

Forcheri, P., Molfino, M. T., and Quarati, A. (1999) Teleconferencing tools in enterprises: Constraints and opportunities. *Proceedings of PEG99*, Exeter, UK. 10-12th July 1999.

Forcheri, P., Molfino, M. T., Quarati, A., and Riccio, F. (1998) A computer-based model for continuous training in SMEs. In G. Davies (ed.) *Proceedings of IFIP World Congress, Teleteaching'98* 31st August-4th September 1998.

Hampel, T., Ferber, F., and Muller, W. H. (1988) mechANImateach – A new approach to the teaching of mechanics, In G. Davies (ed.) *Proceedings of IFIP World Congress, Teleteaching'98* 31st August-4th September 1998.

Kommers, P. A. M., Grabinger, S., and Dunlap, J. C. (1996) *Hypermedia learning environments: Instructional design and integration,* New York: Lawrence Erlbaum.

Liao T. T. (ed.) (1995) *Advanced educational technology: Research issues and future potential.* Nato-ASI Series, Springer.

Noss, R. (1995) Thematic chapter: Computers as commodities. In A. A. diSessa and C. Hoyles (eds.) *Computers and exploratory learning.* Berlin: Springer-Verlag.

Rekkedaln, T. (1998) Teaching in the electronic college: Some didactic considerations based on feedback from students. In G. Davies (ed.) *Proceedings of IFIP World Congress, Teleteaching'98* 31st August-4th September 1998.

BIOGRAPHIES

Paola Forcheri is senior researcher at IMA-CNR (Italy). Her current research regards: education and training in mathematics and informatics, technology based educational systems, continuous training in enterprises. Research is inserted in EC and national projects. She has authored over 80 papers and trade-marks, edited special issues of journals and conference proceedings, and organised international and national conferences.

Maria Teresa Molfino is senior researcher at IMA-CNR (Italy). Her research interest are focused on Computers in Education and on Automated Reasoning. She has written more than 80 scientific papers. She edited special issues of journals and conference proceedings; and she taken part in the organisation of international and national conferences. She is the Italian leader of national and EC research projects.

Extending the role of glossaries in a virtual learning environment

Katherine Sinitsa and Alla Manako
International Research and Training Center of Information Technologies and Systems UNESCO/IIP, 40, prosp. Glushkova, 252650, Kiev, Ukraine. kath@umod.kiev.ua

Keywords: learning environment, cognitive tools, hyper-glossary, autonomous learner

Abstract: A virtual learning environment comprises of a combination of tools that facilitate learning experience. For an autonomous learner, it is crucial that those tools provide cognitive support necessary to arrange, plan, monitor and assess learning on one's own. This paper offers some ways to reconstruct a glossary into a cognitive tool and describes its application in autonomous learning.

1. INTRODUCTION

The technological revolution in education is accompanied by the changes of the research focus from instructional strategies to learning support tools, from a teacher-centred to a learner-centred paradigm and further to a *learning-centred* one (Boy 1996). The most recent approaches to learning with an emphasis on cognitive function, provide a common platform for the educational technologies by addressing both children and adults as lifelong learners.

Within this framework, the focus of educational software design shifts from courseware to learning environments, which are aimed at the facilitation of knowledge and skills acquisition, exploration of information resources represented by the different media, support of hands-on experiences (learning by doing), and other learning activities. A combination of tools available to a learner via telecommunication facilities forms a virtual learning environment (VLE), which 'enable the full information, exploration, communication and feedback, as if you are in a well-organised classroom.' (Kommers and Zhiming 1998).

VLE opens new horizons in learning and training, and a variety of approaches and implementations are still waiting for systematisation and classification. We will focus further in this submission on learning environments for an autonomous learner, that is, we will not consider collaborative learning, or instructor's guidance and support. In contrast to the instructional design, which arranges both content and control of learning, an environment for an autonomous learner should support a learning cycle defined and managed by a learner themself.

We consider an 'autonomous learner' as a person seeking additional information, trying to enlarge their knowledge, skills or capabilities for successful professional activity. Thus, learning needs and requirements are defined by learners themselves, who must also:

- determine the current status of their knowledge in relation to a task;
- set some learning objectives, describing the amount of the content that should be learned, procedures that should be mastered;
- find necessary information sources, tools, services;
- select appropriate units for learning, taking into account both external (technical, economic) and internal (learning style) preferences and restrictions;
- arrange activities to practice in application of the newly acquired knowledge;
- monitor, control and sequence learning;
- master new knowledge and incorporate it into mental model;

assess their own understanding.

VLE, organised as a set of inter-operable and communicating systems, may add value to each of its components by the integration and extension of their roles in a learning process and the introduction of cognitive support for a learner. This issue is further explored in more detail with the production of a glossary, which historically is considered in education as a complementary tool for storage and retrieval of short factual information.

The introduction of the hyper-text technology for navigation along the cross-references in a glossary does not change the overall attitude. For the domains with an extensive terminological base, a glossary naturally plays a more important role and can be turned into a support tool for self-learning and self-assessment.

In the following sections we will consider some ways to turn a hyper-glossary into an intelligent tool and propose some narratives of the new roles of a hyper-glossary in a learning environment for an autonomous learner.

2. COGNITIVE SUPPORT FOR THE AUTONOMOUS LEARNING

In a classroom learning environment, a tutor keeps the balance between new and known components, defines granularity of learning units, plans, schedules, and monitors a learner's activity, thus allowing a learner to focus on the subject matter. An autonomous learner has to perform both roles simultaneously, which requires reasoning at both subject level and meta-level (control and planning). Their main activities include:

- setting learning goals;
- navigation in the information space and search for relevant information;
- selection and sequencing of the information units;
- mastering separate units;
- assimilation of newly acquired knowledge, its integration into the existed mental structure, update and modification of the structure;
- monitoring their own progress and self-assessment.

To facilitate effective learning, a VLE should provide cognitive support for all of the mentioned activities. Cognitive tools empower learner's mental abilities, engage them in an active creation of the new knowledge structures, and facilitate reflection and focusing (Kommers, Jonassen, and Mayes 1991). In domains containing extensive factual information, such as natural sciences, medicine and some engineering disciplines (such as telecommunications, Internet), the main cognitive load is put on search and combination of the information pieces.

The role of a glossary can be naturally extended from an auxiliary information storage to an intelligent assistant, which keeps the knowledge of the particular details and is able to share it with the user on an indirect request, to communicate or demonstrate the structure of its knowledge, and to assist in search of a specific portion of data. By the indirect request we mean the absence of the unique indication of the information portion that may be relevant. A hyper-glossary empowers the user's ability to grasp a new concept by the well-structured description, convenient interface and comprehensive framework for presentation of the conceptual units in the relation to each other.

A concept-based hyper-glossary with extended visualisation can be considered as a reflection of the conceptual structure of the corresponding domain. It can serve as a backbone for the autonomous learning by support of the following activities of the learner:

- search of information (by providing explanation of selected term, assistance in search of an adequate name for a concept);
- local learning (by the presentation of the structured information about a concept, the features of the correspondent entities, its use.);

- integration of knowledge (by the opportunity to compare the concepts within a class, to trace the relations between the concepts, to explore the related concepts);
- self-assessment in terminology and structural knowledge of the domain (by the construction of generic tasks over structured glossary entries);
- navigation and planning of learning (by the elaborated visualisation).

In the above description, an analogy can be traced with the concept maps (Novak 1990) that were suggested as support tools for knowledge synthesis and navigation, facilitators and mediators of knowledge exchange, and a hypermedia authoring framework. In contrast to a concept map, which contains units of any size linked to each other by arbitrary labelled relations, a hyper-glossary contains units corresponding to the terms that are linked by the pre-defined relations. These restrictions and its specific structure extend potential applications of a hyper-glossary by adding new functions – the search of a concept name and self-assessment support.

3. A HYPER-GLOSSARY IN LEARNING

A hyper-glossary content is represented as a network of information nodes connected by the links of various types. Some of these links are directed, others are not. A node corresponds to a traditional glossary entry, though its content is structured according to more fields, for instance, 'used', 'structure', 'more specific' are added (Sinitsa and Mizoguchi 1998). Therefore, a hyper-glossary contains two types of information: an explanation of each term, and a description of an overall conceptual structure, which can be retrieved either as a text or a graph. In the text mode, a user can access data about the selected concept only, References to the related concepts are highlighted as hyper-links, and a type of relation between the current concept and a concept related to it is specified by a name of the corresponding description field. This is a basic mode, which provides a traditional view of the glossary content. In a neighbourhood mode one can see concepts related to a chosen one on a kind of a map. A user can browse the conceptual vicinity of a term along the links, getting more detailed information in the supplementary text-mode windows.

3.1 Local learning

Local learning is ensured by the hyper-glossary representation as a collection of entries with layered structured information. Layers correspond to the definition, contextual description (related concepts), explanations in various levels of details, references to other electronic sources. An elaborated structure of the hyper-glossary entry complemented by a layered content enables a user to extract appropriate information according to their preferences, qualification and a purpose of information retrieval. It also allows them to choose an appropriate level of detail, definition style, presentation mode, visualise conceptual network corresponding to the glossary terms, and to obtain references to further instructional sources.

3.2 Integrating knowledge

A hyper-glossary presents not only isolated concepts, but also their links and combinations, providing a 'stained glass view' to the domain. Each unit of information has its own value and at the same time contributes to the reflection of the whole picture. Therefore, both glossary content and structure affects its application as a knowledge acquisition support tool. The representation of a hyper-glossary as a networked structure, connected by the links of several types, facilitates the integration of learning content, allows them to place acquired pieces into the structure, to connect them to already known concepts, trace relations between concepts, compare them, reveal common features, and study their use in particular context. Conceptual structure of the domain reflected in the hyper-glossary forms a skeleton for combination of the extended multimedia learning content around the basic concepts (Elliott, Jones, and Barker 1996).

3.3 Search of information

Traditional syntactic search (manual search in a glossary index and automatic search of an exact term) is enriched in the hyper-glossary by approximate syntactic search. Approximate search means an extraction of syntactically related terms and is useful both in case of successful exact search and in a situation when the requested term is not found. Syntactically-related terms in a glossary often belong to some concept hierarchy, enabling a user to trace more general, more specific or 'sister' concepts for the chosen one. Failure of the exact search can be caused by a misprint, a spelling error or an incorrect extraction of the term. Approximate search then offers a user a list of similar terms obtained by partial matching with the entries in a glossary index. They may be, for instance, some terms with a common root: test, testing. This function for separate words is incorporated in the spell-checkers, it can be further elaborated to treat collocations. Its value for the glossary depends on the structure of domain terminology.

More elaborated semantic search helps a user to find a term (a concept name) by its tentative description. Unlike the approximate search, which can be implemented in hyper-glossary with isolated entries, semantic search algorithms require special representation of the hyper-glossary content as a network structure with the multi-sorted links between nodes. For semantic search, a notion of a 'neighbourhood' of a concept is introduced. The neighbourhood comprises of concepts that are most tightly related to the chosen one. These concepts are distributed along some 'dimensions', or belong to categories describing the common context, for instance, 'communication protocols' or 'web page design'. The most specific or concrete concepts have neighbourhoods that are rather narrow (consist of a few concepts) and 'plain' (have few dimensions), which is a reflection of the restricted number of contexts in which the term can be used. More general (and more vague) concepts have many more facets and sometimes require terms to be ordered within a certain context to show conceptual distance.

A search of an unknown concept from its description starts with the definition of the terms belonging to its neighbourhood and contexts in which it can be used. In the simplest case, tracing is executed among descendants of the known generic concept(s) of the target concept. Semantic search for the inexperienced glossary users can be guided by a system, for instance, by the introduction of the main categories represented in a hyper-glossary and prompting a user to select appropriate one(s).

Suppose a user is looking for the name of the communication protocol used for a certain type of information exchange. In this case, a generic concept is a 'protocol'. A description of the generic concept defines an 'upper bound' for search of the required concept, i.e., it may be found among the descendants of this concept. For 'protocol', the number of descendants may still be too large for manual search, so additional information about the conceptual neighbourhood may be helpful to cut search space until the number of candidates becomes reasonable for browsing.

Another option to facilitate concept searching is to ask a user for a couple of **Keywords**, which are related to the target term or describe it. These concepts can be considered as a user's description of the concept neighbourhood that defines some 'boarders' for browsing. If a user is unable to name the appropriate concepts, a service engine may offer some candidates for them to mark as 'relevant' or 'irrelevant'. This keyword-based search is similar to the syntactic keyword matching. The difference is in a way of treating the **Keywords**, which are considered as the semantically connected concepts rather than syntactic units.

3.4 Self-assessment

Approximate syntactic search may not only prevent possible lost of motivation caused by the search failures but also facilitate an active knowledge construction, as well as may be used in a self-assessment. To check their understanding, a learner can compose their own definition of some glossary term using examples of the corresponding concept, a description of features of the related (in particular, generic) concepts, and other partial information. The user-constructed definition can be then compared with the actual entry, revealing discrepancies important for planning of further learning.

Besides the above, a number of other 'hyper-glossary reconstruction' tasks can be performed: to draw a conceptual structure (network) for selected glossary entries; to name a concept by its definition; and to group related concepts or to list concepts from the vicinity of a given one. They can be combined with typical exercises to reinforce conceptual knowledge, to recognise examples of the concepts, to distinguish concepts, and to classify objects according to given features. All these activities are based on the specific internal structure of a hyper-glossary and elaborated functions intended to support learning. Assessment and evaluation is done by a learner and is aimed at providing a feedback on learning results.

3.5 Navigation

The network representation facilitates natural navigation along the links of the chosen type, and directed search via hierarchical layering of concepts. Semantic links between the glossary terms support both user-guided and system-guided browsing. One can distinguish two types of browsing: a vertical one (along a hierarchy of concepts) and a context one (within a neighbourhood). Exploring hierarchical relations, a user is travelling along 'a kind of' or 'part-whole' links, exploring more general or more specific concepts. At any moment a user's view is focused on some current concept. In the vertical browsing, all concepts situated one level above and one level below along the chosen link are displayed. Selecting one of them, a user changes their focus of attention and sees a picture from a new viewpoint.

In browsing a neighbourhood, a user explores a group of the related concepts by choosing a specific context. New facets of the current concept are revealed by moving from one context to another. A user can further explore any of the related concepts by selecting it as the current one. Visualisation of the information structure and opportunity to follow links of a certain type enables better orientation of a learner in information space and facilitates individual planning of learning, allows them to master content from the most specific concepts to the general ones or backward, to browse a contextual vicinity of the selected concept, and when necessary to study examples.

4. BASIC INTERNET GLOSSARY AS A BACKBONE FOR RESOURCES COLLECTION

As a part of the first distance course on Basics of the Internet run in 1997, a questionnaire was offered to the participants, which contained a self-evaluation and reflection part. The members of the course were diverse in age, educational background, current professional activity, acquaintance with computers and learning goals. Information extracted from 342 questionnaires provided a picture of the telecommunication use, pointed to the potential bottlenecks for distant education in Ukraine, mirrored users needs in tools, services, and information support. Many participants expressed a wish to have a kind of hand-book on the Internet, which can be addressed for the particular inquiries, and would contain references for further exploration. This idea was taken into account when working on the STACCIS project.

STACCIS is aimed at dissemination of information about telecommunication applications, tools and techniques in Community of Independent States (CIS) countries through the network of so-called 'information and demonstration centres' (IDC). An IDC contains its own collections and a number of electronic catalogues comprising references to electronic publications, software, tools, services, distance courses and other remote resources. We are currently designing the Basic Internet Hyper-Glossary as an IDC component. It is intended to assist novices in telecommunications in their search of relevant topics and facilitate professionally-oriented learning.

The Hyper-Glossary will include terms related to the networks, protocols, data interchange devices, search and navigation, and Web-pages design. Its role is two-fold. Firstly it will provide explanation in Russian for terms entered either in English or in Russian. Currently, glossaries in popular editions does not include English terminology which is needed for those users who work in original environments. On the other hand, online Internet glossaries provide explanation of English terms in English only.

Secondly, it will connect separate terms by the context cross-references and will refer to the other sources at the IDC where additional information can be found. The electronic sources intended for instructional purposes (for instance, texts of distance courses) will then be linked back to the Hyper-Glossary entries. Thus, the Hyper-Glossary will be used both as bilingual glossary and as an explanatory dictionary for study of the Internet-related concepts.

Despite a relatively large amount of the online dictionaries explaining abbreviations and terminology related to the Internet, telecommunications and networks, as well as the existence of other sources oriented to the different types of users, the content of the Hyper-Glossary could not be easily compiled. The reason was that in many popular editions the explanation style is oversimplified, the choice of terms is not well-grounded and concepts are explained in isolation. Thus, the Hyper-Glossary creators had to proceed with the whole cycle of the glossary design, including: the choice of concepts; design of the specific concept map representing the relations between the concepts; composition of the definitions and explanations of the concepts; tracing cross-references; ensuring consistency of the glossary as a whole; and arranging references to the additional instructional sources.

The above described design stages will hopefully ensure the quality of the Hyper-Glossary, which is the most critical issue for the emerging digital resources. We also hope that a more rigorous and scholarly style of presentation will correspond to the national traditions in education that ensure the understanding of what an entity is, its connection to other entities, and the overall principles of its functioning. Modern digital sources inform mostly only the usage or purpose. The concept-based approach of information presentation may be preferable for adult people educated according to the local traditions. Moreover, it could diminish a load over memory, and make learning more time-intense, as well as decrease the influence of negative psychological factors revealed in the adult training.

5. CONCLUSION

The rapid introduction of technological innovation into educational applications should be accompanied by reconsideration of pedagogical and cognitive importance of proposed novelties. The same way as hyper-books are incorporating features first introduced in research on intelligent tutoring, adaptive interfaces and user modelling (Brusilovsky and Schwarz 1997), VLE should update the functions and features of its components. Discussion of the hyper-glossary role illustrates the idea that there is a large potential of educational applications even within a restricted technological base.

REFERENCES

Boy, G. (1996) Learning evolution and software agents emergence. In C. Frasson, G. Gauthier, and A. Lesgold. (eds.) *Intelligent Tutoring Systems*, Lecture Notes in Computer Science 1086, 10-25.

Brusilovsky P. and Schwarz E. (1997) User as student: towards an adaptive interface for advanced Web-based applications. In A. Jameson, C. Paris and C. Tasso (eds.) *Proceedings of 6th International Conference on User modelling,* Sardinia, Italy, 2nd-5th June 1997. Berlin: Springer Verlag.

Elliott G.J., Jones E., and Barker, P. (1996) Authoring semantic hypermedia: A concept mapping approach. *Proceedings of ED-MEDIA'96 World Conference on Educational Multimedia and Hypermedia.* Charlottesville, USA: AACE.

Kommers, P.A.M., Jonassen, D.H. and Mayes, J.T. (1991) *Cognitive Tools for Learning*; NATO ASI Series Vol. 81. Berlin: Springer Verlag.

Kommers, P. A. M. and Zhiming Zhao. (1998) Conceptual Support with Virtual Reality in Web-based Learning. *International Journal of Continuing Engineering Education and Lifelong Learning.* 8(1/2), 184-204.

Novak J.D. (1990) Concept mapping: A useful tool for science education. *Research in Science Teaching.* 27, 937-949.

Sinitsa, K, and Mizoguchi, R. A (1998) Structured hyper-glossary as a cognitive tool for computer-based learning. *Proceedings of CATE-98, International Conference on Advanced Technologies in Education.* Mexico, 1998.

BIOGRAPHIES

Both authors, Katherine Sinitsa and Alla Manako, obtained their PhD. Degrees in Computer Science from Institute of Cybernetics and currently are senior researchers in the Dialogue and Tutoring systems Department of IRTC.

Katherine has been engaged in many projects related to computer-based training, authoring systems design, research in the field of intelligent tutoring systems and user modelling. She has worked as a guest researcher in Germany and Osaka University, Japan. Currently her primary interests are focused on tools and environments for lifelong learning, and virtual education. She is also involved in standards activity in the field of information technology terminology in Ukraine and chairs Glossary Working Group in IEEE Learning Technology Standards Committee.

Alla's research interests are data bases, cognitive aspects of courseware creation, multilingual support for education and training, distance learning, and creation of digital resources and repositories. She was the designer of the first Ukrainian distance course on "Basics of the Internet", and the designer and Web-master of the STACCIS Information and Demonstration Centre in Kiev. Currently she is a participant of a COPERNICUS project and is involved in the creation of the Centre of Distance Education which will be designed as a virtual organisation and hosted by IRTC.

Virtual environments in educational networks

Christos Bouras, Agisilaos Konidaris and Afrodite Sevasti
Computer Technology Institute-CTI, Kolokotroni 3, 26221 Patras, Greece. bouras@cti.gr
Department of Computer Engineering and Informatics, University of Patras, Greece.
Department of Computer Engineering and Informatics, University of Patras, Greece.

Keywords: virtual environments, educational networks, network services

Abstract: The field of Virtual Environments (VEs) is rapidly evolving into a new means of communication and accessing information, likely to overcome many existent technologies. However, being a new field makes the design and implementation of educational VEs an important aspect for scientific research in their educational potentials and the exploitation of existent technologies. New technologies in the field of VEs have appeared the establishment and combination of which, is yet to be investigated. This paper makes an effort to approach the issue of developing educational VEs introducing new aspects in the issues of interface, interaction with the user and functionality.

1. INTRODUCTION

These days, the use of Information Communication Technologies (ICT) has become essential to every learning procedure. New means are making themselves available to the teachers in order to make it easier for them to teach and make their knowledge available to their students. One of the most promising and most recent technologies in this field is the implementation of Virtual Environments (VE).

The term Virtual Environment is used to represent a computer-based interface that simulates ordinary every day activities and provides well-known computer and network services through it. The way that VEs can play a role in educational procedures is starting to appear. By using a virtual environment instead of a contemporary interface, you can easily help people (students and teachers in our case) access all of the available computer and network services without them being expert computer users. Thus, a VE is the best candidate to play the role of the intermediary between basic and advanced services and the inexperienced end user.

2. INTERNATIONAL PROJECTS

The development of educational VEs has been the goal of many projects around the world. We attempt to show the present situation on VE development with this indicative list of projects (Table 1).

Table 1. Educational VEs in projects around the world

Project Name	Participating Countries	Goals
VES [VES98]	Austria, Italy, Greece	The development of a comprehensive resource of teaching material for secondary school education using virtual user interfaces.
ON LIVE (ON Line Interactive Virtual Educator)	European Countries	Contact for groups of teachers in different schools with an innovative telematic service, permitting the students to learn thanks to a personalised "educator" in the form of an 3D character close to the learning thematic desired.
SAELN (Students Across Europe Language Network)	Germany, France, Spain, England	The development of a virtual interactive language and culture education resource for students to communicate with each other.
VIRLAN (Foreign Language Virtual Environment for Primary School Children)	UK, Finland, Germany, and Greece	Creating a virtual world in which children can learn by interacting with foreign children as if they were physically present in the same place.
VRLEARNERS (Virtual Reality Learning Environment for Network of Advanced Educational Multimedia Resource Centres, Museums and Schools)	European Countries	The use of advanced multimedia technologies in the schools environment and to promote co-operation between educational multimedia resource centres, cultural institutions, educators, scientists and schools with the aim to improve learning and training systems in Europe.
Quebec English Schools Network	Canada	The development of a virtual classroom and a virtual staff room.
TIPP (Technology Incentive Partnership Program)	Canada	Development of educational resources that can be shared among school boards across the province, through virtual user interfaces.

The resulting idea from this survey is that the field of educational VEs' development is beginning to be realised as a very important tool in the educational procedure [VES-WP398]. VEs will soon become integrated in every educational process and will be considered a major breakthrough in education.

3. DEVELOPMENT OF A VIRTUAL ENVIRONMENT

There are certain basic concepts on which someone should rely in order to develop a fully functional educational virtual environment (Waters 1996; Turoff 1995). The basic characteristics of the design of an educational VE, as we propose them, must be the following (Earnshaw 1995).

- The VE that will be developed must be user friendly, that is, easy to use. Since the main goal that is to be achieved by developing the VE is the promotion of the educational procedure and since the users of the VE are mainly students this must be the fundamental characteristic of the VE.
- The VE should be simple and comprehensible in its concept (Stuart 1996; Weishar 1998). It must be able to give the user the ability to navigate easily inside it. This can be achieved by developing the VE in such a manner that it simulates environments that the user is used to, such as every day environments. The user must be presented with the capabilities of the basic and advanced network services but this presentation must give him the illusion that he has used them before even though he hasn't. For example the basic network service of sending email can be simulated in the virtual world by the use of an ordinary mailbox. The user will be given the ability to send email by just clicking on a virtual mailbox in the VE instead of having to use a much more sophisticated mail client.
- The VE should be equipped with the ability to provide help at any moment that the user might find it useful. Sometimes even though the developer is aiming at simplifying the network services provided as much as possible, the user might come to a situation where he will not know how to proceed or how to use certain object in the VE. In such a case the VE should be able to guide the user through the problem. There are several scenarios that can be selected for providing help. One is the provision of help whenever a user right-clicks on an object in the VE. Another is the constant provision of help in a separate browser frame. The second even though may seem elementary is much more efficient since it does not demand any action by the user in order to provide help.
- Our proposal for the architecture of the virtual environment is to follow a tree-like structure, where the first two levels will be handled by the

virtual user interface and the other two will be handled by a combination of the services embedded in the user interface and some auxiliary browser frames. This architecture is apparent in Figure 1.

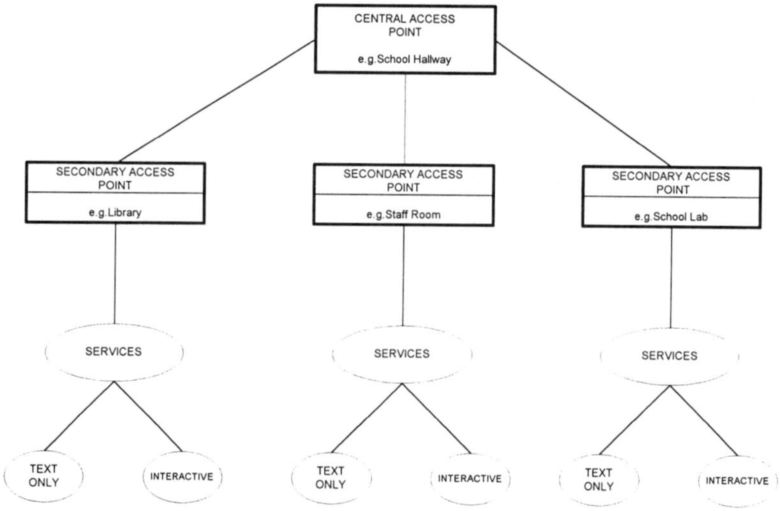

Figure 1 The proposed tree-like structure for the architecture of the virtual environment

4. DESIGNING THE USER INTERFACE

4.1 Browser layout

The educational VE that we propose, and that will be able to provide basic and advanced network services to inexperienced users such as students, will consist of three unequal frames into which the browser window will be divided. The VE will be shown in Frame 1. In Frame 2 we will provide constant help to the user and Frame 3 will be used to interact with the user (see Figure 2). Through Frame 3 the user will be able to pass information that will be required at some point from the VE and see the results of his actions.

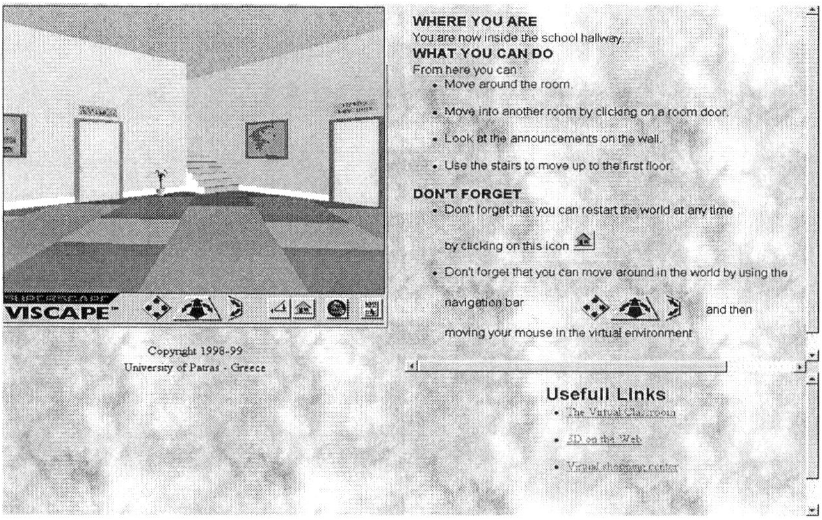

Figure 2. An instance of the central room of the school in the virtual user interface, with Frame 1 on the right, Frame 2 on the top left and Frame 3 on the bottom left of the browser window [VRT for Windows 98].

After the VE has been loaded the user will find himself in front of a big building that will be the virtual school. At this point the user can navigate around the school but he will not be offered any significant services. The user must make his way to the school door and enter in order to take advantage of the full potentials of the VE.

As soon as the user passes through the main school door he will find himself in the central room of the school (Figure 2) which resembles the school hallway. Around the room the user can see other doors that lead to other rooms. These are the staff room, students' room, library, computer laboratory and other rooms where specific lessons are supposed to be taught, such as Geography and History. The user at this point may select a door and enter into the room that he decides. The main room of the VE provides the certainty that the user is presented with all the abilities of the VE at once and he can choose at his convenience.

4.2 The teacher room

This room will address the user's need to access information concerning the school's teachers. Through symbolic assimilations, the user will be able to access a teacher's personal web page, if any, personal information about teachers and the lesson that they are teaching as well as perform trivial searching activities among the teaching staff. The user can also find out the lesson timetable of the school and exchange off-line messages with the teachers.

As the user enters this room he will find himself in front of a set of cabinets through which the subdivision of the school's directory service containing the teachers' entities will be provided. The searching procedure to be followed is: select the cabinet which holds the first letter (from A to Z) of the surname of the teacher to be found, click on the appropriate teacher's name from the ones beginning with the specific letter, which appear as hyperlinks in Frame 3 and then receive information on the teacher and the lessons that he teaches, on Frame 3 again. This information will be available in the form of a card (like a library card) which will consist of a photograph, information and several functionalities such as a button on which the user can click and send email to the teacher, by using Frame 3 again. At any moment the user will be able to return to the VE and recommence his trip.

The teacher room will also be equipped with a desk that will have an interactive book, containing the school timetable, and a computer on it. The computer will provide an alternative means for accessing the teachers' division of the directory service as if one was using a normal web based search. The user will be asked to input the information and receive the results of the search in Frame 3. A bulletin board in the teachers' room will contain any recent announcements concerning the school, for the user to read.

4.3 Student room

The student room will be very similar to the teacher room with some extra features. The user will be able to find a student of the school as described in the teacher room section, using the same two alternative approaches. The bulletin board will be enriched with announcements on student activities such as a school newspaper or maybe some sport activities.

4.4 Library room

The library room will simulate the environment of a real library (Figure 3). When the user enters he will find himself in front of libraries full of books. Above every section of the library the user will be able to see a sign that will indicate the category of the books that are below. When the user chooses a category he will be able to move towards the specific section of the library and look at the subsections of the specific category written on the selves. By clicking on a subsection the user will be able to see in Frame 3, information on all the books available in the school library that concern the specific subsection.

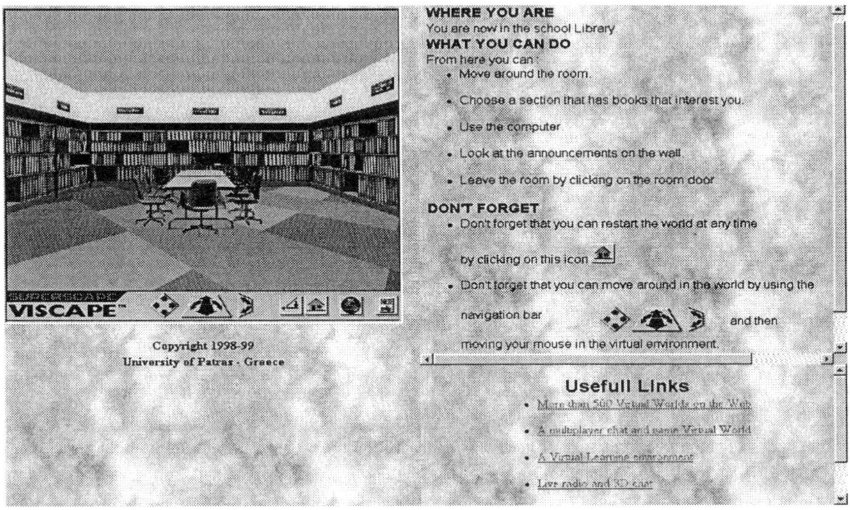

Figure 3. Instance of a specific room's user interface: The Library Room

The library room will also have a bulletin board where the user will be able to get information on the library working hours and where he can send email to contact the librarian.

4.5 Laboratory room

The lab room will be a simulation of the school lab. The user will be able to see desks with all of the school's equipment on them such as computers, faxes etc. By clicking on every piece of equipment the user will receive information on its configuration, its last use and, in some cases, use it by sending faxes and messages to the other users of the computers in the school lab, through Frame 3.

4.6 Specific lesson rooms

The specific lesson rooms will be dedicated to giving information about specific lessons that are taught at the school. These rooms will be divided into three sections.

- The library section that will be a subsection of the whole library and the user will be able to choose titles that concern only the specific lesson. The library will be the same as the one described in the library room section, only smaller.
- The computer section. This section will consist of a desk where the user will be able to use a computer to make queries concerning books on a specific lesson (depending on the room that he is in). There will also

exist an information book, by clicking on which, the user will be able to receive other available on the Internet resources concerning the specific lesson, accessed by hyperlinks in Frame 3.

- The specific lesson section in form of a bulletin board, where the user will be able to see all the information concerning the specific lesson at the school. This information may be the timetable of the lessons, the teachers that teach the specific lesson and the subjects that the specific lesson covers.

The walls of the specific lesson rooms will be decorated with relevant pictures. For example the in the Geography room the user will be able to see maps, by clicking on which, he will be able to see the books that are available in the library about a specific geographical region.

5. CONCLUSIONS – FUTURE WORK

The basic concluding remark after designing and implementing the VE is its potentials are almost unlimited. Future work is suggested on the subjects of linking databases and making them co-operate with the virtual environment (Bouras 1998) as well as creating educational Distributed Virtual Environments (DVEs) (Snowdon et al. 1996). Both of the above will raise the functionalities of such environments to such a level that many established current technologies will become obsolete and be replaced (Schneiderman 1997).

It is important to mention that a VE, which integrates all the network services that are mentioned above, requires constant update and maintenance. The procedure of integrating all these services will surely be lengthy but the result will be a major breakthrough in the educational procedure.

The VE will help the educational community come much closer and will of course promote the exchange of ideas between different cultures. It can provide the forum for meetings and all types of communication.

REFERENCES

Bouras, C., Fotakis, D., and Philopoulos, A. (1998) *A distributed virtual learning centre in cyberspace.* Paper given at 4th International Conference on Virtual Systems and Multimedia, VSMM98, Gifu-Japan, 18-20 November 1998.

Earnshaw, R. J. and Vince, J. (1995) *Computer graphics: Developments in virtual environment.* London: Academic Press.

Schneiderman,B. (1997) *Designing the user interface: Strategies for effective human-computer interaction.* Reading, United Kingdom: Addison-Wesley.

Snowdon, D., Greenhalgh, C., Benford, S., Bullock, A. and Brown, C. (1996) A review of distributed architectures for networked virtual reality. *Research Development and Applications* 2(1) 155-175.

Stuart. R. (1996) *The design of virtual environments.* Blacklick, Ohio: McGraw-Hill.
Turoff, T. (1995) *Designing a virtual classroom.* Department of Computer and Information Science. New Jersey, New Jersey Institute of Technology.
VES (1998) The Virtual European School, ANNEX I – Project Programme, January 1998. Der Buchhandel, Wirtschaftskammer Osterreich.
VES-WP3 (1998) D3.2 Technology Monitoring Report, August. Brussels:EU.
VRT for Windows (1998) *User guide.* Santa Clara, USA: Superscape.
Waters, R., Anderson, D., and Barrus, J. (1996) *Diamond Park and Spline: A social virtual reality system with 3D animation, spoken interaction and runtime modifiability.* Cambridge, Massachusetts, Mitsubishi Electric Research Laboratory.
Weishar, P. (1998) *Digital space: Designing virtual environments.* New York: McGraw-Hill.

BIOGRAPHIES

Dr. Christos J. Bouras is the Head of Research Unit 1, Computer Technology Institute (CTI). His PhD is from the Computer Science and Engineering Department of Patras University. He is currently working in the area of networks, educational technology, telematics and new services. He is experienced in the design and analysis of networks and protocols, and their use for medicine and education. He has been in various research and development projects, including RACE and ADAPT. He has published a number of papers is a co-author of two books.

Agisilaos S. Konidaris is an R&D Computer Engineer. He is now doing PhD studies in the Computer Science and Engineering Department of Patras University. His research interests include telematics and new services, database design, implementation of managed bandwidth services and video-on-demand algorithms. He has participated in projects such as ELECTRA and ODYSSEAS and is now involved in project TODAY'S STORIES.

Afrodite V. Sevasti is an R&D Computer Engineer, at the Computer Technology Institute, Patras, Greece. She is now doing PhD studies at the Computer Science and Engineering Department of Patras University Greece. Her research interests include telematics and new services, virtual reality services, Database design, implementation of managed bandwidth services, and video-on -demand algorithms. She has participated in R&D projects such as ELECTRA, and ODYSSEAS and is involved in project TODAY'S STORIES.

Issues and discussions around networked learning

Reports from discussion sessions

1. INTRODUCTION

A key feature of the Conference was the use of Panel Sessions designed to foster discussion amongst the participants. As a contrast to paper sessions, presenters spoke briefly pointing out the key issues in their work, to stimulate discussion by all in the room. Thus discussion was further encouraged by the comments from reactors and also the chair. This active involvement of all conference attendees in the debate is a feature of IFIP working group meetings and conferences. The seriousness with which the community takes these discussions is evidenced by their inclusion in this book. The notes and reflections from the rapporteurs of these five sessions – collaboration in learning, virtual school, teacher education and pedagogic reflection, Internet and the teacher's role, and envisioning the challenges for future teaching.

2. COLLABORATION IN LEARNING

Chair: Raymond Morel, CH
Presenters: Lasse Lipponen, FI, Paul Nicholson, AU and Anne McDougall, AU
Rapporteur: David Squires

2.1 Promoting educational change with computer-supported collaborative learning

This presentation by Lasse Lipponene was based on the findings of a series of case studies of the use of computer-supported collaborative learning in Finnish elementary schools. The challenges for innovation identified through this work include overcoming technical problems, coming to terms with new pedagogical approaches, and organising schools so that they can realise the benefits of computer-supported collaborative learning. An interesting concept of 'cognitive responsibility' was introduced. In collaborative environments learners have joint responsibilities. As such they need to consciously consider how they can help each other and contribute to the common learning aims. In this context the behaviour of 'lurkers' and dominant group members is critical.

2.2 Linking science thinking and learning with software

In this presentation the use of a collaborative hypertext environment for learning science was discussed (*MetaMap*) by Paul Nicholson. The design of this cognitive tool is based on an extension of the idea of a concept map to three dimensions. It is claimed that this extension attends to problems inherent in conventional concept maps: they are hard to up-date, interpret, relate to other concept maps, concept clusters are often 'off screen' in complex maps, and the complexity of maps is often confusing. The role of the map is to act as a 'voice' for learners, providing a mechanism for them to articulate and express their ideas. These expressions can then be used in collaboration with other learners (and teachers) to provide a framework for debate and collaborative learning.

2.3 Issues in learning with new technologies

The idea of the interface as a partner in learning was explored in this session by Anne McDougall. A simple example of drawing a circle was used to illustrate this idea. The conventional way to draw a circle is to use a compass. The use of this physical 'interface' to the act of drawing implies at least an intuitive appreciation of the concepts of radius and circumference – with the consequent implications for mathematical understanding. This approach was contrasted with two computer based techniques for drawing a circle. First the use of Logo to programme procedures for drawing circles was considered. Procedures can be written which utilise the concept of radius. However, the more natural approach, which resonates with the 'differential geometry' inherent in Logo is the well known 'poly procedure' approach, which does not invoke the concept of radius. Second, the use of a drawing tool, based on the direct manipulation of a square envelope, was discussed. In this last technique there is no implicit mathematical content, as defined in conventional mathematical curricula. Is the use of such tools counter-productive in encouraging and supporting learning, or has the nature of knowledge (in this case the structure and construction of circles) been changed by the advent of ICT?

2.4 Some issues for consideration

2.4.1 Collaboration in learning

Collaboration for learning is a complex idea, and dimensions of this complexity emerged in the discussion. First, there was agreement that the experiences of collaborating learners are often different. An unattractive feature of some collaborative ventures is that major and minor roles may be assigned (sometimes unconsciously) to group members, e.g. a less dominant/able member of a group may be assigned the task of acting as typist when a small group of learners is using software. Issues of concern here are a realisation of cognitive responsibility, with more able dominant members of a group accepting mentoring and supporting roles for other members. In a distributed context anonymity is an important aspect – anonymous discourse can lead to a 'level playing field' environment in which all members have an equal voice and responsibility during collaboration.

Second, there is an issue of whether collaborative learning is simply an environment for individuals to learn in, providing scope for learners to develop their own personal conceptions by 'bouncing ideas' off other people. In this conception, the group does not learn as such; rather individuals are assisted to make personal developments. In contrast, notions of distributed cognition open up the idea of the collaboration resulting in the group learning as whole, with knowledge and an understanding developing in the 'spaces' between the collaborators.

It may be a matter of semantics, but it could be helpful to distinguish between collaboration and co-operation as a way of highlighting these issues. Collaboration is characterised by an awareness of cognitive responsibility and an acceptance of conceptually defined learning owned by a group of collaborators. Co-operation is characterised by a focus on personal idiosyncratic conceptual development with the assignment of roles (beneficial or otherwise) to group members.

2.4.2 Assessment

Assessment in collaborative contexts is problematic. Well rehearsed concerns are typically focused on who did the work, and who should get most credit in a group. Of course, this implies an outcomes oriented approach to assessment, and fails to realise the scope for personally tuned formative assessment focused on learning processes. However, if collaborative learning is to become a 'respected' mainstream approach to learning, summative evaluation needs to be addressed. In this context, the notion of group assessment in which all members grades are moderated in terms of the average grade obtained by the group is interesting. In such approaches, in a group that does well as a whole, all members will benefit, perhaps leading to an awareness of the benefits of cognitive responsibility. Of course, the reverse moderating effect holds, also making possible highlighting the importance of cognitive responsibility.

2.4.3 Software features

A strong point was made that 'fitness for purpose' is very important – the appropriateness of software design depends on what you intend to do with the software. Thus if you want to draw many circles of different colours and sizes to represent balloons on a poster, the use of a drawing tool makes sense. If you are a mathematics teacher trying to teach the concept of radius, the use of a compass or purpose designed procedures in Logo makes sense. In fact, a useful teaching technique may be to give students different procedures, which reflect radial and non-radial definitions of circles.

A subtle but important point emerged in the discussion about the non-neutrality of computer interfaces. It was claimed that the *MetaMap* software provides a collaborative voice to learners. In a sense this implies that the learners are using the software much as a ventriloquist would use a dummy. However, software is not a dummy – it has all sorts of features and possibilities inherent in its design. In fact some writers would go so far to sat that it has intrinsic intelligence of a sort. Thus, the collaborative voice of the learner will be interpreted in this frame of designed inherent possibilities. The consequent potential and limitations determined by the frame need to be taken account of. This leaves us with an important question: Who is driving the design of software designed to support collaboration: the designer (and by implication the commercial producer), the teacher, or the collaborator?

3. VIRTUAL SCHOOL

Chair: Peter Bollerslev, DK
Presenters: David Passig, IL, Wolfgang Weber and Annemarie Hauf-Tulodziecki, DE
Reactors: Doug Brown, UK, and Anne McDougall, AU
Rapporteur: Brian Samways, UK

3.1 Virtual reality and a new media for learning

In the first paper, David Passig and Aviva Sharbat reported on their research into the views of 50 experts on the future of virtual reality (VR) in education. Although it was an ad-hoc group, it did have persons from 11 different countries most of whom held key positions in universities, research institutions or industries involved in educational virtual reality. Five key themes emerged from the paper: VR is a powerful breakthrough and needs an alternative classroom structure; VR is cognitively different but can solve existing problems; VR offers new learning styles; VR has great potential in science and language learning; and teachers require specific training for VR.

The second paper given by Wolfgang Weber and Annemarie Hauf-Tulodziecki focused on media literacy. The concept, based on their research findings, is a framework within which schools can find their own developmental position. On completing their action plans for media literacy the project team were able to identify gaps. These were filled by bringing the ideas of different schools together and supporting the interchange. Four key themes emerged from the paper: new media for learning; analysis of planned use across the whole school; sharing good practice between schools; and bringing schools together and encouraging joint working.

3.2 Reactors

Doug Brown stated that clearly these are exciting times and there is an increasing need for collaboration. It is interesting to note that we often over estimate impacts of new technology in the short-term when predicting the future, but under estimate these in the long term. We need to re-visit 'what is education' more frequently, as all too often we use our own experiences as a base and these quickly become out-of-date with the fast developments. Do we react and respond to the technology or use the new technologies to deliver our educational choice? We too should ask ourselves whether or not we are addressing the use of the new media and how we integrate these into our already overloaded curriculum.

Anne McDougall said that there is a really strong message that it was correct to put these two papers together on the conference programme. The second speaker Wolfgang Weber is talking about virtual reality as can be clearly seen in his diagram on Work Area. We researchers must be aware that the next steps are often defined by the 'doers' but that the vision from the second presentation provides a very strong pointer to the ways in which virtual reality might be implemented.

3.3 Key issues in discussion

The audience was reminded that in 1983 it was reported that there was disappointment in the introduction of IT into education in that it was only a continuation of 'chalk and talk'. However, that was IT in two dimensions and with VR we now have a three-dimensional approach and this will ensure the future breakthrough. We must also go forward using evolutionary steps and not revolutionary ones. It was also said that over the years we have 'poured' computers into schools but they still are not being used effectively. Currently we are trying to use our research to develop the future by creating a vision.

The implementation of such systems must be made as simple as possible; for example, 'one button' operations. In the German project 'Schools to the Net' showed the potential of the Internet and how computers can be used sensibly when connected. New Media has over 4000 programmes but only about 100 have the potential to improve the quality of learning. Teachers still use the 'drill and practice' press button type, but they are trying to get them to integrate the computer in the learning process. Delegates could visit the 'Fairy Tales on the Web' site (in English) at: http://www.learnline.de

Personal; experiences supported the discussion. One delegate related two of her own experiences. In one she used a computer chemical model but found it offered no more than a real model which could be used in the classroom. In the other she viewed a VR art gallery and in one mode it was possible for her to experience the exhibition in the same way as the partially sighted creator. The second experience could not have been experienced in any other way.

Those present were reminded that the 'biro' when first invented, was sold with the promotion that it could write under water. It was a very useful invention but we still do not write under water. In the same way virtual reality has great potential but the promotion of it may not indicate the future direction.

4. TEACHER EDUCATION, PEDAGOGICAL REFLECTION

Chair: Peter Bollerslev, DK
Presenters: Gail Marshall, US, and Don Passey, UK
Reactors: Harriet Taylor, US, and Rosa Maria Bottino, IT
Rapporteur: Brian Samways, UK

4.1 Connecting teaching and learning

In the first paper Gail Marshall emphasised the need for teaching to 'make meaning' and she gave several examples where ICT could complement good pedagogical practice. She reminded the audience of the need to create a 'web' between teaching and learning using the tools of the mind. She felt there are four 'technologies' of the mind, which were generally not being addressed in today's technology equipped classrooms and finished with a concern for those teachers who because the work was hard for their pupils often did the thinking for them. Two key themes emerged: there is a need to create a web between teaching and learning; and there are four technologies of the mind – planning, memory, representation and inference.

Don Passey continued the connection between teaching and learning, in his paper but from the need for a vision, a plan and implementation. In the UK links between schools and community are being encouraged; there are resources being created for the web; the new national curriculum is reviewing the need for ICT skills; and both pre-service and in-service teacher education are being re-examined. However there is no support at present for a 'connected learning community'. Four key themes emerged: the need for a vision, a plan and implementation; teachers, pupils and parents can be extended; laptops between school and home are beneficial; and a connected society will place greater demands on all of us.

4.2 Reactors

Harriet Taylor said that clearly we have to capture the models of use where it is being done well and transfer these ideas to our work. More resources need to be allocated, but in ways which will be successful. Big ideas and big projects have done well, but translating that to our small individual work is difficult, and as always the politicians want results as soon as the hardware is in place. Using ICT we need better models, and in the light of the useful questions that have been posed by our speakers we now need the answers. The experts are probably here at this conference and we should discuss seriously the out-of-school learning.

Rosa Maria Bottino suggested that the 'Connected Learning Community' is a good way to describe a learning society and we have firstly to convince teachers of the benefits of connecting learners. There has to be a new professionalism in using ICT tools across the curriculum with a view to addressing cognitive skills. Couple this with the need for awareness of the role that ICT can play in the teaching and learning processes it is clear that the form, content and practice of teacher training needs to be revised. In the end schools must use ICT effectively, support pupils, parents and the community and develop ways of supporting the school-home connection. Clearly roles are changing, learning evaluation is changing and new models of analysis (hopefully using ICT) are necessary.

4.3 Key issues in discussion

Two questions were raised how and where do we try to motivate pupils? Similarly with the difficulties raised in the second paper, as we cannot rectify all of these in one full swoop. But often there is enough excitement and enthusiasm to keep the changes going. If changes are meaningful they will continue and we do not need to continually control. Also we have evidence that teachers do not have to be school connected. Nearly half are already down the path in the State of Jersey. We need evaluation but some of these proposed changes are not great. For example, homework set by teachers is often not related to current schoolwork. We must somehow make schoolwork and homework more related. It is important to work on a small scale at school level and with the local community. The new curriculum in the United Kingdom is not technologically originated; it does emphasis the "I" in ICT. When ICT is put in the hands of children their competencies increase enormously. Two years' advancement has been shown in secondary education and three years in terms of desktop applications for year 6 in elementary.

However concern was also expressed that harnessing students' out-of-school time is Fascist, and that it is important that we not only create students that fit into society but that we encourage informal learning at all times. Using the description 'learning in the wild' she felt that homework should be loosened from schoolwork. Another remarked that it is difficult enough to be a good teacher, let alone a good parent. We should make more use of other local organisations such as public libraries with their professional staff. Parents are not professional and are pulled in many different directions by advertising for example.

It was added that in ICT it is the style of learning and the approach to the computer that are important. Some approaches do not capture the hearts of teachers, only their minds. Those teachers who listened on the other hand would certainly buy the message and their children would take it home, adding the caveat that this is not the whole answer. Yet learning is at the centre of importance today and that to be able to work with the 'big' ideas in learning, one must have 'big' ideas in both content and process. The audience was asked to think of what kind of support they would *not* want to give. The audience was also reminded of small-scale projects and the local research into such initiatives where the results challenge the national picture. These have a technical contribution to make to the larger picture.

In conclusion we may have lots of 'vision' but as yet not enough thought has been given to the strategic planning. But head the mistake in tackling the alphabet, a letter at a time and missing the enormous advancement of seeing it as a whole. "We must be careful not to jettison good directed pedagogy for the sake of using ICT".

5. THE IMPACT OF THE INTERNET ON THE ROLE OF THE TEACHER

Chair: David Benzie, UK
Presenters: Petra Wager, FI, and Yvonne Buettner, CH
Reactor: Helene Godinet, FR
Reporter: Paul Nicholson, AU

5.1 Teachers' roles

The use of the Internet in education is growing rapidly, and its application to the curriculum has broadened to cover all curriculum areas. This rapid change and growth in usage has been largely driven by external influences, rather than by pedagogical or educational needs grounded in the classroom. It has had a major impact on teachers and school systems who are not necessarily prepared for the challenges this presents.

Petra Wager discussed the role of the teacher and the emergence of distance education in Finnish schools. A sociological analysis of the role of the teacher in Internet-based classrooms shows that teachers' work has undergone significant changes in response to the demands of the medium, requiring a wide range of competencies beyond those of the traditional classroom. In particular, the teacher is no longer 'just' a teacher but must adopt a multiplicity of roles such as developer, technician, curriculum developer, and secretary, In order for effective implementation to occur, issues specific to each of these new roles must be addressed.

Yvonne Buttner discussed how new skills and competencies are required in addition to those acquired earlier. Teachers need extensive support in implementing these new technologies. It is essential that educators determine the role and value of the Internet in education, and develop appropriate pedagogical and ICT skills in order to facilitate its effective implementation.

5.2 Key issues

The impact of ICT and particularly the Internet has been to significantly change the nature of teachers' work, not only within the classroom, but also by creating new demands on teachers' time outside of the classroom and school. The role has been broadened from a focus on delivering pre-packaged curriculum content to the students, to becoming – a secretary (managing information); a content creator; a researcher or consultant; a curriculum developer; a publisher; a technical expert; or a student (need to keep learning simply to do their job with the new media).

There is a major professional concern about how much can be expected of an individual teacher. Should the demands of the technology require them to undertake unpaid work out of school simply because developing resources for the Internet is so time intensive? If not, then how will school systems fund such development at the local level? If they can't provide funds, is it ethical to expect teachers to do it for free? What industrial and professional issues and pressures need to be raised here?

In distance education, there is the additional issue of distributed expertise, for example, in working with remote schools, who should determine the nature and content of curriculum materials – the local school or central provider? Is it important to draw on local (school-based) expertise, or should a central agency be responsible for all decision making? In either case, what is it that the teachers in each location have to know, and must be able to do with the technology? The critical issue here is that if individual teachers are expected to create, publish, and deliver content, how will they be supported in acquiring the necessary competencies and time?

These issues require real solutions. For example, it is quite likely that teachers will not be able to teach effectively, if at all, with ICT if they do not have access to a computer and current software at home so that they can become 'Internet literate' through personal exploration of the Internet's potential outside of the workplace – they need to have an opportunity to explore the medium in the same way as they developed their traditional pedagogical skills by working in classrooms. The common assumption that traditional pedagogy can simply be transferred to the Internet is not realistic: there is a strong need to know what works, and what does not work well, in online course delivery, and so be able to create appropriate learning activities and learning environments. Of particular importance in this regard is the need to develop communicative processes and strategies so that learning is facilitated by human communication and interaction rather than relying solely on the technology to do the teaching.

5.3 Conclusions

It is clear that effectively addressing the issues above requires extensive support to allow the teacher to develop the required competencies. This has significant financial implications, and even with the best of financial support, may not lead to effective change because of the individual teacher's inability to commit the time needed to conceptualise, create, and publish Internet-based curriculum materials

It is recommended that a workgroup approach be adopted in which the school, and not the individual teacher, becomes the focus for support and development. This may simplify financial considerations, and provide a more durable development model. Within a school, different staff members may acquire specific skills and knowledge that will support the educational endeavours of the whole school. In this way individual teachers are not burdened with the need to acquire a diverse range of skills, but can call on colleagues when specific support is needed. In addition, the distributed nature of the knowledge in the school means that the loss of a single teacher does not remove the whole set of skills and knowledge from the school. The school therefore becomes both a learning community of its own, with its own experts to assist its teachers, and the facilitator of an external learning community. In this way, support structures and processes become a normal part of its structure, and so serve to sustain the changes that prompted their development.

6. THE CHALLENGES FOR FUTURE TEACHING

Chair: Sindre Rosvig, NO
Contributors: Petra Fisser, NL, Andrea Kö and Andras Gabor, HU, and Larry Miller, CA
Reactor: Giovanna Gazzaniga, IT
Rapporteur: Rosa Maria Bottino, IT

6.1 The challenge of change

The first two papers, by Petra Fisser and Andrea Ko, stressed the necessity that education, and, in particular, higher education have to meet the requirements of the networked society. Opportunities offered together with some disadvantages were discussed and examples of good practice were proposed.

For example, the University of Twente has a long tradition in the use of telematics applications and, at present, the task force 'Telematics application in education' has been formed with the aim of stimulating and initiating new projects. The aim is to use telematics to support the learning process and not to go in the direction of a virtual university. Petra Fisser emphasised that the vision which is at the basis of this project at present is that the industry sector has the need for university graduates who are prepared in using information and communication technology in their future profession. The objective of the work done at the University of Twente is to offer more flexible learning environments which are not meant to replace the instructor but where their role progressively changes – from lecturer to guide. Of course this passage is not a simple one and the teachers have to be supported in this change and in using ICT applications: the 'Telematic Studio' has been established at this regard. More details about this quite innovative project could be found at: http:/teletop.edte.utwente.nl

Andrea Kö started from the same assumption of Petra, that education cannot be separated from the business and economy; it is influenced by market and by the new changes in technology. It has to consider the strong need that industries and companies have of ICT skilled persons. Of course, university, and education, in general, could not be only concerned with the present interests of the occupational market but need to have a strategic vision of the future knowledge society. Schools and educational institutions need to radically re-engineer their traditional activities. Andrea suggested two main streams that seem her decisive at this regard: the individual learning through the lifelong studies, and the remote/virtual college.

Larry Miller presented a vision of the future teaching that is grounded into a different background, that of primary education. From this perspective he outlined two possible views: a) the curricula embedded in software seen as a lever to move teachers toward new approaches to teaching, and b) the curricula, designed by experts, embedded in software, and then delivered to students using classic programmed instructional principles. Different premises and visions of future teaching can suggest different answers to some crucial questions: The technological refusal is a guilty of teachers? Who is in charge of technological innovations? Will technology make schools and teachers irrelevant?

6.2 Reactor

Giovanna Gazzaniga reacted to these contributions and outlined some possible problems and possibilities. She started from the consideration that using ICT in education is mandatory now and that teachers must face the problem of how to introduce ICT in their teaching activity. This brought her to some initial questions: are we sure that teachers are well informed about new possibilities? Can we consider the scenarios presented by Petra and Andrea as 'normal'? And, generally speaking, how ICT can be introduced in the teaching activity? As far as this last question is concerned, she delineated three different situations: i) teachers who work alone and simply adapt their usual approach to teaching to ICT environment ('Internet tolerant curricula') ii) teachers who work alone and try to exploit some of the new opportunities offered by ICT, and iii) teachers who work relying on the support of expert institutions. Each of the three outlined situations has both positive and negative aspects, and, often, teachers cannot choose among them.

Some of the questions that Giovanna then raised considered not only the teacher but also the learner's point of view. Is it always good for students to handle new technologies even if ICT are merely used as a substitute of a quite traditional approach to education? Could students refuse ICT if they perceived them as a way for saving money or teachers time?

6.3 Discussion

The discussion that followed these briefly sketched issues and questions involved all the audience, conveniently stimulated by the chairman, and mainly developed around the following questions.

Teachers should be prepared to the fact that students have competencies in ICT uses and opportunities to use them by their own. School is usually slower than external reality.

How can we give to the students all the support they need for effective learning through the use of ICT with short time at disposal? The use of ICT do not usually saves time but instead increases the time required.

Can computers become a discriminating media? Do we adequately consider gender problems? Are different attitudes sufficiently valorised?

Is it now teachers or student time?

PART 4

COGNITION AND LEARNING

Cognitive development in ICT contexts

Pamela Gibbons, Kathryn Crawford, Susan Crichton and Robert Fitzgerald
Australian Catholic University, PO Box 968, North Sydney, NSW 2059, Australia.
p.gibbons@mackillop.acu.edu.au
University of Sydney, Australia
School District #10, British Columbia, Canada
Australian Catholic University, Australia.

Keywords: cognition, context, individual differences, designing learning environments

Abstract: New, dynamic, virtual learning environments are presenting opportunities for more diverse types of learning and cognitive social activity than have been previously available in formal educational settings. Some consequences of our understanding of how learning occurs include newly recognised forms of learning, how these can be nurtured, and how this new knowledge can be applied to the design of virtual social contexts that encourage new approaches to learning and thinking. Also, settings in which ICT are used can be designed in new ways to take advantage of the knowledge that cognition is plastic, active and socially embedded. In this paper, four related investigations are presented which are based on systemic, socio-cultural approaches to the understanding of learning in ICT contexts. Our research indicates, however, that there is also a need for changes in institutional practice if these new approaches are to be actualised.

1. INTRODUCTION

New dynamic virtual learning environments are presenting opportunities for more diverse types of learning and cognitive social activity than have been previously available in formal educational settings. One consequence of our understanding of how learning occurs is that newly recognised forms of learning can be nurtured. It is also now possible to apply our knowledge of learning to the design of virtual social contexts that encourage new approaches to learning and thinking. A second consequence of our understanding of how learning occurs is that settings in which information and communication technologies (ICT) are used can be designed in new ways. That is, the social practices and physical design of settings in which humans learn can be designed to take advantage of the knowledge that cognition is plastic, active and socially embedded. Our research indicates, however, that there is also a need for changes in institutional practice if these new approaches are to be actualised.

In this paper, a range of research-based perspectives on the dynamics of learning in ICT-rich contexts is presented. Merleau-Ponty (1962) showed that our knowledge is dependent on being in a world that cannot be separated from our body, our language or our socio-historical settings. This embodied or emergent view suggests that meaning has its origin in the activity of the semi-autonomous agent and recognises the fundamental plasticity of cognition. Emerging neuro-evolutionary views such as the Theory of Neuronal Group Selection (TNGS) (Edelman and Tononi 1995) also entertain the plasticity of cortical function at the level of neuronal groupings and consider perception as an active and creative act. Socio-cultural theorists (Luria 1973; Vygotsky 1978; Crawford 1996) recognise the plastic and active form of higher psychological function. While important work has been done on the situated (Lave and Wenger 1991) and distributed (Hutchins 1995) nature of cognition, both of these approaches tend to marginalise the activity of the thinking subject (Nardi 1996) and the role of individual differences in cognitive function. The real challenge for research is to investigate individual difference constructs within situated human activity frameworks that entertain the dynamic relationship between learner and context. Systemic, socio-cultural approaches to the understanding of learning in context therefore form the basis of the explorations discussed herein.

The first study presented explores the development of a practice-based model of cognitive style for studying the interaction between individual learners and context. This research suggests that cognition and context are not closed independent systems but rather open-ended and dialogic. The second study, also investigating individual differences in cognitive style in an ICT context, proposes the exploitation of such knowledge to design computer programming learning environments which actively encourage the development of those cognitive abilities which are required to progress to intermediate and advanced programming.

The last two studies investigate the above themes at a more 'macro' level, that is, that of institutions. The third study reports a three-year study of online learning in which data support the notion of an inter-relationship between the institutional contexts and instructional design and practice. The final study investigates informal learning by staff in a university setting. The data confirm the strong positive relationships between individual agency involving conceptions of technology, personal visions and goals of future uses of technology and emerging capabilities. The implications for the design of workplace practices to support learning and development are discussed.

2. DESIGNED INTERACTIONS: TECHNOLOGY AND LEARNERS

Luria's integrative work on the brain (1973), still well regarded in contemporary neuropsychology (Goldberg 1990), provides the theoretical foundation for a model of cognitive style that underpins this study. Luria identified two different types of intellectual activity: simultaneous processing (involving the organisation of discrete elements into an integrated group or whole) and successive processing (involving the ordering or chaining of successively arriving elements). An executive control function has also been identified. In the study reported herein, two groups of learners were selected on the basis of an identified marked asymmetry with respect to their levels of simultaneous and successive processing, it being hypothesised that a strong stylistic approach would be evident for these groups. One characterisation of these two groups is as *procedural* (successive) and *relational* (simultaneous) thinkers. It is important to note that these models are conceptual and are used as objects to think about cognitive practice.

Integrated Learning Systems (ILS) are computer-based systems that manage the delivery and evaluation of instruction. A recent evaluation of an ILS found that procedural/verbal thinkers gained more per unit time than relational/visual thinkers on computer-based mathematics and reading tasks ($F(3,62)=4.55$, $p<.006$, effect size=.18) suggesting the instructional design of the system was better matched to procedural/verbal thinkers (Fitzgerald, Hughes and Fitzgerald 1996).

This research also explored the possibility of 'situated interventionism' with the aim of "creating new forms of practices" (Engestrom and Cole 1997:308) by manipulating the setting of children's problem solving. One setting was developed to be more open-ended and relational requiring children to solve co-variation problems by trying to find the 'pattern'. The other setting was more closed and rule-based requiring children to solve similar problems by closely following the instruction they had been given. The data showed interesting context effects suggesting procedural thinkers worked better in the rule-based settings ($F=2.542$, $p=.058$) whereas there was no context effect for relational thinkers. There were also strong suggestions from the data that children could describe their problem solving in more complex and sophisticated ways in open and relational settings.

This study demonstrated the utility of this practice-based model of cognitive style for studying the interaction between learner and context. We have seen that cognition and context are not closed, independent systems but are fundamentally dialogic, open-ended and directed towards the future. We have also seen that with knowledge of cognitive style it is possible to manipulate contexts in ways that can make new practices possible. Beginning with an analysis of individual differences, this research strongly suggests the importance of moving beyond the solitary thinker to consider their dialogical engagement with the world and offers a glimpsed potential for a better understanding of *designed interactions.*

3. PROGRAMMING CONTEXTS FOR THE DEVELOPMENT OF COGNITIVE ABILITIES

Also grounded in the work of Luria (1973), this study explored the proposition that the development of mental models of recursion is profoundly influenced, in product and in process, by the simultaneous and successive processing abilities of individual learners (Gibbons 1995). Five case study subjects with specific asymmetric cognitive profiles were drawn from the population. Whilst controlling for the executive control function, subjects were selected on the basis of asymmetric high/low, low/high and high/high simultaneous and successive processing profiles.

Differences in simultaneous and successive processing abilities were observed to be associated with differences in motivation, problem perception, strategy development, selection of tactics, implementation activity, solution discovery, and self-assessment of performance. From this study it has been possible to identify a number of critical factors in the design of computer programming environments that encourage the development of simultaneous processing abilities which are, in turn, crucial to the progression of learner-programmers to more advanced levels of programming.

It was observed that the satisfactory accomplishment of trivial programming tasks through attention to procedural detail contributes to the persistence of successive strategies in the absence of tasks which, unlike recursion, demand simultaneous processing. As high successive learners progress to attempt more complex tasks in novel situations, the likelihood of successful task solution diminishes; this is exacerbated by the reliance of early successes on successive strategies and the resultant reluctance to abandon such strategies. The non-systematicity of high successive learners' conceptualisation may result in their failure to ultimately progress to the development of a sound understanding of complex constructs and their long-term manifestation of cognitive activity typically associated with novices.

The notion of the plasticity of cognitive abilities is therefore supported by this observation that, without the setting of tasks which demand the invocation of simultaneous processing, successive abilities will progressively improve, by default and without deliberate intervention, at the expense of simultaneous abilities.

Knowledge of differences in component cognitive abilities can provide a basis for the informed structuring of collaborative programming teams. Whilst some learners may be capable of individually invoking the concerted activity of simultaneous and successive processing abilities, others may fully realise their potential only in concerted collaboration with others of complementary cognitive profile. The provision of systemic programming supports, i.e. cognitive artefacts (Norman 1991), to supplement simultaneous or successive abilities would serve a similar function and facilitate the realisation of the computer as a collaborator.

4. VIRTUAL ENVIRONMENTS TO SUPPORT LEARNING

This research represents a case study of three years of actual practice of participants in one online educational programme. It was located online in a computer conference hosted by the British Columbia Ministry of Education and the Open Learning Agency – The New Directions in Distance Learning programme (NDDL). Participants communicated via an electronic conference and email system, and instruction was supported with audiographic conferences. It was an expectation of the project and an assumption of the initial research design that a rich community of learners would form online. However, what emerged from the research was the realisation that the organisational structure of the educational programme had a substantial affect on the learning potential, becoming as much of an artefact for the participants as the technology and the curriculum.

Developed from this research is a theoretical model of an organisation for learning, informed by action and intentional learning. This design recognises that the organisation into which an innovation is placed is a critical variable in the adoption of the innovation. Three attributes of an organisation for learning were identified: personal mastery (individual activity), social interaction (collaboration), and systems thinking (holistic understanding). The model developed from this research suggests that any learning activities, especially those existing in lean, socially impoverished environments such as cyberspace (Walther and Burgoon 1992), must incorporate opportunities to develop personal mastery, social interaction, and systems thinking into their designs. The assumption that those three attributes might be inherent in a model was found not true in this case study.

If virtual learning environments are to support higher order thinking, designers and educators must consciously build the three attributes of organisations for learning into the model. Activity Theory must be incorporated into the school experience, allowing all learners (students and educators) to grapple with activities to develop personal understanding and demonstrate learning, allowing schools to develop as organisations for learning.

Most notable in this research was the effect that the organisational structure had on the participants' ability to maintain the virtual communication network. While there were many confounding variables that appeared to affect online communication, the organisational structure (size, developed hierarchy, increased bureaucracy, etc.) was identified as having a major impact and, over time, was able to modify an innovative instructional design, which utilised most of the promises of computer-supported conferencing, and return it to the traditional design of direct instruction.

5. LEARNING AND INFORMATION TECHNOLOGIES IN CONTEXT

The fourth study describes research which was carried out at the University of Sydney (Crawford and Crawford 1997) to investigate the factors influencing emerging conceptions, capabilities and patterns of use across several disciplines and in the administrative sector. The project aimed to elicit information about:

- staff conceptions of the opportunities and constraints of the university context with respect to ICT;
- the impact of job definitions and role expectations on the use of ICT;
- staff access to and use of ICT at work and at home;
- the relationships between these variables.

The research identified strong positive relationships between individual agency, evolving conceptions of ICT, personal vision and goals for future use of ICT and emerging operational capabilities in the use of ICT. There were wide differences in access to and use of ICT at work and at home. Earlier indications of the impact of differing local contexts on emerging conceptions and capabilities were also confirmed. There were marked differences between groups in capabilities, conceptions and patterns of use.

The data indicated that emerging operational capabilities in the use of ICT and frequency of use were positively associated with:

- the reported agency of subjects, i.e. the extent that they felt able to act independently to resolve problems and make change;
- the extent that subjects had a positive personal vision of their future involving the use of ICT.

High levels of agency and a personal vision of a changed future involving the use of ICT were positively associated with workplace settings where:

- personal or group agency and independent action were rewarded (e.g. research);
- there was consensus about the functionality of new technologies in the valued activities of the group (e.g. role of ICT in discipline-based activities);
- group (i.e. department or section) identity and goals for future activity included the use of ICT.
- Capabilities and conceptions were negatively associated with:
- highly regulated contexts (e.g. administration);
- feelings of distress about change;
- feelings of lack of time.

The last two factors were positively associated with age, years of employment at the university and level of employment. They also appear to be associated with a persistence of well established operational (successive) strategies that are unquestioned and sustained even when it is obvious that they are not strategic in the new situation. This result is similar the behaviour of successively oriented programmers described above. Within the university setting, personal agency was clearly used in two opposing ways according to individual conceptions of strategic action:

- to resist changes associated with ICT;
- to enhance communication, co-operation and the use of ICT in research and administration.

This research supports Wenger's (1998) assertion that people occupy multiple roles in multiple communities and their learning and their activity in each role are influenced by the dynamics of the particular context. Within a large organisation such as a university, informal learning is influenced substantially by the socio-cultural rules, roles and conceptions of staff and these in turn are influenced by localised conditions with variation from group to group and according to ascribed roles within each group. In the sample, people appeared to respond strategically in different ways according to the socio-political contexts in which they worked. These different responses were associated with differing conceptions of, and operational capabilities associated with, ICT.

6. SYNTHESIS AND CONCLUSION

The first study observed that to better realise the new opportunities offered by technology we need to develop more reflexive theoretical accounts of learners acting in contexts of practice. Studying technology-rich environments in the context of cognitive style has allowed us to *recognise* dimensions of the interaction between learner and context and with this knowledge *act* to *design* future interactions. Similarly, the second study, in proposing the design of learning environments to foster complementary collaboration, not only recognises, but seeks to actively exploit, the intellectual richness afforded by the social distribution of knowledge and cognition between individuals and artefacts.

The latter two studies extended these propositions into institutional contexts revealing the crucial role of social settings in affecting the outcomes of designed learning environments. The third study discovered that, even when using leading edge telecommunications technology in an attempt to move beyond the traditional direct instruction model typically found in most educational institutions, the structure of the learning environment was not consistent with the attributes required to support knowledge-building. The organisational structure of the institution, itself, was found to have the potential to limit innovative practice and replace it with the traditional methods even when there had been an attempt to modify these methods through the use of new technologies in the first place. The last study supports the notion that the dialogic relationship between people and technology is strategic and personal. Capabilities and frequency of use of the ICT environment were positively associated with personal identity, goals and relationships with the institutional arena that were consistent with learning informally in order to accomplish meaningful goals through strategic use of technology.

The fourth study also supported the observation that there is a need for changes in institutional practice if new approaches to learning with ICT, and working with ICT, are to be realised. New technologies offer the possibility of changes in the scope and distribution of human activity and experience. In any place where people work together, however, learning how to integrate new technologies productively with day to day activities, often with their origins in a previous age, is a major challenge.

From these studies we now recognise:

- the diversity of contexts and human responses in educational settings;
- that learning contexts are socio-politically situated but always open to change;
- the plastic, active and socially-embedded nature of cognition;
- dialogic and personal inter-relations between context and cognition and related knowledge and capabilities;
- that learning is a natural lifelong process when adaptation to novel situations is necessary.

In the future, we are interested in developing theories which take into account the dynamics of the fluid interaction from which individual and group knowledge and capabilities emerge.

REFERENCES

Crawford, K. and Crawford, S. (1997) *Agency, technology and vision: The dynamics of learning.* Sydney: The University of Sydney.

Crawford, K. (1996) Vygoskian approaches to human development in the information era. *Educational Studies in Mathematics* 31(1-2) 43-62.

Edelman, G.M. and Tononi, G. (1995) Neural Darwinism: The brain as a selectional system. In J. Cornwall (ed.) *Nature's imagination.* Oxford: Oxford University Press.

Engestrom, Y. and Cole, M. (1997) Situated cognition in search of an agenda. In D. Kirshner and J.A. Whitson (eds.) *Situated cognition: Social, semiotic and psychological perspectives.* New Jersey: Lawrence Erlbaum.

Fitzgerald, D., Hughes, P., and Fitzgerald, R.N. (1996) *An evaluation of computer assisted learning in Victorian schools.* Research Monograph. Melbourne: Victorian Directorate of School Education. [http://www.sofweb.vic.edu.au/lt/cal_eval.htm]

Gibbons, P. (1995) A cognitive processing account of individual differences in novice Logo programmers' conceptualisation and use of recursion. *Journal of Educational Computing Research* 13(3) 211-226.

Goldberg, E. (1990) *Contemporary neuropsychology and the legacy of Luria.* New Jersey: Lawrence Erlbaum.

Hutchins, E. (1995) *Cognition in the wild.* Cambridge, MA: MIT Press.

Lave, J. and Wenger, E. (1991) *Situated learning: Legitimate peripheral participation.* Melbourne: Cambridge University Press.

Luria, A.R. (1973) *The working brain: An introduction to neuropsychology.* Middlesex: Penguin.

Merleau-Ponty, M. (1962) *Phenomenology of perception.* Evanston, IL: Northwestern University Press.

Nardi, B. (1996) Studying context. In B. Nardi (ed.) *Context and consciousness.* Cambridge MA: MIT Press.

Norman, D. A. (1991). Cognitive artefacts. In J. M. Carroll (ed.) *Designing interaction: Psychological theory at the human-computer interface.* Cambridge, MA: Cambridge University Press.

Vygotsky, L. (1978) *Mind in society.* Cambridge, MA: Harvard University Press.

Walther, J. B. and Burgoon, J. K. (1992) Relational communications in computer-mediated interaction. *Human Communications Research* 19(1) 50-88.

Wenger, E. (1998). *Communities of practice.* Cambridge, MA: Cambridge University Press.

BIOGRAPHIES

Pamela Gibbons is currently the Head of the School of Business and Informatics (NSW) at Australian Catholic University, based at North Sydney. Her doctoral studies focused on individual differences in cognitive abilities as they relate to students' learning of computer programming.

Kathryn Crawford is a Senior Lecturer in the Faculty of Education at the University of Sydney and also directs the Novae Research Group at the Australian Technology Park. She is interested in investigating the social dimensions of technology-based learning with particular regard to better understanding the fluid dynamics between learner and artefacts.

Susan Crichton works in Schools District #10, British Columbia, Canada where she has been involved the design and evaluation of online education programmes for students living in remote regions. Her current research interests include the investigation of 'screen literacy'.

Robert Fitzgerald lectures at Australian Catholic University, based in the Faculty of Education at Signadou Campus, Canberra. His current research interest lies in exploring the ability of teachers to design technology-rich learning environments to facilitate the development of newly recognised forms of learning.

In the future, this group hopes to continue their collaboration on socio-cultural approaches to the study of learning in information and communication technology contexts. It is expected that the work of Luria and Vygotsky will continue to underpin their development of theories relating to situated cognition and the centrality of socio-cultural contexts in ICT learning environments.

Using ICT to support constructive learning

Chen Qi and Zhang Jianwei
Department of Psychology, Beijing Normal University, Beijing 100875 China.
chenqi@email.bnu.edu.cn

Keywords: dialectic constructivism, word problem, constructive learning environment

Abstract: In light of our dialectic constructivism, we have developed a set of instructional software on word problems in elementary mathematics. We managed to use ICT to create a constructive learning environment from four perspectives: (1) Challenge and support learners' higher-order thinking; (2) Promote learners' deep and flexible understanding on the base of introductory knowledge acquisition; (3) Enhance learners' conversation and collaboration through micro-community; and (4) Facilitate learners' self-regulation during learning. Some principal considerations will be explained in detail.

1. DIALECTIC CONSTRUCTIVISM

Constructivism highlights a potentially more hopeful direction for educational reform including the use of ICT in education. However, some constructivists went too far in some arguments, including overestimating learners' agency at the cost of ignoring the importance of teachers' teaching and guidance and overemphasising that learning should be always situated in authentic and complex environment. On a number of occasions (Chen et al. 1998; Chen and Zhang 1998), we have clarified our dialectic view on constructive learning, to include the following relations which are critical for learning and teaching.

1.1 The view of knowledge

Knowledge does not consist of static reflections of the environment, but dynamic constructions achieved through our acting and thinking on the environment. However, we should not deny the objective world and the truth that reflects the law of outside world even though it is relative and dynamic.

1.2 The learning process

Learners should construct their knowledge through higher-order thinking. On the one hand, since they are still growing human being, they need guidance and help from the teacher and support from the culture and society they live in, especially at the introductory stage of knowledge acquisition. Learners construct their own knowledge. In this sense they are the centres in learning process. On the other hand, a teacher still plays a critical role in the classroom. As the organiser, facilitator, information source and monitor of instruction, the teacher has to co-ordinate all the variables related to the learning and teaching processes, such as, the instructional contents, the student's individual differences, the teaching methods and the learning environments. The teacher is the director for whole instructional practice. This point does not conflict with our argument that the learner is the centre in the learning process. the teacher, their students have to be placed on the centre because every decision needs to be made based on students' understanding, thinking, feelings and actions. While for the classroom interactions, both teacher and students are actually actors interacting with each other and all aiming at the success of learning. Students construct their own meaning with ICT and teacher (courseware designer) providing scaffolding for student's learning.

1.3 Individual or social learning

Neither individual students' activities nor social interactions can be accounted for adequately except in relation to the other. Individual students' activity is always located within both the classroom cultural background and the broader society systems. On the other hand, only when individual learners are involved in active and constructive learning activities, which is the internal base, can social interaction add the external power and enhance their knowledge construction.

1.4 The relation between concretion and abstraction.

Knowing is a dynamic and effortful process, stepping from sensory intuition to essence abstraction, and eventually to the most advanced stage, the materialisation in thinking. Accordingly, certain kinds of abstraction and generalisation are needed for the introductory stage of learning. While at the advanced stage of knowledge acquisition, it is more necessary for learning to be situated in a more authentic and complex environment.

2. FRAMEWORK OF THE LEARNING ENVIRONMENT

In light of Dialectic Constructivism, we have designed and developed a set of CD instructional software on word problems in primary mathematics, including Two-Step Word Problems in Primary Mathematics and Typical Word Problems in Primary Mathematics. We managed to use ICT to create a constructive learning environment from the following four perspectives.

2.1 Challenge and support learners' higher-order thinking.

Lower-order thinking occurs when students are required to receive or recite factual information, or to employ rules and algorithms through repetitive routines. Higher-order thinking requires students to manipulate information and ideas in ways that transform their meaning and implications, such as combining facts and ideas to synthesise, generalise, explain, hypothesise, or arrive at some conclusion or interpretation (Newmann and Wehlage 1994). During constructive learning processes, students are often engaged in higher-order thinking, for instance, solving problems actively and generating new meanings and understandings. Teaching should be done by inquiring at the leading edge 'of the learner's thinking', rather than just telling students what to do and how to think (Fosnot 1989). In this sense, ICT should be used to stimulate and facilitate learners' higher-order thinking, rather than merely to transmit more information. Unfortunately, there has been very little consideration on this point in instructional design in China. Also, it is not very easy for all learners to think actively and generatively. Therefore, we should give them adequate support and guidance in order to ensure their success in problem solving and knowledge construction.

2.2 Promote learners' deep and flexible understanding on the base of introductory knowledge acquisition.

Students with deep understanding can make clear distinctions, develop their own arguments, construct their explanations for related phenomenon, and solve more complex problems creatively. Those with merely some superficial and fragmented understanding can only recall and apply the knowledge in rote ways. Accordingly, there is no doubt that we should promote learners' advanced knowledge acquisition in ill-structured domains (Spiro et. al, 1995; Jonnasen 1993), However, advanced knowledge acquisition needs to be based on learners' achievement in introductory knowledge acquisition stage, in which learners may need more basic training.

2.3 Enhance learners' conversation and collaboration.

Knowledge is socially negotiated. More substantive conversation and collaboration among learners and between learners and the teacher are needed in order to pursue constructive learning and teaching. The importance of a learning community where ideas are discussed and understanding enriched is critical to the design of an effective learning environment (Savery and Duffy 1995). ICT should be used to enhance learners' social interaction, which is another critical perspective of knowledge construction.

2.4 Facilitate learners' self-regulation during learning.

We should help learners to plan and monitor their own learning processes, evaluate their learning outcomes, and regulate their learning activities towards effective knowledge construction.

Word problem solving is an important and relatively difficult part in primary mathematics. Our courseware was focused on general two-step word problems whose solution involving a unknown medium variable, and some typical word problems concerning domain-specific knowledge (e.g. about speed, price). We designed six modules altogether in the courseware (see Figure 1). Two of them are designed for the introductory knowledge acquisition stage, including Sample Word Problems whose function is to help students learn to solve word problems concerning a kind of new mathematical relationship, and Basic Practice designed to strengthen learners' knowledge and skills just acquired. The module of Sample Word Problems was designed mainly based on theory of learning through problem solving, but with more guidance and support. The module of Basic Practice, although looks like training and practice in traditional courseware, was designed to strengthen learners' understanding by modifying the known data and goal in word problems (as will be detailed later). For the advanced knowledge acquisition stage, we designed another two modules: Advanced Problem Solving and Authentic Tasks. Besides, considering children with particular needs, we designed the module of Particular Skill Training to help them from particular perspectives, including representation of word problems and understanding of key words and sentences that can give us more information about mathematical relationships. The last module is Thinking Tools which offers open tools that learners can use to represent, analyse and solve certain kinds of typical word problems, such as those concerning speed or working rate.

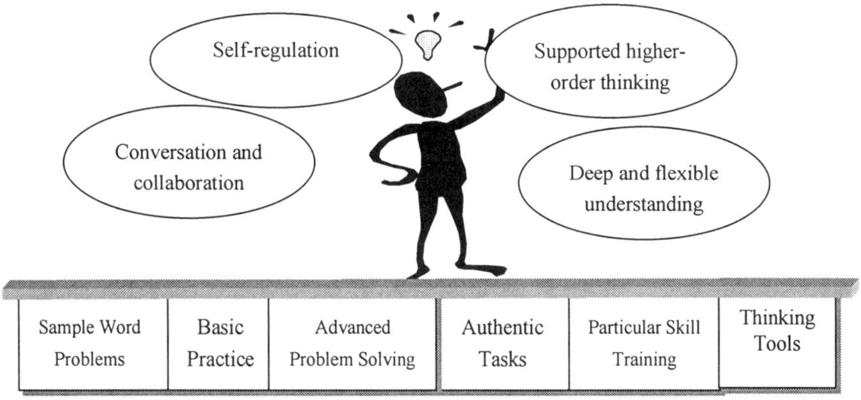

Figure 1. Framework of the learning environment design

3. PRINCIPAL CONSIDERATIONS IN LEARNING ENVIRONMENT DESIGN

3.1 Supported problem solving

In traditional education, we used to regard knowing and doing as two distinct things. Only when students have been told about certain knowledge, can they solve the corresponding problems. Dewey (1933) moved from this tradition and stated the importance of 'learning by doing'. Contemporary constructivists stepped forward from this point to assert that learners construct their own knowledge, and put forward different models for learning and teaching, such as project-based instruction, problem-based learning (Schimdt 1995), anchored/situated instruction, and a cognitive apprenticeship model (Brown et al. 1989). Despite the distinct differences, there is an important common principle across these models: learning through problem solving. During the problem solving process, learners will activate their knowledge to understand the problem situation, make their inference and hypothesis, and generate their strategies. Therefore, problem solving often leads to learners' acquiring new insight into the phenomenon.

The theory of learning through problem solving is also very important for mathematics educational reforms (Hiebert et al. 1996). In our software on word problems, we also designed the module of Sample Word Problems in light of this theory. Rather than simulating a teacher's explanations and demonstrations in classroom, at beginning of learning process, we advise learners to try thinking over and solving the sample word problem by themselves first. Nevertheless, as our dialectic constructivism argued, learning through problem solving does not mean learning all by discovery. External guidance and support, which may be different from those in traditional teaching, are still very important in this circumstance. Therefore, as the learner solves the problem, the programme will keep monitoring their activity and offering various kinds of support and guidance to facilitate their problem solving activities and hence the construction of knowledge on the new mathematical relationships. The supports and guidance include the following.

Thought-provoking feedback and guidance: for example, if a learner types a formula involving a typical error when solving the problem, the software will offer them the corresponding feedback and guidance that may promote their thinking, such as, 'Attention! What is the goal of the problem?' or 'Which number means the total?'.

Tutor-Online: When a learner has tried for three times but still can not find the solution, the software will advise them to click a button, Tutor-Online, where three kinds of supports are available: (1) some corresponding preparatory problems concerning the prerequisite skills and knowledge; (2) a tutor's explanations on the structure of the sample word problem and the strategies to be applied; and (3) the right answer to the problem. A learner can select the needed supports from the above ones by clicking buttons. Whenever they feel that enough support have been received, they can return to continue solving the problem by themselves. Some low-achievers may need to solve some preparatory problems and get more support, while those high-achievers can solve the problem more by themselves with less guidance. Also, it is likely that learners with different learning styles (e.g. field-dependent vs. field-independent) may like different types of support during their problem solving process. This hypothesis will be tested in our later studies.

Reflection prompts: A learner's problem solving activity does not lead to knowledge construction automatically. As some research has manifested, it depends on various factors, of which learners' reflective abstraction may be the most important one (Gabrys et al. 1993; Hmelo and Ferrari 1997). Throughout problem solving processes, learners need to reflect on the underlying problem structure and the strategies used, and as a result to grasp the mathematical relationship more mindfully and systematically. In our software, as learners try solving the problem, we will give them some questions to prompt their reflection on their problem solving processes. For example, when a student has accomplished the first or the second step during the problem solving process, the programme will ask a question such as 'what's the sub-goal of this step?' to help them rethink over their solutions.

As we have asserted, support and help are necessary and essential for constructive learning and teaching. What more? If a learner really has no intention to work by themself, they can directly start from Tutor-Online to solve the preparatory problems, listen to the explanations, and see the right answers, just as a learner used to do in traditional mathematics classroom. This might meet with some teachers' or students' needs on particular occasions.

3.2 Grasping mathematical relationships by modifying the word problem

For constructive learning and teaching, the question is not how many word problem learners have solved, but how well they can understand the fundamental relationships in word problems. Since the mathematical relationships will be more obvious in comparison, or say, during its changing, in the module of Sample Word Problems and Basic Practice, we prepare a button 'Change It' to modify the given data or goal in the original word problem. For example, the original problem is: 'There are 24 kg apples in a shop. *Pears are 4 times heavier than apples*. How many pears and apples are there altogether in the shop?' The modified problem is almost the same except that the second sentence has been changed to *'Apples are 4 times heavier than pears'* In order to solve the changed problems, learners have to find out the subtle differences and think over the influence on mathematical relationships. This may help learners understand the structure of word problems clearly and grasp the key information promptly. Asking learners to analyse the differences between two or more cases may help them notice relevant features and prepare them for an explanation about why those features are significant.

3.3 Promoting learning through advanced problem solving and authentic tasks

The problems in the modules of Sample Word Problems and Basic Practice are typical and relatively simpler ones that can help learners grasp the basic mathematical relationships. In order to further learners' understanding and promote the transition from an introductory knowledge acquisition stage to an advanced knowledge acquisition stage, we designed another two modules in the software, Advanced Problem Solving and Authentic Tasks. In the module of Advanced Problem Solving, more complex problems characteristic of ill-structured domains (Spiro et al. 1995) are offered including problems involving redundant data, or concerning two or more knowledge sections and other novel problems that can help learners gain new insight into mathematical relationships. These problems were chosen not because they are difficult and can frustrate learners, but because they can improve learners' understanding about the mathematical relationships in word problems, and hence can facilitate the transfer of learning in broad domains.

Besides, partly based on the theory of situated learning, we designed another module, Authentic Tasks, to further learners' understanding towards the transfer in more general and real situations. This module begins with the animation of a story concerning certain mathematical relationships. For example, two boys carried books for three times. They carried 120 books for the first time and the same for the second time. For the last time, they carried 10 books more than the first time. All the data was embedded in the plots. Then the story breaks off with a question asked by one of the boys, such as 'how many books have we carried already?' The first task for learners is to verbalise the story appropriately as a word problem rather than as a general story. They should choose the most appropriate one from four figures' narratives. The other task for learners is to think over how to solve the problem in the story. We designed four simulated partners (as will be detailed in later section) who have different understanding and strategies over the problem. Learners are required to understand and evaluate the four solutions and choose the right one from them. When a learner has made their decision, the animation will continue to check whether the solution is right or not according to the story itself. The Authentic Tasks may help learners see what the mathematical relationships are actually like in the real world.

3.4 A micro-community to enhance social interaction

It is a pity that instructional software usually does little to enhance learners' social interaction. As a trial in our software, we designed four simulated partners representative of different learning styles to act as learners' partners, for instance, an impulsive boy and a reflective girl. In the modules of Sample Word Problems, Advanced Problem Solving and Authentic Tasks, learners can have a discussion with the four children by clicking a button, Partners-Online (see Figure 2). They can select a child and listen to their explanations of their thoughts on the word problem, and then evaluate these ideas critically. In this way, learners can see several different ways to analyse and solve a problem, and reflect on the distinct differences among these methods. They can also see some typical errors made by the partners in word problem solving. This may help learner in another way. Besides, as we have mentioned, in the module of Sample Word Problems, learners can visit Tutor-Online to seek supports and helps for word problem solving from the simulated tutor. We hope that the interactions among learners and the simulated partners and tutor may function partly as a micro-community in computerised learning environment.

Figure 2. Partners-Online

3.5 Self-regulation through process tracing and advice offering

As masters in learning process, learners need to monitor and regulate their learning activities and manage to make good use of the resource (e.g. time) available in learning process. In order to facilitate learners' self-regulation, we added the function of process tracing in our software. The software can collect real-time data during a learner's learning process, including the time they have spent, the content they have visited, the scores they have gained, and the errors they have made in equations or calculations. Learners can fetch this valuable information about their learning when they need it. This may help learners to reflect on their learning accurately and hence regulate their learning effectively. In addition, the software will give learners some advice based on this information. As years of research on CAI has proved (Chen 1994), it may be more effective to let learners control their learning process under some guidance than programme-control or learner-control single-handedly. Whether these real-time data and suggestions can support learners' self-regulation needs to be proved by further research.

In addition, some other considerations are also of great significance in our learning environment design, such as enabling learners to represent word problems appropriately, and supporting learners' problem solving with thinking tools. They can not be detailed here for the limitation of length.

4. CONCLUSION

Educational reform based on constructivism should enable a step forward from traditional education, which still has its own advantages although confronted with great challenges. The design of a constructive learning environment needs to focus on learners' needs in foregoing learning processes, and to try to facilitate and support their higher-order thinking and deep understanding. It is important to engage learners in reflective problem solving and enhance the interactions in a micro-community to achieve the above goals. Particularly, we should take learners' different learning styles and levels of capability into account, so that we can create a learning environment that is open and supportive for all learners.

REFERENCES

Brown, J. S., Collins, A., and Duguid, P. (1989) Situated cognition and the culture of learning. *Educational Researcher* 18(1) 32-48.

Chen, Q. and Zhang, J. (1998) Constructivism as a learning theory: Essence and comments. *Journal of East China Normal University* (Educational science edition) 1, 61-68.

Chen, Q. (1995) Effects of learners' characteristics and instructional guidance on computer assisted learning. In D. Tinsley and D. Watson (eds.) *Integrating information technology into education.* London: Chapman and Hall.

Chen, Q., Liu, R., and Zhang, J. (1998) Creating a constructive environment for learners to explore word problem solving. In Tak-Wai Chan, et al. (eds.) *Global education on the net; Proceedings of ICCE'98.* Beijing: China Higher Education Press and Springer-Verlag.

Fosnot, C. T. (1989) *Enquiring teachers, enqruing learning: A constructivist approach to teaching.* NY: Teachers College Press.

Gabrys, G., Weiner, A., and Lesgold, A. (1993) Learning by problem solving in a coached apprenticeship system. In: M. Rabinnowitz (ed.) *Cognitive science foundations of instruction.* New Jersey: Lawrence Erlbaum.

Glover, J. A., Ronning, R. R., and Bruning, R. H. (1990) *Cognitive psychology for teachers.* New York: Macmillan Publishing Company.

Hiebert, J., Carpenter, T. P., Fennema, E., Fuson, K., Human, P., Oliver, A., and Wearne, D. (1996) Problem solving as a basis for reform in curriculum and instruction: The case of mathematics. *Educational Researcher* 25(4) 12-21.

Jonassen, D. H., Mayes, T., and McAleese, R. (1993) A manifesto for a constructivist approach to uses of technology in higher education. In I. M. Duffy, J. Lowcyk, and D. H. Jonassen (eds.) *Designing environments for constructive learning.* Berlin: Springer-Verlag.

Kintsch, W. and Greeno, J. G. (1985) Understanding and solving arithmetic word problems. *Psychological Review* 92, 163-182.

Marx, R. W., Blumenfeld, P. C., Krajcik, J. S., and Soloway, E. (1997) Enacting project-based science. *The Elementary School Journal* 97(4) 341-358.

Newmann, F. M. and Wehlage, G. G. (1994) Five standards of authentic instruction. In K. M. Cauly, F. Linder and J. H. McMillan (eds.) *Annual editions: Educational psychology 94/95.* The Dushkin Publishing Group.

Savery, J. R. and Duffy, T. M. (1995) Problem based learning: An instructional model and its constructivist framework. *Educational Technology* September/October: Vol ( ) 31-38.

Schimdt, H. G. (1995) Problem-based learning: An introduction. *Instructional Science* 22, 247-250.

Spiro, R. J. et al. (1995) Cognitive flexibility, constructivism, and hypertext: Random access instruction for advanced knowledge acquisition in ill-structured domains. In L. P. Steffe and J. Gale (eds.) *Constructivism in education.* New Jersey: Lawrence Erlbaum.

BIOGRAPHIES

Qi Chen, Professor of educational psychology in the Department of Psychology at Beijing Normal University, is the vice president of the Educational Psychology Committee of the Chinese Psychological Society. Qi Chen was a visiting scholar in Psychology and Education at UCLA during 1980-83 and has been researching educational computing for more than 15 years. She believes that with more understanding about student learning, ICT could be more effectively integrated into education.

Jianwei Zhang, majored in educational psychology in the Department of Psychology, Beijing Normal University. He is researching learning through problem solving, science learning, and learning environment design.

Computer-based communication in the classroom

Rosa Maria Bottino
Consiglio Nazionale delle Ricerche, Istituto per la Matematica Applicata, Via de Marini 6 16149 Genova, Italy. bottino@ima.ge.cnr.it

Keywords: communication, collaborative learning, problem solving, multi-environment systems, context of use

Abstract: This paper is based on a study aimed at investigating the potential of collaborative learning in mathematics problem solving using computer-supported learning environments that incorporate communication opportunities. The specific context in which the study was undertaken involved the use of the multi-environment system ARI-LAB, which was implemented to develop problem solving abilities in primary school students. On the basis of the results obtained from long-term experimentation with this system, some research problems are discussed with the purpose of investigating factors which influenced the nature and type of student interaction. The final aims are to support the design of effective computer-based instructional materials that incorporate communication opportunities and in particular to stress the importance of establishing a well-designed context of use for the technology.

1. INTRODUCTION

In the 1970s, educational computing research began exploring ways to support educational instruction. This culminated in the 1980s in sophisticated (but still basically drill-and-practice) integrated learning systems, which, in general, had a limited impact on school practice. In response, research over the past decade has begun to show the practicability and efficacy of alternative approaches whose presuppositions lie in the pedagogic theories that have steadily been gaining credence (such as constructivism and situated learning). The aim has been to build learner-centred systems where learning in a particular field is based on active exploration and personal construction rather than on a transmissive model. From the point of view of Human Computer Interaction, the reference metaphor is that of the workspace. Modern graphical user interfaces and interaction opportunities have developed from this paradigm.

Current research in new environments, new competencies and collaborative and co-operative learning have led to the belief that the workspace concept, as an interaction metaphor, cannot adequately take account of the opportunities that information and communication technology is rapidly making available, and so it needs to be coupled with a new interaction model: the communication space. This new way of looking at human-computer interaction on the one hand, and educational computing on the other, is reflected in the dialogue between different conceptual models and research agendas. We make reference to Vygotsky's socio-cultural theory, Leont'ev's activity theory and the model of human activity developed by Cole and Engeström (Bakardjieva 1998).

The strong interaction between different points of view, theoretical perspectives and new communication possibilities offered by technological advancements is opening up new scenarios, and educationalist face the need not only to understand the technical and management problems related to the use of this technology but also to consider how these new possibilities influence or change the nature of the underlying pedagogy and its relation to theory and practice.

Too many projects seem to focus on the technical innovations and opportunities offered by communication and networking rather than on their role or use (Watson et al. 1998). In order to deal with this last perspective, at least three classes of problems need to be tackled in an integrated manner.

a) The design of potentially rich open-learning environments: How can communication opportunities be integrated? How can an environment that supports communication influence the processes involved in the acquisition of given knowledge? What is the relationship between communication opportunities and the whole learning environment?
b) The role of the context of use: How can effective communication be promoted? What factors influence the nature and type of student interaction? What are the students' needs in this area? How can a balance be reached in communication between users engaged in a partnership? How can cross fertilisation among them be promoted?
c) Analysis of the communication activity: How can we analyse the communication activity? What forms of learner interaction resulted from systems that explicitly integrate communication opportunities? How does the learners' dialogue and communication patterns support the learning activity?

On the basis of a specific example, I analyse some aspects related to these areas. The aim is to contribute to the outlining of a methodological approach that may be adopted to tackle the problems described.

2. INTEGRATING COMMUNICATION OPPORTUNITIES

This paper reports a research project that aims to integrate the use of ICT into mathematics teaching at compulsory school level (students aged 6-14 years). The research concerns the development comprehensive testing of a computer system, called ARI-LAB (Bottino and Chiappini 1995), which is designed to assist students in arithmetic problem-solving. ARI-LAB is an open-learning system comprising a structured and connected set of environments combining hypermedia and network communication technologies. Its main environments are: a *microworld environment,* a *solution environment*, a *communication environment* and a *database environment*. The *microworld environment* features several microworlds with dynamic and graphic representation. These include: 'coins', 'abacus', 'calendar', 'simplified spreadsheet', 'histogram', 'quotition division', 'partition division' and 'art bits'. To make an example, in the 'coins' microworld it is possible to generate coins (in Italian lire), move them on the screen, withdraw coins, change coins and replace them with other coins of the same value, etc. When the user interacts with a microworld and obtains a visual representation (e.g. a set of coins grouped in a given manner) that fits her/his goal, s/he can copy it into the solution environment. In the *solution environment* the student chooses an arithmetic problem from a set prepared by the teacher, and builds up a solution by using verbal language and graphic representations obtained through interaction with the microworlds. In the *communication environment*, the student can share messages and solutions with other students, while in the *database environment* the student can look up problems previously solved and stored, either by the teacher, by her/himself, or by another student.

When designing ARI-LAB we drew on various theoretical approaches. These include the socio-cultural approach to thinking and learning and, in particular, Vygotsky's notion of cognitive tools, i.e. objects provided by the learning environment that allow students to incorporate new auxiliary methods or symbols into their problem solving activity. Moreover we considered the model of human activity that Engeström has built on Leont'ev's 'activity theory'. This interprets human learning as a systemic formation, taking into account its tool-mediated, object-oriented nature and its grounding in community practice. From the point of view of mathematics education research, we have taken into account research on applied problem solving, on situated learning, on the role of visual representation and on interactive learning. We start from the pedagogic consideration that primary school students, and often secondary school students, usually have serious difficulty tackling arithmetic problem solving and that teachers have trouble assisting them adequately. In the school tradition, symbols are used as mediating tool even in the very first approach to problem solving. Basically, traditional teaching relies on the early introduction of arithmetic symbols and written computation algorithms as the only way to describe the solution process and to obtain the result.

This approach seldom works well, as is witnessed by the fact that too many students, when solving a problem, try to guess what operation is necessary: they are not able to give meaning to the arithmetical signs in relation with the situation described in the problem. The introduction of arithmetical symbols and written computation, can be introduced fruitfully when children have already experienced the potentialities of a numbering system, and are able to enact informal strategies within concrete problem situations. It has been shown (Lesh 1981) that symbols which are not completely arbitrary but present some analogical connections with the reference objects can assume a very important role in the learning process. Representation systems such as coins, calendars and histograms can act as mediators between the situation described in the problem and the mathematical ideas, relations and processes involved in the solution. A number of such representation systems have been implemented in ARI-LAB's microworld environment, exploiting the graphical and interaction possibilities of the computer. In this way the mathematical ideas involved in problems of additive and multiplicative structure are made more accessible to students, by means of perceptive-type control, grounded in the children's extra-school experience.

In designing ARI-LAB, an alternative architecture to the one usual present in traditional education systems (student-computer) has been adopted. At least three agents have been brought into the learning process (student-computer-collaborative partner). For this reason, we have integrated into ARI-LAB a communication environment that has been designed so that users can engage in problem-solving within a social interaction process. This can change students' attitudes towards the problem, their assumptions on how to solve it and the validation context in which the resolution process is set. In the following chapters we will analyse how this has been made possible. ARI-LAB offers the user various communication opportunities: distance communication through a network or via a modem connection, or communication with the teacher or with classmates through a local network. There is also a variety of interaction modes. The user can choose the partner to communicate with at a given time, exchanging written messages and problem solutions. Moreover, the user can decide whether or not to read a message or solution as soon as it is received, store a received solution in the database, display the entire dialogue held with a partner. From the interface viewpoint, the microworld, solution and communication environments are presented simultaneously in the same display frame so that the user can easily switch from one to the other at any time. The reason for this is that communication must be an integral part of the problem solving activity and students must develop a synergy between communication and the other activities performed (building a representation, explanation of a solution).

If all the opportunities foreseen in the design of the system are to be effectively exploited the system must be used within suitable contexts of use that are planned and implemented within the overall education strategy. In the following, I briefly discuss an example to show ways in which ARI-LAB has contributed the restructuring of teaching and learning activity in the classroom. These examples are taken from the experimentation performed with the system over the past few years.

The experimentations had been performed in various school situations with children, some of whom were deaf. With one class, in particular, experimentation was carried out through almost the whole cycle of primary school, from the second to fifth grades; in this case the system was integrated into most of the mathematics syllabus. The teachers of the classes involved were present throughout all the experimentation and participated actively in following the students' work on the computer.

3. DESIGNING A CONTEXT OF USE

A number of possible strategies may be used for promoting and supporting collaborative learning activities based on computer-mediated communication (Slavin 1996). These strategies have a strong influence on learner behaviour and subsequent learning outcomes. In experimentation with ARI-LAB, an itinerary of classroom activity was planned to serve as a catalyst for collaborative learning. Tasks were included for which communication and co-operation among users might be meaningful for the specific object of the activity, namely a learning objective. The objective in this case was the development of abilities in the use of the decimal positional system and in solving additive and multiplicative problems. In my experience, at least with young students, the best tasks appear to be those which provide a method and allow a context for collaboration to be built. These tasks must scaffold the activity, that is, provide assistance at critical times offering methods and links to previous knowledge and experiences that the students themselves are unable to apply.

In the research with ARI-LAB, three strategies have been investigated in particular that have shown strong potential. These are pairing students with symmetrical roles and tasks; giving responsibility and control to them; developing investigative and open-ended tasks without single answers. Due to space limitations, I cannot discuss and exemplify all three strategies, so I chose to briefly analyse one example involving the first two.

During experimentation with ARI-LAB second-year primary school students were set the following task, to be performed communicating in pairs:

> *The teacher chooses a given amount of money and tells the whole class. Each student generates coins to make up the given amount and then, by means of the communication environment, has to send his/her classmate a message indicating the amount obtained and the coins used to make it up (e.g. one 1000 lire note; three 100 lire coins, etc.). The interlocutor has to check if the solution received is correct and then make up the same amount in another way. Then s/he in turn sends her/his solution to the other student as in the previous manner, and so on until one of the two students makes an error or is unable to find a new combination of coins. The rule is that it is not possible to propose previously used representations. If one of the students' representations is wrong (with respect to the amount given) and the interlocutor identifies the error, the latter wins the game.*

This game was proposed to students who had already developed experience in counting and in using the 'coins' microworld of ARI-LAB to make up given amounts. It was proposed at a stage which is critical for the development of the number concept, i.e. when students must progress from a view of the number as the result of a counting process to a view of the number in its relationships with the other numbers, relationships which can be functional to the solution of a problem or of a class of problems. The game pursues this objective inside the framework of monetary equivalence, which is meaningful for students since it allows them to draw on their extra-school experience. Playing the game, the students explore different ways in which an amount can be formed and are required to co-ordinate representation by means of coins on the one hand, and the representation in written language necessary for communicating with the partner on the other. The game develops through the written dialogue between the two interlocutors.

The game structure calls on the students to plan representation strategies that are increasingly articulated and complex. In doing so, the student can rely on the assistance given by the 'coin' microworld. The game structure fosters the need for the students to evaluate their own personal strategy as well as that of their interlocutors. Moreover, it promotes the co-ordination between the representation of the given amount by means of coins (in the microworld), its verbal representation together with coin representation (in the solution environment), and the indication in verbal form of the structural components of the number (in the communication environment).

The communication context of the game motivates and assists co-ordination of this activity in both the production and strategy evaluation phases.

4. ANALYSIS OF THE COMMUNICATION ACTIVITY

The system automatically stores dialogues between students and these can be later analysed together with the work that each student performs in the system's other environments, which is also recorded. For example, let us consider an excerpt (translated in English) of a real-time dialogue mediated by the computer between two children tackling the task described in the previous example (the amount to achieve is 2350 lire).

ANNA-M:	2 one-thousand lire banknotes, 3 one-hundred lire coins, a fifty lire coin
MARIO-R:	that's correct
MARIO-R:	2 one-thousand lire banknotes, a two-hundred lire coin, a one-hundred lire coin, a fifty lire coin
ANNA-M:	you did it correctly
MARIO-R:	2 one-thousand lire banknotes, seven fifty-lire coins
MARIO-R:	four five-hundred lire coins, a two-hundred lire coin, a one-hundred lire coin, a fifty lire coin
ANNA-M:	10 one-hundred lire coins, 5 two-hundred lire coins, 3 one-hundred lire coins, a fifty lire coin
MARIO-R:	you got it exactly right. Well done
ANNA-M:	you got it right too

The communication exposes the students to different ways of forming the given amount. When a student receives a solution from their interlocutor, in order to check it, they can reconstruct it in the coin microworld. In this way the student can acquire the partner's strategy and elaborate it in order to obtain a new solution. As the example shows, Mario, starts from the solution sent by Anna and applies single-step changes in order to produce alternative solutions. In this case also the structure of the dialogue (decomposition of the amount into its components in written language) contribute to support this activity.

Anna and Mario approach the goal at different levels. While Mario is able to re-elaborate Anna's solution, Anna, initially reasoned in terms of the coins she wanted to use, drawing on the support offered by the 'coin' microworld in order to obtain the required amount.

The following frames, (Figures 1-4) show how Anna interacted with this microworld to obtain the last amount she sent to Mario.

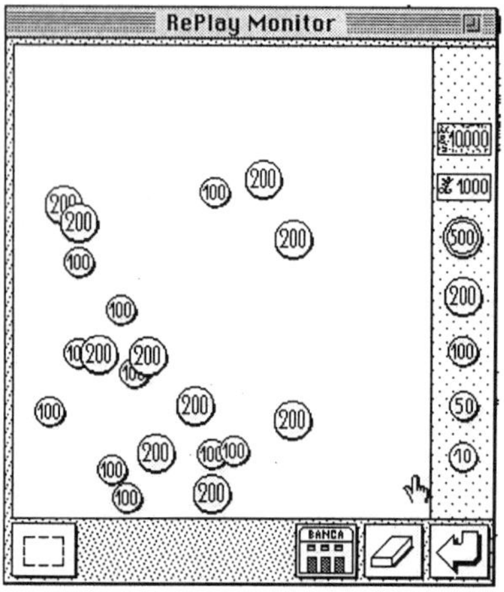

Figure 1. Frame 1

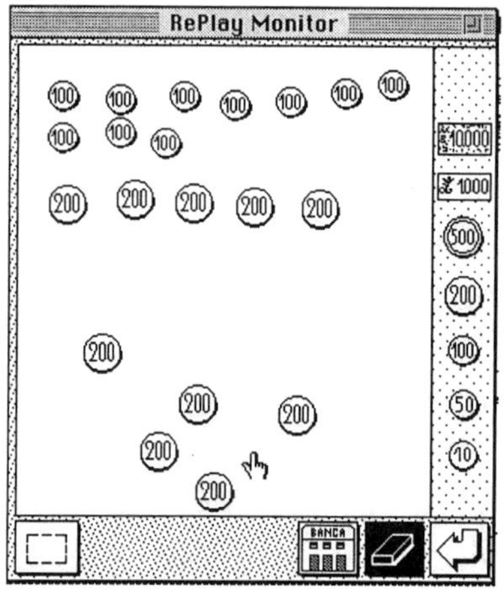

Figure 2. Frame 2

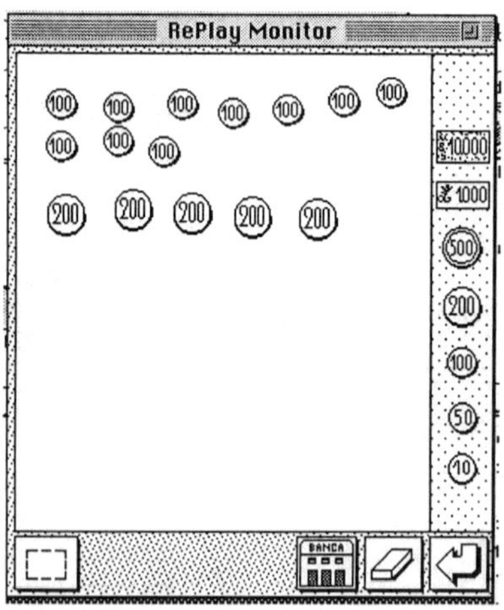

Figure 3. Frame 3

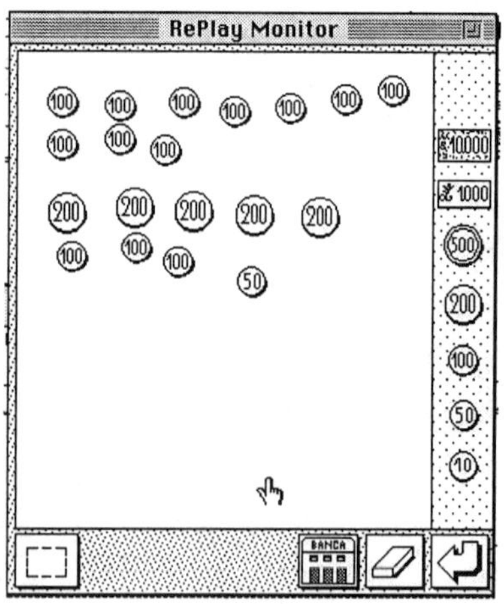

Figure 4. Frame 4

It is clear from Frame 1 that the student is unable to work out the problem in advance. Nevertheless, she begins to apply a strategy: she starts off using the 100 lire coins and applies knowledge about the equivalence of coins (10 hundred-lire coins make a thousand). She then moves on to 200 lire coins, but without taking account of the overall total (Frame 2). When she starts counting (Frame 2), she realises that she has too many 200 lire coins, so she cancels them (Frame 3) and adds the coins needed to make up the total (Frame 4).

It's worth noting that when interacting with the system (generating coins, grouping them in the workspace, and so on) the student is able to adjust her behaviour according to the goal to be reached, albeit in a step-by-step rather than comprehensive manner. At the same time she explores new representations (e.g. five 200-lire coins make one thousand) that can be used later on. Let's see how the communication unfolds:

MARIO-R:	ten two-hundred lire coins, three one-hundred lire coins, a fifty lire coin
ANNA-M:	Exactly right
ANNA-M:	a one-thousand lire banknote, 13 one-hundred lire coins, a fifty lire coin
MARIO-R:	Exactly right
MARIO-R:	11 two hundred lire coins, a one-hundred lire coin, a fifty lire coin
ANNA-M:	That's wrong
MARIO-R:	Why is it wrong?
ANNA-M:	because 11 two-hundred lira coins make two thousand lire, a one hundred lire coin makes two-thousand one-hundred, fifty lire coin makes two-thousand one-hundred and fifty
MARIO-R:	No!!! I tricked you with 11 two hundred lira coins, they make two hundred and fifty
MARIO-R:	I am wrong!! They make two thousand two-hundred.

Checking Mario's solutions was very important for Anna. It reinforced her counting abilities and, as the communication evolved, supported her use of previously seen strategies or facts (e.g. ten one-hundreds make a thousand, plus three one-hundreds – in total thirteen one-hundreds).

The communication context changed the students' attitude towards the problem: they moved from an application of rules which they consider were expected by the teacher to more personal motivations. For example, desire to win the game (as opposed to simply carrying out the teacher's instructions) induces Mario to produce increasingly difficult and tricky solutions that required a high level of mastery. This example offers some hints about the opportunities that close integration of communication and working environments may offer to problem solving activities.

Passing from the empirical materials collected during experimentation with ARI-LAB towards more general concepts, some observations can be made. Communication can be seen as a new mediational means that become a formative component of new systems of activity. These systems can induce and motivate more complex and articulated uses of knowledge that are supported by the close integration of communication with activities in other working environments. Conceptualising and modelling these activity systems as complex sets of learning objects and objectives, rules, roles and tools, rather a narrow focus on the technical aspects, is therefore the actual challenge facing the design and implementation of computer-based learning systems.

5. CONCLUSIONS

The purpose of this paper is threefold – to investigate some of the issues facing educational computing research as a result of the new opportunities made available by communication technology; to support the design of effective computer-based instructional materials; and especially to underline the importance of establishing well designed context of use of the technology (Oliver et al. 1998).

Outcomes from the ARI-LAB research project suggest a number of ways in which environments incorporating communication opportunities and related learning activities might be designed to enhance learning. Specially-designed tasks are needed for which communication and co-operation among users would be meaningful in relation to the learning objective of the activity. For example, in the reported experiment, the development of the number concept is supported by a communication task (a game), through which students can explore the different ways a given amount can be formed, and at the same time co-ordinate different representations for expressing it. These tasks must provide a method and allow the building of a context for collaboration. In the reported experiment, for example, the communication activity exposes the students to new methods of forming a given amount, supporting the use of previously seen strategies and changing their attitude towards the problem.

These goals can be achieved if attention is paid to strategies which have proved to have particular potential in this respect, such as pairing students with symmetrical roles and tasks, and giving them responsibility and control, as in the case reported. The possibility to implement these and other useful strategies requires that school pedagogy be attentive to the new opportunities offered by communication technology; for example, in the case discussed, the need to reshape the form and status of arithmetic problems has been stressed. Close integration of communication and activities performed in other working environments (e.g. microworlds and databases) can induce and motivate more complex and articulated uses of knowledge, contributing to the scaffolding of the activity by providing assistance at critical times and links to previous knowledge. This integration can be promoted also at the interface level, for example, by presenting within the same display frame the different workspaces made available by technology.

REFERENCES

Bakardjieva, M. (1998) Collaborative meaning-making in computer conferences: A socio-cultural perspective. In T. Ottmann and I. Tomek (eds.) *Proceedings of ED-Media and ED-Telecom 98*, Association for the Advancement of Computers in Education.

Bottino, R. M. and Chiappini, G. (1995) ARI-LAB: Models, issues and strategies in the design of a multiple-tools problem solving environment. *Instructional Science* Vol. 23(1-3) 7-23.

Lesh R. (1985) Conceptual analyses of mathematical ideas and problem solving processes. *Proceedings PME* 9(1) 73-96.

Oliver, R., Omari, A., and Herrington, J. (1998) Exploring interactions in collaborative world wide web computer-based learning environments. *Journal of Educational Multimedia and Hypermedia* 7(2/3) 263-287.

Slavin R. (1996) Research on cooperative learning and achievement: What we know, what we need to know. *Contemporary Educational Psychology* 21(1) 43-69.

Watson, D., Blakeley, B., and Abbott, C. (1998) Researching the use of communication technologies in teacher education. *Computers and Education* 30(1/2) 15-21.

BIOGRAPHY

Rosa Maria Bottino is a Research Scientist. Her research interests are in the role of information and communication technologies for improving teaching and learning processes, mainly in the field of mathematics and computer science. She is the author of many scientific publications in both national and international journals, books and conference proceedings, and guest editor for journals, and conference proceedings. She has organised conferences and promoted projects both at national and international levels. She has been involved in the design and experimentation of educational software for primary and secondary school.

Mathematical website constructions for prospective elementary school teachers

Jack Carter and Beverly J. Ferrucci
California State University, Hayward CA 94542-3092 USA. jcarter@csuhayward.edu
Keene State College, Keene NH USA

Keywords: pre-service teacher education, mathematics education, websites

Abstract: This study explored the performance of pre-service elementary school mathematics teachers who created, modified, and uploaded web pages for a future classroom site. Results showed the prospective teachers were successful: (1) using a web page editor, images, and links to prepare their individual website projects; and (2) completing examination items related to website construction. More than 70% of the future teachers indicated they enjoyed the project, and an equal percentage reported they had learned web page editing skills. Suggestions for enhancing the changed curriculum included increasing the emphasis on mathematics learning and better integrating content on spreadsheets and websites.

1. BACKGROUND

Recent research reports have directed attention to important considerations in using the World Wide Web (WWW) for instructional purposes generally and in designing and implementing website projects for pre-service teachers particularly. Shotsberger (1996) surveyed existing efforts at using the WWW for instructional purposes, pointed out innovative uses of the web, and suggested ways instructors could optimise the design of instructional sites. Since most of the instructional sites that were surveyed functioned as adjuncts to the classroom, Shotsberger found that such sites were mainly archival in nature and their primary purpose was to reinforce instruction. Moreover, three considerations appeared to constitute good WWW document design: (1) more and shorter web pages having few links were generally better than a small number of long pages with many links;

(2) pages that included options to enhance navigability, and paragraphs and lists that had common formats were exemplars of consistency in website design; and (3) winnowing a site of inappropriate, extraneous, or redundant material was necessary to ensure the site did not become rich in visual enhancements but devoid of real content. Finally, Shotsberger noted that student work, the centrepiece of any course, was prominently displayed in better instructional sites.

The recent literature has also emphasised the WWW as an important platform for pre-service teacher education. Halpin and Kossegi (1996) included WWW searches in courses for prospective teachers and measured their attitudes on the use of the web with a questionnaire. The results indicated that the students believed that web technology was apt to be a major and positive influence in their future teaching.

Mathematics teacher education on the WWW was the focus of Jiang and McClintock's 1997 research report on how future teachers used web resources to organise, analyse and share data. Particularly, the authors noted that the pre-service teachers recognised that using web resources was an effective way to learn mathematics. Also noteworthy was the fact that students in the study sent solutions or comments to the sites they had explored, and thus became experienced at sharing ideas with people across cities, regions and countries. The authors noted that their research subjects expressed the need to create their own web pages and recognised the value of term projects and electronic forums to answer questions or seek support when learning difficulties arose. These findings were reiterated by Charland (1998) in a recent article for practising teachers on classroom homepages.

Gerber, Shuell, and Harlos (1998) explored how the Internet might be used in a classroom mathematics project and investigated how students learned in this instructional environment. Results showed that the students mainly regarded the web as a source of information and a means to communicate with others.

2. PROCEDURES

Based on the preceding reports there is ample support for website assignments for prospective elementary school mathematics teachers and for a WWW project as part of a mathematics content course for these future teachers. The preceding studies also point out that students regard the web primarily as a valuable source of information and a means for communication. Consequently, a reasonable focus for a project for the future teachers could be a review of mathematical content commonly encountered in elementary school programmes. Along with this mathematical review, the authors made the decision to incorporate web pages within the assigned project to illustrate and emphasise the importance of both Internet and content skills. The authors further decided to make topics in descriptive statistics the focus of the content in the websites that the pre-service teachers created. This content selection was particularly motivated by the fact that descriptive statistics constitute a major portion of the initial half of the content course into which the web project was to be incorporated.

Since the study by Jiang and McClintock (1997) found that pre-service teachers see the need for experience in creating web pages, it was also decided to make the construction of web pages a main emphasis of the prospective teachers' project. Following the guidelines established by Shotsberger (1996), it was further determined that the project would provide exemplars of good website design within an easily navigable website. Also, following the examples provided by the preceding research reports, the decision was made to document this curricular change by conducting an exploratory study of the resultant student performance outcomes. Thus, the purpose of this study was to explore pre-service elementary school teachers' performance in a mathematics content course as they used the WWW and website software to create, modify and upload web pages for their individual, future classroom sites.

The website activities for the study consisted of three 110-minute computer sessions using software to construct, modify and upload websites. Following the computer sessions students completed a website project and then an exam on the website software they had used. After the exam the prospective teachers completed a questionnaire about the project.

The activities for the study spanned two weeks with the computer sessions on days 1, 6, and 8, and the exam and questionnaire administered on day 13. website projects were also completed by day 13.

Prior to the first session at the computer, students received details of the website project along with a sheet of information about URLs, account numbers and passwords. The project required the future teachers to customise a website that contained class information along with a statistical review for the prospective teachers' future students. After customising the website, the students also needed to upload the site.

An individual folder of each student's partially completed website was prepared on a diskette and an electronic discussion forum was established for the class members and instructor to use in facilitating communication and networking. This communication and networking component enabled the participants to discuss questions about the project, to solve problems that arose, to give advice on URLs and other web-related resources, and to check on the overall progress of the project.

During the computer sessions the pre-service teachers received instruction about the website software and completed activities using the software and the Internet. The first computer session focused on locating background graphics and mathematical title graphics on the Internet, saving images, and creating a table within a web page to display and describe images. The second computer session was devoted to the topics of modifying text and backgrounds, uploading modified websites, and making links to pages within a website. The third class session emphasised searching for and saving graphic images, inserting images into web pages, and creating links to the Internet. During the third computer session students were also reminded of the need to consider both grouped and un-grouped data in reviewing statistical measures of centrality and dispersion.

The pre-service teachers were afforded an opportunity to communicate and network with each other via their websites' internal electronic discussion forum. Also, the students' websites contained pages for classroom information and pages on which each prospective teacher was to prepare a review of elementary concepts from descriptive statistics.

The website projects were scored on a scale from 0 to 150 with 50 points being the maximum possible score for completing the web page(s) that reviewed each of the three statistical concepts of mean, median, and interquartile range.

The exam on the website software included questions on the edit, preview, and source modes for viewing and modifying web pages. Other questions related to the use of dialogue boxes and pop-up menus that students used to insert background graphics and to change font colours for text and links within web pages. Still other questions on the exam dealt with website files and with the creation and use of links in websites.

After completing the exam the prospective teachers were asked to complete a questionnaire about the website project. Particular questions asked whether they liked the project, what they learned from doing the project, and why they selected the material they used in preparing their web pages. A final question asked the future teachers whether the project helped them to see classroom applications for websites and to give examples of such applications.

3. RESULTS

Twenty-one of the prospective elementary school teachers completed the website project. In all, the project accounted for approximately 8% of the students' grade in the course and the students' average score was approximately 87.3%. Scores on the project ranged from 66.7% to 100%.

Table 1 shows the 21 prospective teachers submitted a total of 89 web pages, 59 background images, 80 graphic images, 85 in-site links, and 28 WWW links in the sections of the website they completed. The number of web pages prepared by the pre-service teachers ranged from 3 to 8 and the median number of pages prepared was 3. The number of images (both background and graphics) used by the future teachers in completing the website project ranged from 3 to 11 with a median number of 7. Also, the number of links (both in-site and WWW) created by the prospective teachers ranged from 2 to 14 with 7 being the median number.

Table 1. Online elements submitted in Completion of Website Project

Element	Number
Web Pages	89
Backgrounds	59
Images	80
In-site Links	85
WWW Links	28

A count of images and links showed the future teachers completed an average number of 2.8 background images, 3.8 graphics images, 4.0 in-site links, and 1.3 WWW links in the web pages they created. In particular, the number of background images that were used ranged from 0 to 4 with a median number of 3. The number of graphics images used ranged from 2 to 7 with 4 being the median; the number of in-site links ranged from 0 to 11 with a median of 3; and the number of WWW links used varied between 0 and 3 with a median number of 1. Figure 1 shows that the average number of web pages, images, and links used by the pre-service teachers in completing the project was 4.2, 6.6, and 5.4, respectively.

A total of 22 of the pre-service teachers completed the five items on the course final exam related to the creation and modification of web pages. The overall average score of the future elementary school teachers on these items was 73.6% while the overall average score on the future teachers on all items on the final exam was 68.7%. The most difficult of the final exam items that dealt with web pages was an item about the types of files that produce illustrations on a web page. Twelve of the 22 pre-service teachers correctly answered this item, while all except one of the future teachers correctly answered the easiest item, an item concerning the mode to use when inserting background images into web pages.

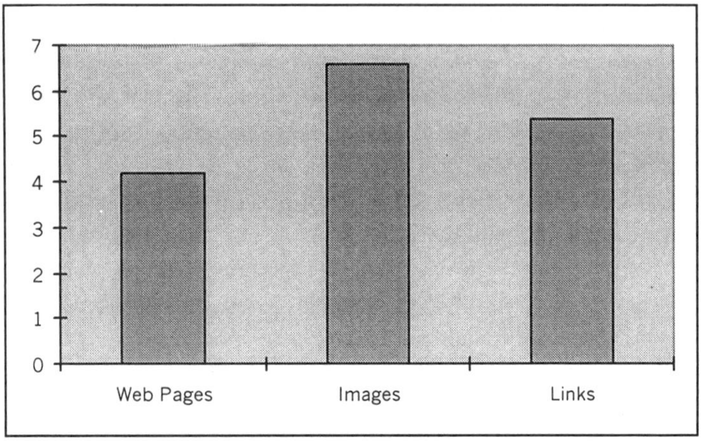

Figure 1. Average Number of Web Pages, Images, and Links Submitted

Nineteen of the 22 pre-service teachers took the final exam together and these students were asked to complete the questionnaire about the website project. A total of 17 completed questionnaires were received from these 19 prospective teachers.

In response to the first questions on the questionnaire: 'Did you like the website project? Why or why not?', a majority (71% or 12) of the students indicated they enjoyed the project. As reasons given for enjoying the project, the students indicated they enjoyed looking at their work on the web or surfing the Internet to view educational sites, or learning about making web pages or computers. Among those students who wrote that they did not like the project, the predominant reason given concerned a lack of time to work on the project. Other negative comments related to hardware problems, the difficulty of the project, lack of help by computer lab staff, and the need for more information on the website editor or web research.

The second item on the questionnaire was 'What did you learn from doing the website project?'. Most the responses (12 of 17) related to the use of the web editor software or to creating and uploading of websites. A few students also wrote that they learned about teaching ideas or about how much time was required to build websites.

Item 3 on the questionnaire, 'Why did you select the material you included in the web pages on the mean, median, and interquartile range?', generated replies that mainly focused on the desire for simplicity, clarity, pertinence, a high level of interest, and attractiveness. Several students also reported that the material they used was the best they could find given the time constraint.

The last item on the questionnaire asked the future teachers to describe the ways they might use websites in the classroom. Most of the prospective teachers described one of three uses: as a source of information for or about classroom assignments, as a source for online help with homework, or as a source of games that help in learning mathematics. The remaining respondents related that they might use websites in the classroom to enable parent-teacher or teacher-student communication, or to teach topics related to the use of technology, or to present enrichment, review/re-teach topics, or deliver instruction by means of a 'different and fun activity'.

Students' use of their websites' internal discussion forum was also investigated. Initially, the discussion forum was set up as a means for students to inform one another of helpful or interesting websites. This objective was met when students posted the URLs of mathematical websites or pertinent graphics for their projects. However, the forum rapidly evolved into a networking tool when students began to post questions, provide advice, and suggest other directions for the projects. Students were encouraged to interact on the forum, and many students later remarked on the value and usefulness of the discussion forum and on its ease of use. As a result, it often appeared that the forum allowed students to explore a variety of valuable and interesting Internet sources and to compile a list of these resources for future use. Perhaps more importantly though, the forum engaged students in discussions about the quality and mathematical content of websites, and these discussions allowed students to gain insight into both teaching approaches and current technology.

For example, one forum discussion revolved around the discovery and sharing of a statistical website. Several students first wrote about their excitement in locating the site, but as the discussion progressed, two students questioned the quality and computations within the site. One student indicated that without this shared experience, she would have been impressed with the surface features of the site, but unaware of the shortcomings and errors within the site.

4. CONCLUSION

Based on the overall average score of 87.3% earned by these pre-service teachers on the website project and the overall average score of 73.6% they earned on website items on the final exam, there is good evidence that website construction can be an appropriate and reasonable part of the mathematics curriculum for prospective elementary school teachers. The preliminary task of uploading partially completed websites for each of the pre-service teachers to modify and upload required a substantial amount of preparation time and three, busy, 110-minute class sessions. Having a teaching assistant to help the instructor with both the preparation and the hands-on computer sessions would be a tremendous asset in facilitating future small classes, and such assistance would probably be an absolute necessity for larger classes or even multiple small classes.

Student performance on particular website projects showed that the completed sites contained, on the average, approximately 4 new web pages, 7 graphics, and 5 links. This data again provides evidence that the project was an appropriate and reasonable undertaking for these future teachers, since the assignment simply asked that they replace the 3 given pages with web page(s) and that they create their own graphics, text, and links within these pages. About 42% of the graphics in the completed websites were used as background images and about 25% of the links in the completed websites were links to pages outside the website. These figures likely reflect the technically more difficult natures of (1) making background images for web pages, as opposed to inserting a graphics image in a web page, and (2) making a link to the WWW, as opposed to making a link to a page with the same website.

Some completed websites appeared to make better use of images in creating a unified appearance for those pages that reviewed a particular topic. For instance, one prospective teacher's site contained the same background image for each page along with a small graphic of a fractal. Using such a consistent design scheme appeared to unify the entire site and imbue a sense of dependability, predictability, and reassurance to the content as was earlier observed by Shotsberger (1996). Future projects involving the construction of instructional websites in mathematics may wish to emphasise this design consideration.

More than 70% of the future teachers indicated that they liked the website project in responding to the post-project questionnaire, and the majority of those who indicated they did not like the project cited time limitations as the reason. The fact that the project was due on the last day of classes for the term may have contributed to the time pressures that were referenced by both those who liked and disliked the project. Other negative comments related to hardware problems or the lack of available help while at the computer. Some hardware problems appeared to be defective machines, but others were likely caused by overloading communication links to the computers hosting the student accounts. For example, in demonstrating how to upload a website there was no success when all students attempted to upload almost simultaneously, but all students were able to upload their sites when this task was later completed individually. Knowing in advance these and similar hardware pitfalls should provide future instructors with instructional time to give more attention to online help features thereby alleviating some concerns about the availability of help at the computer.

More than 70% of the pre-service teachers also indicated on the questionnaires that they learned technical skills related to web, but few of the respondents indicated they had learned about mathematics. In retrospect, it appears that a greater emphasis on the mathematical content of the project can be achieved by providing more details about the mathematics to be put on the web pages. This type of revised assignment could, for example, specify that the review of the median should include both grouped and ungrouped data, both odd and even amounts of data, and exercises that involve conceptual understanding as well as problem solving rather that simple computational skills.

Analysis of the last two questionnaire items revealed that these prospective teachers foresaw their future classroom websites to be primarily sources of information, albeit information that is understandable, clear, pertinent, and attractively and interestingly presented. A few respondents did express expectations of using websites more as a interactive tool, either as a helper with homework or as a generator of spreadsheet-based mathematical games. These responses may have been due to the fact that immediately prior to the website project the pre-service teachers completed a unit on using spreadsheets in mathematics. Greater integration of the content on spreadsheets and websites in courses for prospective elementary school mathematics teachers is apt to further enhance awareness of the potential of the web for instructional interaction.

The present study also provided the future teachers with several examples of links to WWW sites that illustrated the conferencing potential of the web (Foley and Schuck 1998). In the tally of the links submitted by the future teachers in their completed website projects, approximately 25% of these links were to web locations that functioned, at least partly, as conferencing or interactive sites. As a result, it appears likely that these future teachers will come to rely, perhaps more than they anticipated or verbalised in this study, on learning approaches that are enhanced by web-mediated interaction.

REFERENCES

Charland, T. S. (1998) Classroom homepage connections. *Technological Horizons in Education* April 1998, 62-4.

Foley, G. and Schuck, S. (1998) Exploring the potential of a web-based conferencing tool in mathematics education. *Proceedings of the International Commission on Mathematical Instruction – First East Asia Regional Conference on Mathematics Education* 3, 167-179. Korean Society of Mathematical Education, Seoul.

Gerber, S., Shuell, T. J., and Harlos, C. A. (1998) Using the Internet to learn mathematics. *Journal of Computers in Mathematics and Science Teaching* 17(2/3) 113-132.

Halpin, P. and Kossegi, J. D. (1996). *The WWW, pre-service teachers and their mathematics courses.* Paper presented at the Summer Conference of the Association of Small Computer Users in Education, June 1996. North Myrtle Beach, South Carolina.

Jiang, Z. and McClintock, E. (1997). The World Wide Web – A powerful learning tool for preservice mathematics teachers. Paper presented at the National Conference on College Teaching and Learning, April 1997, Jacksonville, Florida.

Shotsberger, P. G. (1996). Instructional uses of the World Wide Web: Exemplars and precautions. *Educational Technology* March/April 1996, 47-50.

BIOGRAPHIES

Jack Carter received his doctorate in mathematics education from the University of Texas at Austin. Since 1981 he has taught in the Department of Mathematics and Computer Science at California State University, Hayward. His research interests include teaching and learning undergraduate mathematics, comparisons of national systems of mathematics education, and the use of technology in mathematics instruction.

Beverly J. Ferrucci is Professor of Mathematics at Keene State College in Keene, New Hampshire. She received a doctorate in mathematics education from Boston University and a doctorate in psychometrics from Boston College. She is the editor of the New England Mathematics Journal, and her research interests include pre-service and in-service education of teachers in mathematics, technology and cross-cultural studies of prospective mathematics teachers.

PART 5

NATIONAL AND SYSTEM-WIDE PROGRAMMES

Information and communication technologies in Finnish education

Elaborate strategies and the rugged reality

Matti Sinko and Ella Kiesi

Ministry of Education, P.O.Box 293, FIN-00171 Helsinki, Finland. matti.sinko@minedu.fi
National Board of Education Helsinki, Finland.

Key words: information and communication technologies, use, national policies, primary education, secondary education, teacher in-service training, electronic learning materials, lifelong learning

Abstract: This article is based on the ComNEd presentation given by Matti Sinko together with Ella Kiesi. It reports findings from recent national research funded by the Finnish National Fund for Research and Development, Sitra. Generally, the findings are positive. Schools are generally well-equipped with the technical infrastructure to support pedagogically meaningful uses of information and communication technologies. Most teachers and students have indicated their willingness to use ICT to a greater extent within constructivist paradigms such as collaborative learning and genuine problem solving. Information and communication technologies are integrated into the curriculum more often in studying foreign and mother tongue languages and in information technology studies. Factors which have prevented more efficient use of ICT are teachers' confidence in their skill levels, in-service training which provides both pedagogical and technical support, and a paucity of electronic learning materials. Suggestions for future improvements are made.

1. BACKGROUND AND MILESTONES OF THE NATIONAL ICT POLICY DEVELOPMENT

Information society strategies were first formulated by the Finnish government in 1994 and the first version was updated through a process delegated to the Finnish National Fund for Research and Development, Sitra producing the report *Knowledge, Competitiveness and Quality of Life* in 1998.

Parallel to this process corresponding strategic documents were drafted in the area of education and research under the auspices of the Finnish Ministry of Education. The implementation of the first National Information Society Strategy for Education and Research 1995-99 was begun in 1995 and was subjected to the evaluation of ICT in Finnish education initiated by the Finnish Parliament and funded by the Finnish National Fund for Research and Development, Sitra in 1997-1998 (Sinko and Lehtinen, 1999).

The focus of the evaluation was broader than just the implementation of the national strategy and resulted in several reports. Shortly after the publishing of these reports and the delivery of the report *Knowledge, Competitiveness and Quality of Life* to the prime minister in December 1998, the then-Minister-of-Education Olli-Pekka Heinonen set up a task force to draft the second National Information Society Strategy for Education and Research 2000-2004, which was published in April 1999 and the first copies of the English-language version were disseminated at the ComNEd 99 conference.

Based on these documents, reports and processes I will try to draft in this paper an overall picture of the uptake of and the pedagogical use of information and communication technologies in Finnish education focusing mainly on primary and secondary education but addressing to a certain extent issues of tertiary education and lifelong learning outside formal education establishments.

1.1 The strategy for 1995-1999

The information society strategy in the area of primary and secondary education was implemented through a programme called Information Society Programme for schools 1995-1999. In its aims it emphasised the provision of basic ICT skills and knowledge to all students and also the perspective of lifelong learning was held important. All schools and libraries were to be provided with access to the Internet by the year 2000. Teacher education was considered to be a first priority. Measures were proposed to stimulate and enhance domestic production of digital learning materials.

2. METHODS USED IN EVALUATING THE ACTUAL USAGE OF ICT IN EDUCATION

The evaluation was grounded in the fairly extensive review of reviews of research literature of the impact of ICT in education and complemented with various national and comparative international evaluations or assessments carried out in recent years. For this evaluation several inquiries were completed by all players in the education field (education officers, head-teachers, IT co-ordinators, teachers, and students). A substantial number of case studies of experiments and practices claiming to be innovative were carried out. All this was complemented through administrative data from schools gathered by National Board of Education.

2.1 Infrastructure

It may be useful to provide a concise summary of the technical ICT provision of Finnish schools to be able to understand the environment in which teaching and learning in Finnish educational institutions take place at present. The figures indicate, that the access of students and teachers to computing and networking resources is broadly on the same level compared with other highly developed information societies. The student per computer (minimum 386) ratios can be seen in Table 1 and student access to the Internet in Table 2.

Table 1. Computers per School and Students per Computer in 1999

Level	PCs/school	Students/PC	
		1999	2000*
Primary	9	12-13	10
Lower secondary	26	11-12	8
Upper secondary	26	9-10	6
Vocational	82	5-6	3-5

It has to be noted, however, that there are vast deviations from these average figures. One of the most decisive factors seems to be the size of the school: the smaller the school the better equipped it tends to be. Since primary level schools are more often smaller than secondary schools, this explains a slightly surprising finding that primary schools are quite well equipped.

Table 2. ICT provision of the Finnish educational institutions

Students	Internet connection
Primary	22
Secondary	21
Vocational	5

The technical and material infrastructure has developed fairly favourably in recent years. The aim of connecting all schools to the Internet has been nearly achieved. Approximately 90% of primary schools, 90% of lower secondary schools, 95% of upper secondary schools and 100% of vocational schools are now on the Internet. Local area networks have been installed in all schools, except small village schools.

The technical solutions to provide access to Internet can be seen in Figure 1. It shows that the network capacity is sufficient for fairly technically demanding Internet tasks. The majority of schools has a bandwidth of at least 128 kB per second.

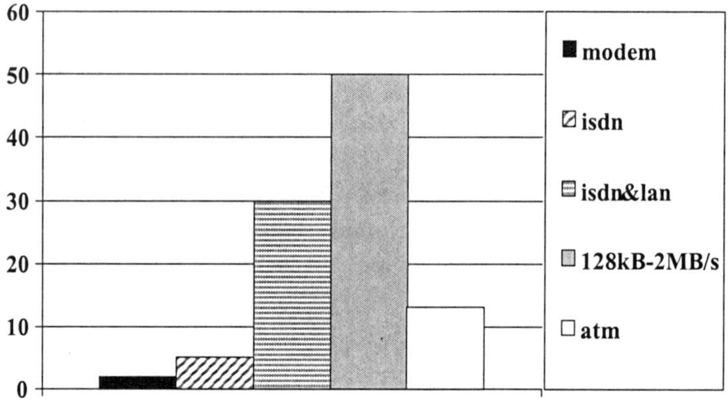

Figure 1. Technical standards of schoolnets

Table 3 summarises the personal access of students and teachers to ICT resources compared with the average figures for all citizens. It shows that the access to ICT of the educational community as a whole has reached levels that provide ample opportunities for utilising these resources for educational purposes. According to Statistics Finland (1997) families with children attending school have higher uptake of personal computers than families on the same economical level with no children attending school. ICT resources available for members of educational communities, libraries provide also an important increment.

Table 3. Personal access to ICT

	PC		Internet	
	M	F	M	F
Teachers	83	83	30	30
Tertiary students	81	67	34	19
Secondary students	90	79	60	
Primary students	76	74		
Homes	40		20	

2.2 Knowledge and skills of teachers

According to our study (Sinko and Lehtinen, 1999) only 20 % of teachers feel confident with their present ICT skills and with their pedagogical competence to use ICT. Two thirds of teachers expressed their willingness to get more pedagogical and technical support and training in the use of ICT. Questions were also asked about how teachers perceive new technologies from the viewpoint of emerging constructivist pedagogical paradigm. See Figure 2.

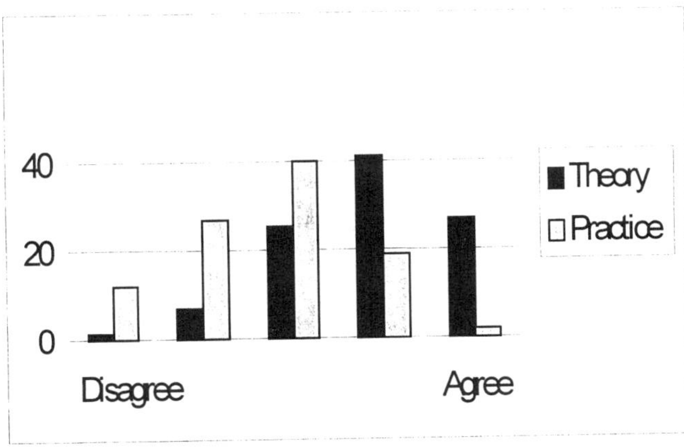

Figure 2. Use of ICT in solving genuine problems according to Finnish teachers

Again two teachers out of three considered ICT very useful in trying to implement these ideas but only few had tried to do so themselves. The results were very similar when answering to the statement "Collaborative learning can be supported by computers". See Figure 3. The reasons for this vast discrepancy can be quite understandable. Teachers may genuinely share the opinion they expressed even though it may be socially acceptable to express that kind of opinion in a survey but lack the resources to implement it. There are in many cases not enough computers available and most teachers also lack necessary skills and competencies to venture into such an activity.

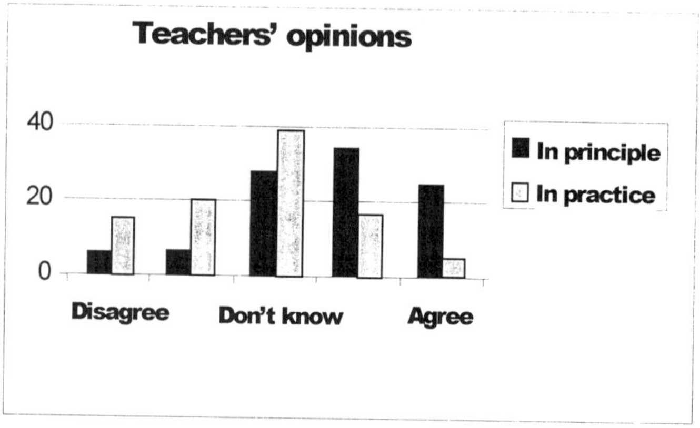

Figure 3. Collaborative learning can be supported by ICT

2.3 Student achievement

The ultimate test of the success of educational ICT policy is of course how students can benefit from these investments. We were able to test that only in a limited way. Mainly we had to be content with surveying pupils' and students' opinions of their own skills and competencies. When the skills reported by students themselves were compared with their actual skills, the differences were fairly small. So listening to students' own voices may be useful. When compared with the results of the use reported by teachers of their use, the educational use of ICT can be very concisely presented in the Table 4 and Figure 4.

Table 4. Types of educational use of ICT in Finnish schools

Types of educational use
Word-processing in preparing study reports and research reports
Web-browsing for information search
Email for communication with peers
Graphics
Learning about ICT

Word-processing has been by far the most common type of use of computers in schools. Now the phenomenal proliferation of the Internet has brought usage of browsing tools up to the second place. The use of ICT for learning about it was not asked but all other evidence shows that it is one of the main rationales behind much of the use of ICT in schools.

When looked at across the curriculum the addition of C in the acronym of ICT in education becomes justified. ICT seems to be most frequently used in studying languages and mother tongue in addition to IT studies itself. Paradoxical, however, is how many students, about 25 % report that ICT is "never" used in IT!

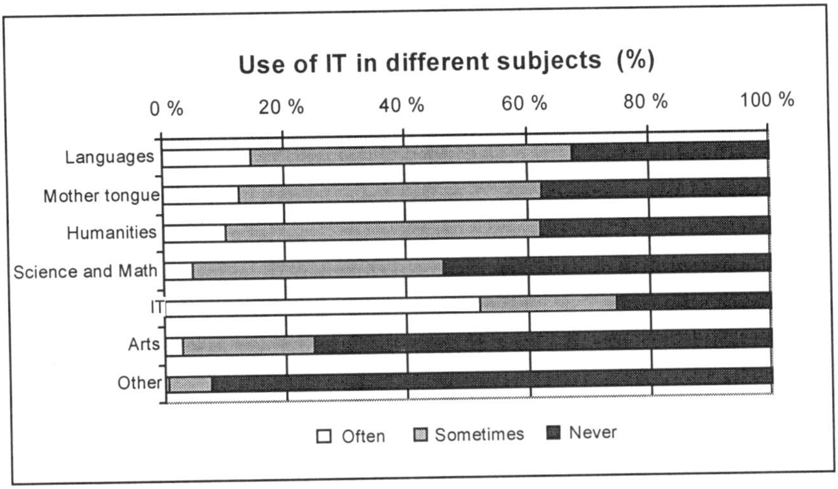

Figure 4. Actual use of ICT in Finnish schools according to students

Students are not too often asked when decisions concerning their working environment are to be changed or reformed. One should – at least in this case. They are eager proponents of increasing the integration of ICT in their learning environments. We should be able to better capitalise on that support readily given by students as shown in Figure 5. And that indeed has happened. Many schools, especially on secondary level are actually dependent on exploiting students' IT expertise. Students maintain computers, servers, and networks, install software, supervise computer labs, support and advise fellow students and teachers, sometimes even train teachers. Some national funding has been allocated to schools for them to be able to acknowledge excelling student achievements by awarding them grants. Sometimes students get also paid for their contribution.

In the national assessment we were able to identify a group of students, about 4 % who could be classified as young IT professionals. They met the criteria that normally are used to identify expertise: they were frequently asked for advice, they provided help, they were paid for their services, they communicated with other professionals in the field.

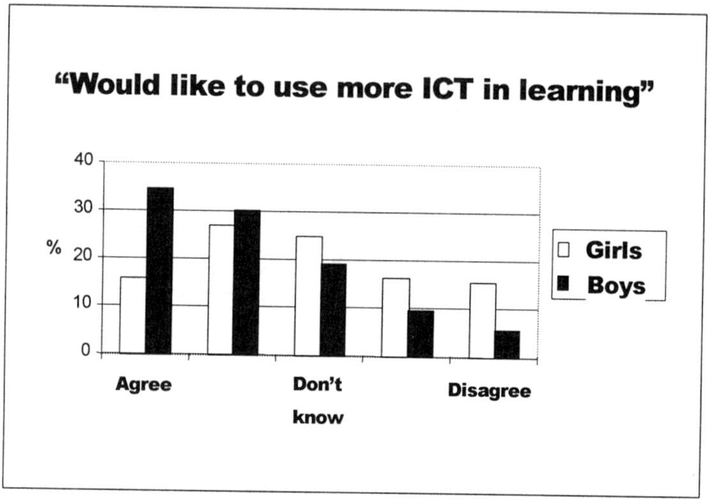

Figure 5. Willingness of students to use ICT in learning

2.4 Materials and services

The shortage of relevant electronic materials is a well-known fact throughout the world, and especially so in the countries of small language constituencies like Finland. The commercial providers of traditional educational materials have been quite slow in adopting these new technologies as a means of providing materials for schools and homes. The new media companies on the other hand have lacked resources for long-term investments in development work necessary for a sound and solid basis of materials' production lines. New constellations between old and new businesses take time to be formed. In the meanwhile National Board of Education has supported production of educational multimedia titles thus continuing its role established in supporting the production of so called computer-aided learning (CAL) materials. There has been considerable and sustained efforts to capitalise on the broader Nordic education market through collaboration of Nordic education authorities and companies in design, exchange and dissemination of electronic learning materials. Despite these efforts, the uptake and usage of specific electronic learning materials is extremely low.

2.5 Curriculum development in schools

We asked IT co-ordinators and head-teachers, how is determined the use of ICT in schools. The answer was a bit surprising: in almost all of the schools (96 %) reported that it is up to the teachers themselves to decide whether they apply ICT or not in their teaching. This can be considered as a supreme example of professionalism highly appreciated in the Finnish education system. It can, however, be questioned if it is in accordance with the national curriculum guidelines, which do not constitute IT as a compulsory or even a voluntary subject to be offered by schools. The guidelines strongly suggest IT being integrated in all teaching and also to be offered as a specific subject if so desired.

There are specific IT courses in the curriculum in 64% of the schools. IT skills requirements for all students have been listed in 46% of the schools. But IT use is defined across the curriculum in 26% of the schools only. So much remains to be worked out in schools to provide information society skills for students in a systematic and comprehensive way.

3. SUMMARY OF POSITIVE OUTCOMES

The state of ICT in Finnish education can be summarised as follows. Throughout the education community attitudes are in general very positive and confident towards implementing new technologies in education. There has been no significant opposition to this intense prioritising of investments in educational technology. Indirectly, one can see passive opposition especially by teachers with strong humanities orientation, who tend to weigh investments in computers and networks against ailing school libraries and cuts in public library acquisitions. Teacher unions have also been reluctant to fully support in-service training schemes which require teachers to invest their own time when at the same time many teachers have been laid off or made redundant, not to mention cuts in fees and teaching hours. Thus it can be recognised a high level of dedication to enhance the use of ICT by all stakeholders on the education scene.

Basic ICT skills have been adopted widely in education establishments. There were no difficulties in identifying plenty of innovative cases in schools on all levels. Many cases indicated also genuine collaboration across the curriculum within a school as well as between two or more schools.

Technical infrastructures are gradually approaching pedagogically appropriate levels. It was also evident that introduction of ICT had clearly been catalysing pedagogical paradigm change in many schools.

Access to ICT resources offered by schools and libraries to students seem to equalise access to and use of ICT provided by homes.

3.1 To be addressed or improved

It is clear that on the national level the expenditure for the educational technology has not yet reached sustainable cost levels. On the one hand the public money spent is not sufficient to guarantee a pedagogically meaningful technical platform for efficient use of new technology in schools, even though there is enough computers at present to make pedagogical experiments feasible. The most burning shortage concerns especially electronic materials on domestic languages and pedagogical as well as technical support and training for teachers.

There is need to raise the present level of research and development of high-level learning environments. The real challenge for the Finnish education community is to solve the problem of scaling up the results achieved in small-scale well-supported experiments and to disseminate successfully emerging good practices. Furthermore we should not forget the apparent needs to cope with the paramount and constantly growing many-faceted issues of equality.

The rhetoric of school reforms in general and with regard to the information society in particular seem to lead to a fundamental discrepancy between the aims and the actual outcome of reforms. One reason for this is the difficulty in distinguishing between technical and social innovations. What is technically possible and can be achieved in well-supported and designed small-scale experiments may fail to materialise on a larger scale because of a failure to overcome chasms between innovators and the majority of people inherent in any social innovation. It is easy to get innovators and early adopters to pick up new innovations but it takes much more careful planning and social engineering to make the majority adopt useful innovations if this requires changing old behavioural patterns and investing time and money for benefits not immediately at hand. The history of technical innovations is full of failures to make them socially successful. The short history of educational IT and ICT reforms suggests that we have underestimated this social inertia. This seems to be a universal fact. (Cf. Moore, 1995.)

Unfortunately, our recent evaluation of ICT in Finnish education largely confirms this hypothesis. There are a number of innovative experiments and projects going on all around the country, but it is sometimes difficult to consolidate good practice in the schools participating in the projects – let alone to disseminate the results to other schools. The great challenge is still to accomplish lasting pedagogical changes on a large scale, a challenge which has to be addressed with much more attention in the future than has been the case in the past.

3.2 New information society strategy for education and research

A new national strategy for education and research in the information society for the years 2000-2004 has been recently published. It has been largely based on the evaluation outlined above. From that perspective it is not surprising that the proliferation of so called information society skills was chosen the first priority to be addressed. Those skills and competencies can best be pursued by raising the skills and competencies of teachers through intensified and improved teacher pre- and in-service education.

More and better ICT and so-called new media professionals are also needed. Investments in physical networks can be justified only if the networks will be effectively used. That means need to develop extensive online education system and services based on one of the best education network infrastructure in the world.

The network capacity will be quite poorly exploited if we fail in enhancing production of electronic learning materials. And as shown earlier the present technical level of education infrastructure needs still strengthening of support structures. All this cannot be achieved through public sector but requires a careful and innovative orchestration of collaboration between public and private sectors.

REFERENCES

Ministry of Education, Finland. (1995) *Education, Training and Research in the Information Society. A National Strategy.*

Ministry of Education, Finland. (1999) *Education, Training and Research in the Information Society. A National Strategy for 2000-2004.*

Moore, G. (1995). *Crossing the Chasm.* Harper Business, New York.

National Fund for Research and Development (Sitra), Finland. (1998) *Knowledge, Competitiveness and Quality of Life.*

Sinko, M. and Lehtinen, E. (1999). *The Challenges of ICT in Finnish Education.* National Fund for Research and Development (Sitra), Finland.

BIOGRAPHIES

Matti Sinko is Senior Adviser in Ministry of Education, Finland, Manager of the project evaluating ICT in education initiated by Finnish Parliament and funded by Finnish National Fund for Research and Development, Sitra, Member and secretary of the task force responsible for The National Strategy for Education and Research in the Information Society 2000–2004.

Ella Kiesi is the chief technologist of the National Board of Education, who has been in charge of implementing the first national information society strategy for education and research for 1995-1999 for primary and secondary education. Ella is also a member of the task force drafting the National Strategy for Education and Research in the Information Society 2000–2004.

Preparing teachers for the connected learning community

Don Passey
Department of Psychology, Lancaster University, Lancaster LA1 4YF, UK.
d.passey@lancaster.ac.uk

Keywords: strategic plans, national development, ICT strategy, connected learning communities, teacher training needs

Abstract: The United Kingdom (UK) has embarked on an ambitious path – it intends to develop a connected learning community that links and involves schools, libraries, museums, business, industry, and community centres. The first stages of the plans to achieve this vision are laid and being put in place – a strategic vision has been developed, a plan which includes targets and funding for physical resources has been produced, funding and support for teacher training will be available, and resource development on the Internet is under way. The ultimate vision is concerned with the opportunities and abilities that will exist for learning at times in and out of, and in and beyond, school. Curriculum documentation is being put in place to specify the future student, and teacher curriculum (presumably to support this plan). But the mechanisms to support teachers in developing the means to help students learn across and in the school-home-community continuum are not at this stage identified. Is this a basic flaw in the strategy, or a symptom of timely and phased planning?

1. INTRODUCTION

The European Commission, in their paper entitled Learning in the Information Society: Action plan for a European education initiative (1996), outlined the concept of a learning society for the European Union (EU). A part of that concept was the belief in the benefits of connecting learners in school with learners in other places. The document stated that "the Commission supports the extension of 'public access' to the Information Society. This includes especially the connection of schools, universities and libraries". The United Kingdom (UK) response to such ideas was to initiate a programme of pilot developments, in schools, Local Education Authorities (LEAs), and colleges (DFE 1995b). The results of these pilot developments were evaluated and reported in detail (Scrimshaw 1997). Subsequently, a consultation document, entitled Connecting the Learning Society – National Grid for Learning: The Government's Consultation Paper (DfEE 1997), was produced by the Department for Education and Employment. This outlined the proposed strategy for developing a learning society.

A number of terms have been used to describe the concept of developing a learning society. The term 'connected learning community' is one such term, which contains potentially three different elements that can be separately considered, each one implying something rather different:

- connected community (implies compatible physical links at least);
- learning community (implies some level of agreed purposes for learning, over perhaps a potentially long period of time);
- connected learning (implies some common or agreed purpose and resource).

The challenge for all individuals involved in education is to enable provision for all of these elements. The challenge for those not involved in education is to consider whether involvement would be useful, and how to develop meaningful links. In the case of teachers, they need to develop understandings of what the system might offer, and how it can be used successfully, not just within the school, but also between and across the home, school, and community domain.

2. WHAT IS NEEDED

At a strategic or national level, to put into practice such a long term goal, it requires a strategic vision, a strategic plan, and an implementation plan. The Stevenson Report (1997), provided a strategic vision of ICT use in schools, a part of which was a development towards a 'connected learning society'. The report stated that "We wish to see a society within ten years where ICT has permeated the entirety of education (as it will the rest of society) so that it is no longer a talking point but will be taken for granted – rather as electricity has come to be". The Superhighways Evaluation Synopsis (Scrimshaw 1997) gathered evidence and reported outcomes from a range of 25 different projects that were implementing aspects of 'connected learning' across the UK, and gave a message that "The notion of a learning institution emphasises the need to change internal relationships and processes ... The notion of the learning community complements this by directing attention towards the ways in which schools or colleges establish links both to other educational institutions and to the local community."

As a result of these two reports, and others, the UK Department of Education and Employment produced a strategic plan, which was published as a consultation document. The National Grid for Learning Consultation Paper (DfEE 1997) stated that the plan would in part provide for the development of a Grid that would be "a way of finding and using online learning and teaching materials", "a mosaic of inter-connecting networks and education services based on the Internet which will support teaching, learning, training and administration in schools, colleges, universities, libraries, the workplace and home".

So, a strategic vision is set, and a strategic plan is laid. But what of implementation? And what of implementation at the level of the teacher? Already a range of some of the likely needs for implementation by teachers have been identified by a number of authors. For example, Visser and Jain (1997), in a paper on building open learning communities, stated that "While learning is an individualised effort, it is also a social activity. Teaching must be conceived of in terms of a larger social exercise of connecting learners (and, in the process, building communities) to each other and to the world around them. The process of connecting learners involves creating dialogue among diverse groups of learners that allow them to understand and appreciate the differences as well as the similarities that bond us as human beings. This means that teachers must be committed to understanding their learners and the communities that they come from". Cornu (1997), in a paper which considered what teachers will face in terms of implementing future uses of ICT, stated that the experiences in France suggested that teachers will need to accommodate to "the fact that more and more, he (she) will have to manage the access to knowledge, to help students organise the knowledge, hierarchising the knowledge".

The need for teachers to be able to use ICT effectively in schools is a clear need, but their need to be able to support students, parents and the wider community in practices that enable a 'connected learning community' to function are clearly needs that are just as vital, and needs that will be likely to be more difficult to develop, since little practice exists already.

3. HOME-SCHOOL-COMMUNITY ACTIVITIES

Evidence shows that children are using ICT at home, often regularly, for educational reasons and educational (Passey 1995; Passey et al. 1997; Sanger et al. 1997). Children use ICT at home, for example, to:

- write stories and poems;
- create works of art and to design materials;
- develop presentations in visual, text, and sound forms, often integrating these forms together;

- fax and email others to gather information and details;
- access information via the Internet and CD-ROMs.

In many cases these educational pursuits are unrelated to school activities. Parents may be encouraging their children to become involved in such activities, but, again, without reference necessarily to the school situation. Students may take their generated 'home' work into school, but teachers, other than recognising its existence, may do little to further encourage the concept, they do not necessarily capture the potential it offers, and may do little to consider how to utilise possibilities of partnership with the home. In fact, they most often reject its presence since they regard it as being 'elitist' or potentially supporting the 'haves'.

The UK Superhighways Initiative evaluation which focused on home-school links (Passey et al, 1997) showed a range of positive educational and social benefits and gains for parents, teachers, and students after a short period of use between homes and schools. The study reported that "Resources made available via communications technologies enable students to work on materials at home, and enable parents to support their children in this use. Early findings of outcomes arising from home school link developments suggest that the potential outcomes for further developments of this nature could be significant". Other studies and further studies suggest that this is also the case.

Some schools are beginning to consider the school-home-community domain more strongly. In BEON: Facing the future, a document produced by ICL (1997) following one of the Superhighways Initiative projects, it was stated that "ICT offers new opportunities for schools to extend their partnerships with parents and for involvement with the wider community. Many BEON schools are inviting parents into school to share the achievements of their children through the use of ICT. Some have begun ICT-related evening classes and are positive about the contribution they can make to the lifelong learning of the community". Examples now exist of schools in the UK that offer 'breakfast clubs', which provide access to ICT facilities from 7.30am onwards, with a breakfast, for those who 'have not' the ICT facilities at home. Some schools are asking parents to consider investing in laptop computers, so that students may work with them between home and school (as part of the Microsoft UK supported Anytime Anywhere Learning Project). These are all important initiatives – they not only provide a perspective on a range of possible futures, but they provide also the opportunity for the study of how teachers involve parents, how they encourage learning across the home-school-community domain, and how these teachers reassess their own teaching role and methods.

The need exists for mechanisms to capture the results and outcomes of such experiments, to identify, and to share these with others, so that practice can be modelled and developed more widely. The development of ICT practice in schools in the UK has relied, in the past, upon mechanisms to share ideas between schools, and often the ideas have been shared in the absence of a formal mechanism being put in place. The sharing has often, therefore, been ad hoc at best. In this respect our past should enable us to consider the need to build the mechanisms which will serve our present and future needs.

4. WHAT IMPLEMENTATION IS PLANNED

Thus far, developments to implement a strategic plan in the UK have focused on four major areas:

- physical resources to link schools and communities, provided through a phased Standards Fund available to state funded schools through the LEAs and the DfEE;
- resources for use across the physical network, being developed by the British Educational Communications and Technology Agency (BECTa);
- a curriculum to state ICT skills and uses appropriate to students (DFE, 1995), in-service teachers (TTA 1998a), and pre-service teachers (TTA 1998b);
- teacher training, to be identified through a needs analysis resource, and to be provided by lottery funded approved training providers.

However, while the physical resources are enabling some potential linking between schools and the wider community to occur, neither the student and teacher curricula, nor the teacher training analysis and training provision account for the needs of teachers to develop mechanisms to support school, home and community learning.

The current student curriculum (DFE 1995a) indicates that students should develop "an ability to use effectively IT tools and information sources to analyse, process and present information, and to model, measure and control external events". While the student requirements go on to say that this should involve "understanding the implications of IT for working life and society", no statement is made of such need to understand the implications for use of IT to support learning between the home, within the community, and for and beyond the school (even while the student is at school). For the lottery funded training programme for in-service teachers, the TTA (1998a) have identified a range of expected outcomes that should arise from that training. While a great deal of attention is paid to pedagogical perspectives on the use of ICT, no attention in this document is paid to the need for teachers to consider the use of ICT to support teaching and learning across a school, home, community domain. Similarly, the pre-service teacher curriculum (TTA 1998b) makes no explicit mention of the future needs that pre-service teachers might have to support pedagogic practice for teaching and learning in the school, home, community arena.

To develop an ambitious learning society, local, regional, national, and international action will be required.

- Evidence will need to be gathered – about who has what equipment; who uses what applications; about appropriate support to provide.
- Human networks will need to be formed – about who has what interests; who has common concerns and goals.
- Physical equipment may need to be put in place – how 'have nots' will be supported; what resources will provide maximum access; what applications are needed for educational practices.
- Resources will need to be developed – commonly agreed student and teacher curricula; Internet resources to share information and ideas locally, regionally, nationally, and internationally.

In the immediate future, developments and studies of home-school-community practice should consider and identify:

- the technologies and applications used by students to pursue educational endeavours;
- the place and times when educational endeavour is undertaken;
- the form of educational activities undertaken;
- how teachers manage the learning processes and activities involved (when these are occurring over longer periods of time, or at a distance);
- how teachers encourage appropriate educational activities;
- how parents are involved and supported;
- how parents support students in the home-school-community domain;
- how appropriate learning objectives are set and maintained;
- how appropriate learning outcomes are identified and attained (when technology can be used to 'share' to much greater extents);
- how achievements can be used to better inform others;
- what particular educational benefits and gains result;
- what social benefits and gains result.

Many initiatives being developed currently are likely to be too constrained, in certain ways, to school systems – they do not necessarily consider the need for partnership between home, the community, and schools. Often too little evidence is being gathered to inform initiatives. There are exceptions – the States of Jersey is undertaking an island wide survey of schools, colleges, libraries, and youth facilities to find out about the ICT skills of its educational and education-related employees. The States of Jersey Education Department is also involved in an initiative involving laptop use between a school and homes. Different technological trials are being set up across the island to test out potential solutions for island-wide networking. Resources for an island-developed Intranet are being developed. A major programme of training will use a variety of modes of delivery to support all staff employed in education. Accreditation is sought through the European Computer Driving Licence (ECDL), and negotiations are underway to make the ECDL an island-wide qualification available to all its inhabitants. The States government has thus supported and is in the process of producing an ICT strategy that involves all island-dwellers – business and industry, education, social services, and homes. This dynamic development, which considers parallel needs for human networking, physical networking, and resource networking, is concerned with placing the teacher in a position to develop ICT skills dynamically as a part of the learning society development.

5. CONCLUSIONS

Being able to harness effectively some of the 85% of the time that students are not in school (Brighouse 1997), is clearly a notion that has been considered and utilised in the past, since homework is a common prescription of schools for its students. But homework tasks are often discrete and discontinuous elements, related, on occasions, only loosely to work undertaken in lessons in schools. ICT enables us to consider the harnessing of some of the 85% out-of-school time in different ways:

- through developing a continuity of work between school and home;
- at times to meet the possibilities that students can offer;
- related absolutely to that work which has gone before;
- using the support and involvement of the teacher with others outside the classroom;
- with the support and involvement of parents and the wider community.

So how will teachers be prepared for this need, a need which in many cases already exists? And exactly what are those needs? If ‘connected learning communities’ are to become a reality, teachers must be prepared for the support of learning between the school, home and the wider community. It will be to our disadvantage to leave this need unattended. If the potential of home and school links is to be harnessed, these needs must be provided for as a part of our equation of teacher development at this time. Even if the details of what to do, and how to do it are not known, at least the concept should be accessible, so that discussion of its potential can be developed.

ICT provides the opportunity for those using it to extend their activities (see Table 1), but since these activities are fundamentally different (at least, initially) for different groups, then teachers face challenges as a consequence. ICT will offer the potential for students to extend their learning by enabling them to focus on their interests to increasing extents, and by presenting their work in increasingly diverse ways (in visual, auditory, text, and multi-media forms). The consequences will be that some students will be able to extend their achievements to far greater extents.

Table 1. Extending activities

Teachers	can extend their pedagogic potential	but need to know how to use this at a distance, in homes and other environments
Students	can extend their learning potential	but will need to know how and what learning to apply at different times
Parents	can extend their support potential	but need to know how to develop and use this support both locally, and in negotiation with others

The challenge for teachers will be to manage an increasing diversity, so that students are advantaged – so that those who extend their learning attainments are not limited, and those who could achieve more are set appropriate goals through appropriate learning objectives. Teachers will have the potential to more effectively support students in their own learning environments, perhaps at home, perhaps in the shopping mall, but also to support students in their own learning contexts by providing learning opportunities in their individual areas of interest. A focus on a school-based environment for learning will only give access to and provide for a part of the entire potential – if the full potential is to be gained, the access and use of the entire home-school-community domain must be developed, and the abilities of teachers to utilise it are essential elements for this process.

REFERENCES

Brighouse, T. (1997) Speech to NCET Seminar, Coventry, UK. 27 February 1997.

Cornu, B. (1997) Teachers and teacher education facing information and communications technologies. In D. Passey and B. Samways (eds.) *Information Technology: Supporting Change Through Teacher Education.* London: Chapman and Hall.

DFE (1995a) *Information Technology in the National Curriculum.* London: Department For Education.

DFE (1995b) *Superhighways for Education: The Way Forward.* London: Her Majesty's Stationery Office.

DfEE (1997) *Connecting the Learning Society: National Grid for Learning.* The Government's Consultation Paper. London: Department for Education and Employment.

European Commission (1996) *Learning in the Information Society: Action Plan for a European Education Initiative. (1996-98).* Brussels: EU.

Passey, D. (1995) *An Evaluation Study of Teletutoring Methods at Open School, and the Potential for its Further Development in the Education and Support of Children in a Range of Situations and Locations: The Report*. Totnes, UK: Open School.

Passey, D., Forsyth, K., Hutchison, D., Scott, A., and Williams, N. (1997) *Group D – Evaluation of the Projects Focusing Mainly on Home-School Links.* Coventry, UK: National Council for Educational Technology.

Sanger, J., Wilson, J., Davies, B., and Whittaker, R. (1997) *Young Children, Videos and Computer Games: Issues for Teachers and Parents.* London: Falmer Press.

Scrimshaw, P. (1997) *Preparing for the Information Age: Synoptic Report of the Education Departments' Superhighways Initiative.* London: Department for Education and Employment.

Still, M. and Sharp, J. (1997) *BEON: Facing the Future.* Bristol, UK: ICL Education Systems.

The Independent ICT in Schools Commission (1997) *Information and Communications Technology in UK Schools: An Independent Enquiry.* London: The Independent ICT in Schools Commission.

TTA (1998a) *New Opportunities Fund. The Use of ICT in Subject Teaching.* London: Her Majesty's Stationery Office.

TTA (1998b) *Initial Teacher Training National Curriculum for The Use of Information and Communications Technology in Subject Teaching.* London: Her Majesty's Stationery Office.

Visser, J. and Jain, M. (1997) Towards building open learning communities: Recontextualising teachers and learners. In D. Passey and B. Samways (eds.) *Information Technology: Supporting Change Through Teacher Education.* London: Chapman and Hall.

ACKNOWLEDGEMENT

My thanks to Simone Kennett, States of Jersey Education Department, for her kindness in offering comments on an earlier draft of this paper.

BIOGRAPHY

Don Passey has undertaken number of evaluations and research projects, looking at the uses and outcomes of ICT in primary and secondary education, and has worked as a consultant to government agencies, commercial companies, and individual schools He led one of the Superhighways evaluation teams, which looked at the potential development and uses of communication technologies in home and school situations, and is currently leading an evaluation team that is looking at the implementation and learning outcomes of the Anytime Anywhere Learning Programme in the UK and the States of Jersey.

Supporting pedagogical change through teacher development

Joy Murray
New South Wales Department of Education and Training, 3a Smalls Road, Ryde, NSW 2112, Australia. jomurray@ozemail.com.au

Keywords: teacher development, pedagogical change, computer technology, flexible delivery

Abstract: This paper describes an innovative teacher professional development programme, Technology in Learning and Teaching (TILT) developed in Australia by the New South Wales Department of Education and Training. It describes the programme itself which is flexible enough to satisfy individual needs while at the same time providing an introduction to, and practice in, specific skills. The paper outlines the collaborative process of conceptualisation, development, piloting, evaluation and implementation across the state. This collaborative process is reflected in the programme itself and provides its philosophical base. The TILT programme aims to motivate and support teachers as they develop new skills, to give them the confidence and enthusiasm to go on learning after the programme has finished. The paper concludes with an examination of the programme's achievements and implications for further development.

1. INTRODUCTION

A change programme is more than its booklets, equipment, video and audio cassettes and disks designed to convey some identified content. The concepts important to writers, audio and video makers rely on more than words and images to convey their message. In workshops learning depends on a facilitator's creation of an atmosphere of trust, respect, enthusiasm and excitement. An examination of hardware, software and courseware will not convey what the materials *mean* to participants in any useful sense. They will have different meanings to different people in different contexts depending on their current knowledge, skills and disposition and their individual learning needs. A change programme is far more than the sum of the parts.

Learning is built on the relationships which unfold through collegial support networks and in communication with facilitators who provide a context in which the learning can occur. As Stacey says, '"successful human organisation cannot be the realisation of some shared intention formed well ahead of action. Instead, success has to be the discovery of patterns that emerge through actions we take in response to the changing agendas of issues we identify" (Stacey 1992 in Fullan 1993). An effective change programme therefore needs to provide opportunities for the building of relationships through communication and through working together on projects of mutual benefit. A well designed programme will exemplify Banathy's (1988) heuristic system types, systems which he describes as "open to and co-evolving with their environments", fluid enough, and responsive enough, to allow for changes to take place. It will take a learning systems approach to development which, according to Bawden (1994), "allows a series of vital insights into the way organisations deal with the demands of their ever-changing environments – indeed it supports the view that successful organisations – as communities-of-learners – learn to co-evolve along with their environments, rather than simply reacting to the environmental changes forced upon them."

2. DEVELOPMENT AND IMPLEMENTATION OF A CHANGE PROGRAMME

2.1 Technology in Learning and Teaching (TILT)

The TILT programme was developed in 1995/6 in response to a NSW State Government promise to provide training in the classroom use of computer and information technology (CIT) for teachers who were not already using technology in the classroom. TILT is designed for teachers of Kindergarten to Year 12 and across all subject areas. In NSW the TILT programme has been provided for 15000 teachers across the state, which is approximately one third of every school's full time teaching staff.

TILT deals with the development of teacher skills in the use of CIT; it is also a programme about extending teacher choices for what and how things happen in classrooms. It examines a range of hardware and software applicable for a range of age groups and learning areas providing transferable skills and an understanding of underlying concepts. It includes suggestions on how to incorporate computer technology into classroom life and support for teachers in using CIT for administrative and research purposes.

The aim of TILT is to give teachers the confidence and skills to begin using computer technology for administrative purposes, professional purposes (such as research and lesson preparation) and in the classroom. More importantly it is hoped that TILT will give teachers the enthusiasm to continue learning about and with CIT. Behind this is the view that the use of computers and information technology will support a paradigm shift in education from objective to constructed knowledge; from teacher centred to learner centred classrooms; from teaching and instruction to learning; from time and place bound to flexible access (e.g. Papert 1993; Dwyer 1995).

2.2 The context

TILT was developed following the Labor Party's success in the 1995 NSW state election. It was part of an overall whole of government strategy to upgrade technological infrastructure and make the increasing use of ICT a priority. In particular TILT was part of the government's Computers in Schools Policy which included: providing all schools with an Internet machine and if necessary an additional telephone line; linking all schools to the Internet; providing advice on the use of CIT in the primary school classroom and in each secondary school learning area; the rollout of computers to schools to achieve a ratio of at least one computer to 14 students; and the creation of a Department of Education and Training website to include online curriculum based activities for students as well as information and on line development programmes for teachers.

The election promise was to provide a 30 hour technology training course to 'kick start' teachers who were not already using technology in the classroom. The developers of TILT, aware of research around what makes a good teacher development programme and what constitutes good teaching with and about computer technology, had therefore to satisfy the needs of government as well as their beliefs about good professional development. Each teacher was to have 2 days relief from face-to-face teaching (later to become 3 days), the Internet was to feature prominently and teachers were to be introduced to touch typing. The challenge was to convey enough enthusiasm to make a 30 hour course last a life time.

2.3 Development history: consulting with stakeholders

A teacher development programme is implicitly underpinned by the principles which have guided the programme's development process. A programme which respects the learner begins with the developers' respect for a broad range of expertise. A programme which addresses the learner as colleague is developed between colleagues. A programme which allows for diversity (multiple entry points and multiple pathways) is developed in an atmosphere which allows for creative ideas to flourish. Programme and programme development implicate each other.

The development of TILT began with consultation with representatives of stakeholder groups and the involvement of a wide range of people bringing a broad knowledge base to the course development. In all about 30 people attended a two day planning meeting in July 1995. The meeting produced a set of principles which would underpin the programme (flexible delivery; school based learning; individual learning pathways; learning partners; negotiated assessment), a set of desired outcomes for teachers and for students, and a map of the content to be covered. To a great extent the processes employed in this 2 day meeting were reflected in the product. The set of principles respected the learner, the outcomes for teachers and students supported the learner and the content to be covered both satisfied the needs of government and allowed for diversity of participant needs and interests. Systems theory referred to above (Benathy 1988; Bawden 1994) provided the framework for a non-hierarchical networked structure in which the programme would operate.

Concurrently work was continuing on an evaluation strategy and a Principals' Briefing package which was to inform principals of the programme, give advice on identification of participants and ways in which participants could be supported.

2.4 Implementation: the importance of participant feedback

The programme that emerged from the above process consists of 6 one hour interactive satellite broadcasts (now videos), 6 small group hands on workshops and 3 days' in-school follow up activities (see below). The first satellite broadcast and the first 2 workshops were piloted in semester 2, 1995 with approximately 130 participants from 66 schools in 2 metropolitan and 2 rural regions. These pilot workshops were 3 hours long rather than two hours, the third hour being a participant feedback session. At the same time a base data survey was trialled as part of the evaluation strategy. This has been reissued each semester. It seeks EEO statistics and information on previous experience with, and use of, computer technology both in the classroom and at home.

Towards the end of 1995 the TILT facilitators, together with a small number of participants, principals and representatives from the original working group came together for 2 days to evaluate the pilot. This meeting was also attended by the broadcast producers and workshop material writers. Changes were made to the content of the materials and the sequence of components. The original 2 days relief was raised to 3 days for each participating teacher in response to a NSW Teachers Federation agreement.

TILT was trialed in semester 1 1996 with approximately 400 participants from the same 66 schools. The 5 remaining satellite broadcasts were developed and broadcast at two to three week intervals throughout the semester. Course materials were written for the remaining 4 workshops. Meanwhile hardware and software was purchased to support implementation. The Principals' Briefing interactive satellite broadcast was trialed together with a support document. At the end of semester 1 a further feedback meeting was held and further adjustments made to materials, sequence and structure.

In semester 2 the participant group was increased to approximately 800 teachers in 16 districts. New facilitators were trained by the TILT team and the semester 1 facilitators. The training was also attended by district Technology Advisers and Training and Development/Curriculum Co-ordinators to facilitate team building and district planning. In 1997 the programme was implemented in all 40 NSW school districts. Changes continue to be made in response to participant comments invited at the end of each semester. Evaluation results and any changes made as a consequence are conveyed to schools each semester in the TILTed Newsletter. It is considered important that facilitators and participants know that their comments are taken seriously and acted on wherever possible.

3. MOTIVATING AND SUPPORTING TEACHERS AS THEY DEVELOP NEW SKILLS

3.1 Meeting participant needs

The TILT programme is based on the assumption that teachers have different needs at different times and bring different skills and knowledge to any learning situation. Even with a selection criterion of teachers who are not currently using technology in the classroom it is evident that there is a whole range of expertise in any group of participants. TILT takes this into account and provides a range of activities from which to choose. Teachers can access the materials in their own time, progress at their own pace and work with friends and colleagues from their own school or across schools. In all of this they are supported by a trained facilitator.

The TILT folder contains 6 booklets, a journal/workbook, 6 audio cassettes holding recordings of the readings (paper copy is included in the booklets) and CDROM with support activities and sample software.

Participants either work with the facilitator through the workshop material or negotiate a different activity based on their own needs and abilities.

Each booklet includes: a basic workshop (presented by the facilitator) with prompts for reflection; suggested follow up activities; suggested classroom activities; 2-3 self paced extension activities (designed for participants already familiar with the basic workshop who choose to follow an extension activity in workshop time); and readings. Feedback from participants indicates that the TILT folders are well received; the many cartoons by Mark David are particularly appreciated. The inclusion of self paced extension activities makes the folders a valued resource.

The six satellite broadcasts which accompany the workshop materials were shown in semesters 1 and 2 1996, 2-3 weeks apart. In 1997 the broadcasts were provided on video for loan to schools. In semester 1 1997 the broadcasts were also shown as 30 minute programmes free to air on the SBS national series tvED. The satellite broadcasts provide examples from a range of schools where teachers and students are using technology in the classroom. They each feature a studio panel of teacher, community, business or academic experts who address issues associated with the focus of the programme. In addition 2 TILT participants (one primary, one secondary) are visited as they progress through the workshops, they comment on changes to their administration practices; they and their students comment on changes in teaching practice. The satellite broadcasts allowed space for addressing government priorities as well as priorities identified by the development team.

The broadcast is followed within 2 weeks by a hands on workshop. Workshops are conducted locally either in participants' own schools or at a nearby school or technology centre in small groups of between 10 and 12 participants. The workshop begins with afternoon tea and a discussion of issues raised by the broadcast and the sharing of between workshop activities. Most of the rest of the 2 hours is devoted to hands-on work at the computer, or to using other items of hardware, such as a digital camera. The emphasis is on creating a non threatening learning environment in which participants are able to work at their own pace and gain whatever support they need.

Follow up is conducted in the participant's own school at any time throughout the semester. Each participant is allocated 3 days casual relief to be spent, in consultation with the school principal and according to the participant's learning needs. The time can be used to exchange visits with other teachers in their own or neighbouring schools; release another teacher to team teach with the participant; take time out to explore software or hardware; practise skills learned in the workshop; prepare a unit of work; participate in an additional daytime workshop offered by the facilitator or whatever else participants choose in order to follow up on their learning. Participants may invite the facilitator to visit them in their school to assist in follow up work. This could be a one to one session or a group of teachers may have common needs. It is this in-school follow up feature of TILT that gives the programme such flexibility, allowing for multiple entry points, pathways, learning needs and styles.

3.2 TILT facilitators

Facilitators are classroom teachers chosen for their people skills, technological know-how and enthusiastic classroom use of computer and information technologies. Their role is to impart the enthusiasm and confidence needed by participants to continue learning long after the programme has finished.

Facilitators work for a semester across a school district. Each full time facilitator is allocated 70 participants. The participants are organised into workshop groups of approximately 10 people. The role of the facilitator is to conduct workshops, and provide individual or small group support by request as participants take up their 3 relief days to extend their learning.

New facilitators receive two three-day residential training programmes conducted by experienced facilitators and members of the TILT team. The training programmes are approximately six weeks apart to allow time for facilitators to work with participants before coming back together again to discuss issues arising from experience. As part of their training facilitators participate in sessions on presentation skills, adult learning and reflective journal writing. Guest speakers like Toni Downes (1997) and Barbara Lepani (1993) address global perspectives opening discussion around economic, political, cultural, social and equity issues.

Each facilitator has the use of a TILT kit containing: music keyboards, concept keyboards, digital cameras, computer controlled lego kit, scanner, video camera, light projection equipment and an extensive range of software, all of which is available for loan to participants. Two laptop computers are also provided, one for use by the facilitator and one for lending out to participants.

Most facilitators are provided with a station wagon for travel around the district. In country districts these vehicles cover hundreds of kilometres each week, as facilitators travel to isolated schools to provide workshops and in-school follow up support.

3.3 Assessment

Certificates are awarded to TILT graduates provided they have: attended all workshops (or 5 out of 6 with a negotiated equivalent workshop activity for the sixth if necessary); and spent 3 relief days engaged in TILT related activities negotiated with, and supported by, the facilitator, or 2 relief days with an equivalent period of time spent in TILT related activities out of school hours if necessary. Districts hold certificate presentation ceremonies as a way of celebrating completion of the programme and congratulating graduates. TILT certificates have currency at several universities where participants may gain accreditation towards a Masters programme.

4. CONCLUSION

4.1 What have we achieved?

It would seem that TILT has satisfied the needs of government. In 1998 it was Highly Commended by the NSW Premier in the Premier's Public Sector Awards. It seems also to have satisfied the needs of participants: 97% of respondents to the 1997 evaluation affirmed the high quality of their TILT facilitator; 81% commented that the programme was 'well organised', 'thorough' and 'professional'; and 74% commented on the 'excellent follow-up support'. The vast majority reported an increased confidence and a growing use of CIT both for professional and classroom purposes. Changes are occurring in teacher administration and in classroom uses of CIT. A 1998 survey of 402 TILT graduates (1996-1998) across all districts and types of schools revealed that 85% of respondents were now 'using CIT for administrative purposes' at least once a month (60% at least once a week). More importantly 80% of respondents indicated that their students were now using 'keyboarding skills' and 'technology to enhance learning' at least once a month and the majority of participants reported that the TILT programme had assisted them to support students in their use of word processing and selected software packages. Given TILT's aim and target audience this is greatly encouraging. But has TILT in any way supported a paradigm shift in education?

Firstly, any programme can only ever be an *invitation* to change. It can expand options for classroom practice. For those who already support learner centred classrooms TILT offers additional skills in an already familiar context. For others like the teacher who said that TILT had opened up 'a whole new world' and that she was now, 'endeavouring to provide the same enlightenment' for her students, it provides a model for a learner centred process and a catalyst for other changes. In this sense TILT can be said to *support* a paradigm shift. It's strength is in its concern for individual needs, the fact that it takes seriously the knowledge teachers bring to the task, their interests and learning preferences; and it asks for and takes seriously comments on the content and process. Teachers take the *feel* of this with them (and their written comments consistently show this) but are not asked to explicate the parts that make up this particular whole. Secondly although TILT alone will not bring about system wide changes in teaching and learning TILT is just one of a range of programmes for teachers, many of which challenge fundamental beliefs about learning and take teachers through a process that does require discussion of, and reflection on, the parts and the whole.

4.2 What next?

TILT's context is one of changing technology, increasing complexity of the teaching task, and debate about valued knowledge and how it should be packaged and measured. Societies need teachers who can knowledgeably join in the debate and who are willing to continue learning throughout their careers. Requests for follow up programmes indicate that TILT facilitators have succeeded in conveying the enthusiasm and excitement needed for teachers to continue learning. TILT facilitators have deservedly gained the respect and trust of their students. They and we are well placed to work with teachers and school principals to build on these gains. We have already begun the process of consultation. The next four year plan will address: literacy and technology; information skills; values in technology and learning; it will provide school leaders with the knowledge and skills to address whole school planning for continuity in learning with CIT; it will provide an online forum for debate.

For the vast majority of participants TILT has done what it set out to do. The programmes that follow, that build on the skills and invite debate and reflection will be crucial in assisting all of us to understand how we can provide better learning environments for our students.

REFERENCES

Banathy, B. H. (1988) Matching design methods to system type. *Systems Research* 5(1) 27-34.

Bawden, R. (1994) *Learning to Become a More Effective Organisation: A Critical Systems Approach.* University of Western Sydney, Hawkesbury: Hynwest (Consulting) Pty Ltd.

Downes, T. (1997) A matter of equity: Computers in Australian homes. *Australian Educational Computing* 12(1) 7-13.

Dwyer, D. (1995) Finding the future in the past: Readying schools for the 21st century. *Proceedings of the Australian Computers in Education Conference.* Perth, Western Australia.

Fullan, M. (1993) *Change Forces: Probing the Depths of Educational Reform.* London: The Falmer Press.

Lepani, B. (1993) *The Learning Revolution.* Keynote address, The Learning Conference, Department of School Education. Sydney, 16 July 1993.

Papert, S. (1993) *The Children's Machine: Rethinking School in the Age of the Computer.* New York: Basic Books.

5. BIOGRAPHY

Joy Murray is a Senior Project Officer (Training and Development) with the New South Wales Department of Education and Training. Since 1995 she has been responsible for the teacher development component of the State Government's Computers in Schools Policy. Much of her previous work has been in the development and implementation of Literacy programmes at national and state level. In partnership with representatives from six universities in four states she has recently completed a two year study of literacies and technologies in education for the Commonwealth Government.

Schools as partners in creating a learning city

Mike Kendall
Birmingham City Council Education IT Service, Martineau Centre, Harborne, B32 2EH, UK Mike_Kendall@birmingham.gov.uk

Keywords: learning, content, teachers, community, partnership

Abstract: The development of the Birmingham Grid for Learning is the largest schools ICT infrastructure project in the UK. The programme seeks to transform the school system, the role of teachers and to be an agent in the realisation of Birmingham's ambition to be a learning city. The underlying model for the organisation of the programme is to create and manage a creative tension between the people, content and opportunity within a learning gestalt, recognising an inner strength in its connectedness to a wide range of social and political as well as educational initiatives.

1. WHAT IS THE BIRMINGHAM GRID FOR LEARNING?

The Birmingham Grid for Learning (BGfL) is part of Birmingham's programme to realise its education vision and strategy. It is a partnership bringing together the energies of the Local Authority's Education Service, schools and communities with public and private sector partners to accelerate the realisation of the school of the future as the hub of a connected networked community. The Birmingham Grid for Learning provides the opportunity to ensure *all* Birmingham City Council schools are equipped to achieve an established level of information and communications technology, as defined in the Success for Everyone Standards for ICT (Birmingham City Council 1997).

The BGfL builds upon a momentum for the application of ICT to learning and the management of learning established through the work of innovative schools and the Education Department's school improvement programmes. The mutually supportive developments have included: the innovative use of government grants; the development of integrated learning systems; the effective use of management information systems to support school decision making; the production of IT Guidelines; the Year of IT in 1996; and the School of the Future Conference in 1997. The climate in Birmingham created by the Chief Education Officer, Professor Tim Brighouse, has supported risk taking with his belief in the transformative capacity of ICT.

The BGfL is, in the first instance, a four-year programme to be achieved with additional funding from the Department for Education and Employment NGfL Standards Fund Grant (DfEE 1997a and 1998) and the National Lottery New Opportunities Fund (DCMS 1998), complementing planned expenditure by schools and the City Council. The BGfL is one of 10 Pathfinder NGfL projects in the UK. The National Grid for Learning is the UK Government's ICT Strategy for educational infrastructure and content (DfEE, 1997b), a part of the Blair government's vision for '...transforming education' (COI 1998).

The BGfL aims to:

1. provide ready access through which teachers, pupils and the wider education community will be able to access and contribute to a rich diversity of local, national and global learning opportunities (such access will be supported from many points in the community, not just schools, and will be a 24-hour, 365-day service);
2. ensure that all teachers and support staff have the opportunity to become confident and competent to make the appropriate use of ICT for the teaching, learning and the management of learning;
3. provide pupils with the opportunity to accelerate and enhance their opportunities for learning;
4. support schools to extend their roles as centres of learning for their communities;
5. be achieved in partnership with the schools and their communities, as well as public and private sector organisations.

2. THE EMERGING REALITY FOR SCHOOLS

This significant change initiative will impact most visibly on school ICT infrastructure with the provision of whole school networks and high-speed connectivity though the schools Intranet, with all 480 schools connected by August 1999 and internally networked by December 2001.

It is clear that many schools initially see the benefits in terms of more technology, to continue with, even accelerating their current school development plan, and to remove a financial worry. The 89 pilot schools in 1998-99 quickly realised the overall strategy was very different, and they could not just pull out their shopping list of computers; they had to review their overall school development strategy. They had to produce a whole school ICT development plan that addressed the collaborative and shared goals of the BGfL, including a vision statement taking a 3-5 year view of their learning and curriculum development in the school and for the community, including their curriculum and school management ICT systems.

As the programme progresses so are the demands upon schools, with an increasing emphasis upon the schools' capacity to make decisions and to manage change, ensuring processes for continuous change are created, connecting all initiatives currently underway; ICT cannot be a 'bolt-on'. The purchase of computers is usually viewed as a discrete activity and localised in its impact within the school. BGfL is a whole school strategy bringing together changes to learning and the management of learning systems, affecting all the staff and pupils at one time. The emerging reality can be constrained by the '...walls of the mind' (BCS 1998).

The first 89 schools are being established to provide professional support to other local schools as local support centres distributed across 39 electoral wards, as well as becoming Centres of Expertise, using the Birmingham Grid to pooling expertise, making readily accessible and locally owned.

3. DEVELOPING THE CENTRES OF EXPERTISE AND LOCAL SUPPORT CENTRES

The establishment of Centres of Expertise is a key element in the development of the BGfL as schools become centres of networked learning communities and Local Support Centres with teachers readily working together.

The concept of the Centre of Expertise is being developed with the 89 schools receiving intensive support this year. The development is at an early stage with schools meeting again in January 1999 when their infrastructure and Grid connectivity has been established, although some have already started working together. Each of the 89 schools identified an area in which they already had expertise that they could make accessible through the Grid, or could develop once they had received their targeted support.

The Centres of Expertise are developing to:

1. ensure a shared understanding of mutual accountabilities and responsibilities;
2. develop the role of the Local Support Centre;
3. ensure diversity amongst the Centres of Expertise proposals;
4. subject individual centres to peer review/moderation;
5. identify shared professional development needs.

The 89 schools are just the first. All schools have a wealth of expertise that they make accessible to other colleagues and communities. The Centres of Expertise will be developing working methods to make the collaborative working possible. This is a new initiative, with no one having developed a Grid like this before, so the schools and Education Service are all learning together. In time, other non-school Centres of Expertise will be part of the Grid, for example, the local community library and museum.

Traditionally in the UK, schools and their communities had been isolated from their peers, only being accessible as and when special conditions apply, such as inspections and one-off opportunities. The development of the school inspection system and the publication of school examination results in league tables have increased the accountability of schools, as have the perceptions in society that schools had been failing, some if not all of their pupils. It had not been a lack of information about different approaches to learning, or the need to develop a founded rationale for school improvement, it had been its accessibility. Many schools had been isolated, their experiences had been isolating, and the majority of teachers had not had a structured opportunity to ongoing professional development and reflection.

The development of the BGfL is founded on the idea of creating a learning gestalt, whereby all schools are actively working together, sharing the risks and benefits of school improvement initiatives, such that all improve and celebrate their expertise. The approach is founded on the belief that all schools and teachers have areas of expertise that others can learn from, readily supporting each other. Just observe any group of teachers together and they quickly share anecdote and founded theory on this and that. However, many obstacles exist in providing all teachers with regular opportunities to engage in such activities. The BGfL hypothesis is that if all schools are connected, they provide a means for a regular and readily accessible dialogue. It is on this basis the idea of mutual accountability is being tested.

The Centres of Expertise are not purely founded on teachers; they want to recognise the expertise available within communities of the school, whether this is the parents, pupils, support staff, or any other group. They are seen as partners in the establishment of a learning city recognising the broadly based social and economic capital and potential of Birmingham and the wider world.

4. BGFL AND THE CHANGING ROLE OF THE TEACHER

The BGfL raises a number of key strategic challenges for schools and the teaching staff that can be broadly summarised in the working model developed for its implementation. BGfL is based on the premise of developing the people, content and opportunity which together produce a creative environment that can be utilised to develop Birmingham's schools as centres of connected learning communities, as partners of a learning city (see Figure 1). The working model builds on Child's (1987) work on the strategic challenges facing large organisations, adapted by Kendall (1997) in an analysis of ICT innovation risks for Birmingham.

In describing a working model it provided an approach to the overall development strategy and the way they were interdependent, informing the creation of teams of people to work on the development and to provide a coherent sense of purpose.

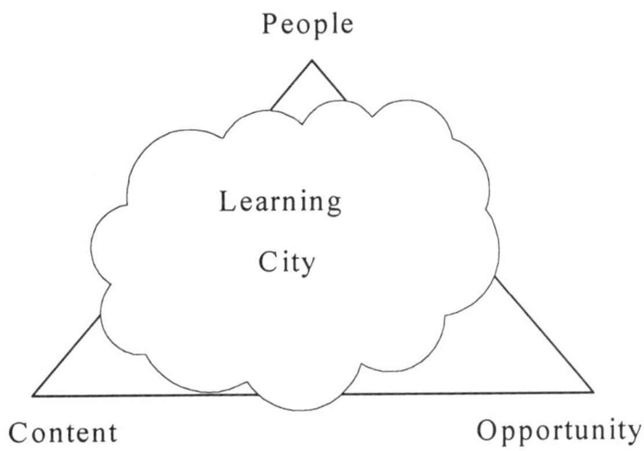

Figure 1. BGfL Development Strategy Model

People: the people who can contribute to and learn via the BGfL will be able to work together, enhancing face-to-face networks, and creating new networks enabled and enhanced by the communications technology. This should include email, bulletin boards, and conferencing, making use of text, voice and image.

Content: the content to enhance the communication potential and opportunity for people, as well as creating new opportunities. We are all content providers, teachers, pupils and the wider community, with knowledge, skills and experiences we can share with others. Commercial content providers will also play a significant role as the creators, publishers and channel of a varied range of resources.

Opportunity: to be able to take advantage of the growing networks of people with whom we share a common interest and need:

> "... multiplying the energy to reach a critical mass of change which will fission out to all schools." Tim Brighouse 27 February 1997.

And to access and contribute to the growing range of content, access opportunities will be required. People, need the opportunity to access content. Initially this has meant providing the technical infrastructure: this is not enough. The ready availability of the technology, will not, of itself, transform the opportunity to access people and content to support their own learning needs and wants. It will be essential that a wide range of structural changes take place, not least for teachers.

Teachers are central to achieving the creative learning community in schools founded in the themes of people, content and opportunity.

4.1 People

The nature of the relationship with teachers in the networked school will change from traditional teaching, people, as learners will be central.

> "The system is focused on how the teacher can do his/her job, rather than on how the students can do theirs, namely to learn. The teacher's first (false) assumption must be that all 30 students are equally interested, ready and willing to learn some *specific* bit of knowledge that the teacher chooses to pass on before the bell rings for the next group of students to arrive." (Jaeger 1998)

Whilst this quote can be criticised as taking an extreme position, the basic premise is widely recognised, it is based on mass teaching of a standard curriculum. It is based on the teacher knowing the answers and channelling the development of the students.

The people who are central to the development of the BGfL are the learners, whether this is the student in the school, or the teachers and other school staff. It is about the notion that the school will provide an environment in which learners are able to access co-learners and learning guides, who understand how to support people learning. In Birmingham, which has promoted multi-faceted, ipsative rather than normative, generalist approaches to learning, this will be very much in-line with the preferred learning styles of the learner, building on Gardner's (1983) multiple intelligences.

Jaeger (1998) proposes a new school system, whose key elements "... must treat students as learning individuals ... where each student plays an active role ... the opportunity for interaction and joint work ... [and] accessible to all students who show motivation and the desire to learn."

The challenge for the BGfL is to build the capacity in people to be able to gain optimally from their learning environment, whether it is in the confines of the classroom or the global village. This will require the recognition that learner and manager of learner is interchangeable, and that at times the traditional student-teacher relationship can be reversed, for the better.

4.2 Content

What is it that people communicate about? This is the premise of teaching and learning, somebody can help somebody to a new understanding and capacity that they didn't have or couldn't express before. This is the content. It can be formal or informal. The question is who provides the content.

Teachers regularly produce content, it is their trade, the presentation of which is their craft skill, weaving an alchemy that engages young people in their learning. However, this content is constrained in traditional teaching by those resources that are readily available, and support the taught curriculum. In the connected learning environment a seemingly limitless resource is available, however unstructured and inaccessible for the learner and teacher.

The teacher as 'content' manager and creator is fundamental to the creation of the Birmingham Grid. Providing the reason why people communicate and learn, and to create more learning content themselves. Content production is a time intensive activity for teachers as is content management: why not use the Birmingham Grid to work with other teachers, educators and learners, as well as community and commercial content providers to avoid duplication and wasted energy.

4.3 Opportunity

Schools have provided the opportunity to access people and content in a tightly structured environment, with clearly defined rules to manage the learner and learning process. The BGfL aims to extend the opportunity for learners to access learning beyond the traditional structures of learning.

One of the key targets is to provide all schools with the technological infrastructure of a connected networked community, obliging people to use it effectively developing new approaches to learning. BGfL must be part of a wider movement to transform education, whether as a National Government or as a local initiative. In the UK the National Grid for Learning is a part of the Government's information society initiative, of which the BGfL is a constituent part.

No matter how many initiatives are planned, launched and even implemented, unless they are part of a fundamental appraisal of learning and its objectives in the learners' locality, transformation in learning will not happen.

5. THE LEARNING CITY – CREATING THE CONDITIONS FOR LEARNING REGENERATION IN SCHOOLS

The BGfL is seeking to create a set of conditions that, it believes, will support the transformation of education in Birmingham. However, this belief needs to set in the broader context in which schools provide a service, learners learn and communities are developed. Birmingham aspires to become a learning city, in which schools and their communities will have a critical role.

> "A Learning City is one which strives to learn how to renew itself in a period of extraordinary global change. The rapid spread of new technologies presents considerable opportunities for countries and regions to benefit from the transfer of new knowledge and ideas across national boundaries." (DfEE 1998a)

> "A true learning (community) is one which develops by learning from its experiences and those others. It is a place which understands itself and reflects upon that understanding … the learning (community) is creative in its understanding of its own situation and wider relationships developing new solutions to new problems." (Landry and Matarasso 1998, in DfEE 1998a)

Fundamentally, schools must be part of a true learning community, a task challenged with the growth of information and communications technology and its impact on learning.

It is fundamental to the development of the BGfL that schools are learning institutions, as opposed to teaching institutions. The school must be connected to its local communities as active partners, rather than as service providers, through this process connecting teachers to their local communities. Schools have always operated as part of a continuum of lifelong learning, but unconnected. As active partners in a learning city they must recognise they are active partners in the task of social and economic regeneration.

Birmingham is establishing two Education Action Zones, areas of social and economic, as well learning, distress to provide the conditions for regeneration, focused around schools. The 6 principles of the Zones are, "… a multi-agency drive … a radical redefinition of how schools function … innovative practice and seeks to extend it … emphasis[ing] inclusive practices … promotes lifelong learning … to share good practice …" (Birmingham City Council 1998). In this redefined world, schools have been provided with a test-bed for innovative new ideas, where the rules that confine the majority of schools to respond to the needs of their communities as they seek to transform themselves, can be dis-applied. An exciting educational initiative to accelerate another exciting educational initiative, the BGfL.

6. CONCLUSION

I have sought to provide an overview of developments in Birmingham as schools become part of a connected learning community and the challenges faced transforming this change programme from a technological initiative into a learning revolution.

The planned transformation of the teachers' and schools role is creating a backlash, with a questioning of the planned levels of expenditure, the training demands upon teachers and its negative effect on children, 'Computers can't teach children how to think' (Williams 1999).

It is early days; the BGfL development only started in April 1998, the Education Action Zones started in January 1999. Many challenges are being faced the transformation has begun. This is the start of a journey, the ambitions are considerable, all stages are not clear. It is essential that a dialogue is maintained with all stakeholders, especially teachers, the uncertainty is unsettling and recidivist. All I can say I am glad I am on this journey and I want to share this excitement and the opportunity with as many people as possible, after all Birmingham is doing what we all have to do to survive and thrive.

Birmingham is not operating in isolation, it is part of the global transformation of education accelerated, or even predicated on the explosion of opportunity through information and communications technology. It is essential for Birmingham that a dialogue is developed, so that Birmingham learns from the global community as it develops it schools, teachers and learning communities.

REFERENCES

Birmingham City Council (1997) *IT Guarantee and Success for Everyone.* UK: Birmingham Education Department.

Birmingham City Council (1998) *Birmingham Education Action Zones.* UK: Birmingham Education Department.

BCS (1998) *2000 and Beyond: A School Odyssey.* UK: British Computer Society.

Child, J. (1987) Information technology, organisation, and the response to strategic challenges. *California Management Review* Fall 1987, 33-50.

COI (1998) *Our Information Age: The Government's Vision.* London: Central Office of Information.

DCMS. (1997) *The People's Lottery.* London: Her Majesty's Stationery Office.

DfEE (1997a) *The Standards Fund 1999-2000.* DfEE circular number 13/97, London: Department for Education and Employment.

DfEE. (1997b) *Connecting the Learning Society. A Consultation Paper.* London: Department for Education and Employment.

DfEE (1998a) *Practice, Progress and Value Learning Communities: Assessing the Value.* London: Department for Education and Employment.

DfEE (1998b) *The Standards Fund 1999-2000.* DfEE circular number 13/98, London: Department for Education and Employment.

Gardiner, H. (1983) *Frames of Mind: The Theory of Multiple Intelligences.* New York: Basic Books.

Jaeger, K (1998) *A New School System: The Jay System.* Bath, UK: International School of America (Bath).

Kendall, M. (1997) *ICT Innovation in Birmingham City Council Education Department.* MBA Project, Birmingham University, UK.

Williams, R. (1998) Computers can't teach children to think. *Times Educational Supplement* 12th February 99.

BIOGRAPHY

Mike Kendall, a teacher of Design and Technology, works on innovative educational development programmes for Birmingham City Council, with responsibility for a range of ICT learning development programmes, including the BGfL. His PhD research focuses upon the roles of ICTs in enabling connected learning communities to develop and to become self-supporting.

PART 6

REFLECTIONS ON RESEARCH IN ICT AND LEARNING

Information and communication technology in education: Desires, promises, and obstacles

Erno Lehtinen
Faculty of Education, University of Turku, Lemminkaisenkatu 1, 20014 Turun Yliopisto, Finland, Erno.Lehtinen@utu.fi

Key words: communication skills, learning theory, social interaction, change, research

Abstract: Rather than a narrow inter-relatationship focused on technical skills, the challenge of ICT for education lies in the new types of knowledge that are opened through the technology. Complex problems in a world of rapid cultural and technological change, a re-consideration of styles of working, and new types of communication challenge both society and education. The focus of research has shifted to the social interaction when computers are used as part of the new learning environment. Yet despite promises of more effective learning, the reality is that learning differences are measurable mainly in experimental or special project classrooms. Change in regular classrooms has proved elusive. Recent evaluations of teachers' responses to the pedagogical challenges illustrate the need for more effective implementation and dissemination strategies.

1. THE INFORMATION SOCIETY AND THE CHALLENGES OF EDUCATION

Education, learning and teaching appear in all recent national and international documents where attempts have been made to outline the road to the information society. Two different approaches to the skills needed in the information society are currently being discussed. The narrow interpretation focuses on the need to train citizens to use technical tools such as computers, information networks, multimedia and virtual realities that constitute the most concretely visible part of the information society. In many countries the official information strategies of education highlight the importance of acquainting students with these new technologies.

Alongside this narrow interpretation of the information society, which concentrates on technical equipment and its use, there is also a wider view, especially when considering the challenges and possibilities in education and training. We must consider the profound qualitative changes in people's lives brought by the information society. Profound changes in the cultures of work and know-how are connected with the rapid construction of the electronic industry, the emergence of a digital and global economy and the revolutional development of different media (Negroponte 1995; Tapscott 1996). It is impossible to predict these changes accurately, but based on the most advanced working life practices and visions provided by futurology, we can outline some trends in the ways work is changing and assess the competence requirements related to these changes.

Knowledge is the most critical resource for social and economic development in the advanced information society, and distributed expertise and networked activities more and more characterise the emerging types of work. Skills of independently searching, producing, and managing knowledge will be essential for thriving in the emerging knowledge society. The skills needed include the ability to solve increasingly complex problems in a variety of knowledge-rich domains, to participate in knowledge work, and to engage in various networked activities. Every citizen will need to be able to engage in education and professional development throughout his or her life.

In the modern knowledge organisations, practices of facilitating knowledge creation and sharing of knowledge are considered to represent the most important competitive factors. Modern organisations do not only deal with content of knowledge (having relevant and updated knowledge) or application of knowledge (using knowledge and innovations in an effective way), but also with the organisation of work with knowledge in a way that facilitates continuous knowledge advancement and supports the sharing of intellectual achievements among members of the community.

As a result of technological development, significant changes in the structures of work are taking place. This can be seen in the growing importance of information-based services in particular, or, to use different terminology, symbolic-analytical services. Although the significance of information-based work will grow, the importance and need for other kinds of activities – routine work and personal services – will remain. On the other hand, some visions of the information society assume "the end of work" (Rifkin 1995), meaning that a relatively substantial proportion of the population will not do salaried work in the traditional sense. Discussions of the educational and training needs of the information society have usually been tied to the demands of information-based work. However, the perspective should be expanded to include opportunities for basic education and lifelong learning also for those who become excluded from this type of work. Some form of selection or tracking is an inevitable part of education, but it is essential that such selection to shorter educational tracks does not effectively suffocate a person's learning skills and motivation and thus exclude these people from the active participation in the information society. As a matter of fact, it is even more important to pay attention to the development of learning skills and motivation for continuous learning among those people who do not have the opportunity to experience learning challenges and to use rich learning tools as a part of their daily work.

The information society is not reflected in our lives only through work, for our entire everyday environment is also undergoing similar changes. Ensuring our development and well-being outside of work requires us to develop our information society skills. When examining the information society, we need to widen our perspective: rather than looking narrowly at information society skills and taking a work-centred approach, we need to broaden our view to take into account the whole spectrum of life. On the other hand, the tools that are brought by the development of the information society offer many opportunities for new kinds of participation and learning taking place outside of educational institutions. People's relationship to ICT can be considered from the perspective of their entire lifespan by looking at the various roles an individual has at different stages of life: in their working life, leisure time, as a member of a family.

By surveying present and future trends, we may identify at least the following four new challenges.

First, managing complex, ill-defined problems and rapid change is emerging as an increasingly central strategy for 'survival'. Increasing information does not unambiguously make our lives more manageable, but in many cases leads rather to growing uncertainty. With the tools provided by technology, people attempt to steer and control their environments with increasing efficiency, but at the same time the social, cultural and economic environment shaped by that technology is becoming more difficult to control and to predict. Formal and precisely defined knowledge alone is not enough for managing this complexity, as we need to be able to combine the knowledge traditionally transmitted through education to the informal knowledge which develops in connection with various activities and which usually cannot be accurately described or defined (Lehtinen and Rui 1996). Rapid changes in social and political practices and in people's social and technological operating environments require that both individuals and organisations flexibly restructure their old practices and thought models and learn continuously. This in turn calls for a more developed understanding of knowledge and how it is constructed in individuals and in social practices. Learners must adopt a learning orientation which aims at surpassing their own expertise limits and acquiring high-quality learning skills that are manifested as the ability to adapt their expertise and learning to the requirements of their present activities (Bereiter and Scardamalia 1993).

Secondly, a new operational model is emerging in production, scientific activities, administration and everyday practices. In it, competence and expertise can no longer be described as the skills of one individual only, but are instead the collaborative expertise of teams and networks, a socially shared cognition. Shared and distributed expertise is different from the traditional model of the division of labour. For one thing there is no 'higher' management which, in principle, has a mastery of the entire problem being solved and assigns various steps to be carried out by different experts; rather, the networking of expertise takes place without any such hierarchical organisation. In addition, networks of expertise often centre on projects. They emerge quickly for the purpose of solving some particular problem, and once the project is over they dismantle. For individuals, the essential skill is the ability to create quickly and spontaneously reciprocal co-operation and communication relationships between experts who represent different types of expertise. For organisations, the essential skill is to be able to create and use the various cognitive 'tools' needed in group problem solving. One such tool, for example, is a body of network-based flexible applications that support communication and the collaborative memory of an organisation or a network.

Thirdly, successful work in an environment based on information networks and increasingly globalised information sources require new kinds of information technology and communication skills, along with the intellectual capacity to control them. For example, it is only data that moves in information networks. Only once data becomes organised does it turn into information. Information only becomes knowledge and wisdom through the interpreting process of a person with expertise. Network technology creates enormous possibilities but demands high levels of skill from its users. The issue is not just technical mastery of network use, but above all the cognitive skills of presenting and developing meaningful questions, and interpreting information by integrating it with previously accumulated knowledge and giving it an appropriate context. One must also be able to critically assess the reliability and relevance of information. Because of these severe demands, the development of information networks may actually lead to the un-democratisation of the acquisition of meaningful information, unless education and training can assure not only sufficient technical skills but also especially the cognitive skills necessary for using information sources. By these skills we mean both the skills needed for processing and evaluating information as well as a well-organised foundation of prior knowledge.

Fourthly, since networks enable rapid interaction between people representing various cultures and professions or people and organisations previously unknown to each other, the challenges of reciprocity and understanding others become even more complex. Network-based operating practices are not just about possessing the skills to use information technology hardware and media, but of possessing more general skills of co-operation, information processing and communication. The essential element in these skills is ensuring that the information acquired through the networks be understood and transferred (by all parties) into usable knowledge by connecting it to meaningful contexts.

A widely experienced concern is how it will be possible prepare future generations to cope with all these cognitive, social, and motivational challenges of the emerging knowledge-based society. In many national and international strategies attention has been directed towards the use of ICT in teaching and studying. The rapid development of ICT has provided education with a rich variety of promising tools and information services.

2. TECHNOLOGY-BASED EDUCATION: DESIRE FOR BETTER LEARNING

In the public information society discourse, the arguments for the use of ICT in education are typically based on various self-evident benefits of information and communication technology. For example, the possibilities for an interactive relationship between the learner and the system are assumed to be beneficial to learning. Similarly, it seems obvious that the multimedia features of ICT that open new possibilities to illustrate learning tasks also facilitate the understanding of the phenomena. The possibility of using ICT in simulating real-life phenomena is one of the features of this new technology that has held out hopes of its educational value. The usefulness of the ICT based simulation has been self-evident in many special training situations, as in training jet plane pilots or nuclear power plant operators. Very fast world-wide access to information sources is currently one of the most promising features of ICT that raises enthusiasm among educators. Educators also rely on the Internet as a useful tool for synchronous and asynchronous communication between teacher and students and among students.

How real are these technology-driven educational benefits of ICT? In spite of the numerous studies on the effects of ICT on teaching and learning, there is not very much specific scientific evidence supporting these 'self-evident' benefits. As a matter of fact, unambiguous evidence of the educational efficiency of the individual technical features of the ICT is unlikely. The effects of ICT depend not only on the equipment but also above all on the pedagogical implementation of technology. Thus, the pedagogical approaches used are, in many cases, more important than the technical features of the applied technology. A successful application of ICT in education always means that many systemic changes in the whole activity environment of the classrooms also take place. This has especially been stressed by Salomon (1994) who has tried to develop tools for describing and analysing these patterns of changes.

ICT has played a noteworthy role in developing new theoretical approaches on learning and instruction. One source of the desires of ICT's impact originates in the current learning research. The adaptation of constructivist epistemological principles in particular has encouraged learning scientists to analyse how technology-based environments would provide learners with new opportunities for exploratory activities which are beneficial for knowledge construction. In the present tradition of constructivism, free, spontaneous exploration and discovery have frequently been stressed. This 'romantic' interpretation of constructivism does not, however, offer an appropriate theoretical basis for designing learning environments for complex concepts and skills (Reusser 1993). Systematic guidance by the teacher is needed, but not in the form of attempts at knowledge transmission. The role of the teacher in the classroom organised on the ideas of constructivism is problematic (Cobb 1994). Thus it is a great challenge to develop constructivism-based models for indirect instructional strategies in which appropriate teacher guidance can be connected with the self-directed explorative activity of the student. Our own research on complex learning in a computer-based environment has shown that it is not an unlimited freedom to act, but a more or less guided sequence of adequate activities that is essential for successful conceptual construction in students (Lehtinen and Repo 1996; Lehtinen and Rui 1996). Experiments with so-called micro-worlds and simulation-based science learning environments (de Jong and Wouter 1998) have shown that information technology can be used in creating new forms of teacher-student interaction in which the spontaneous activity of the student and the teacher's guidance are in balance.

In some computer-based learning environments, the complexity of the content area has consciously been considered. One principle that seems to be common for different approaches is to acquaint students with the structural complexity of the tasks from the very beginning. Instead of teaching sequences of isolated content units, these environments present the students with complex problems while they are studying the sub-elements of problems (Achtenhagen et al. 1993; Lajoie and Lesgold 1992). One of the desires related to the educational use of ICT is that with the help of information technology we can develop environments which present complex problem situations and, at the same time, provide students with a rich variety of tools which effectively support students' attempts to control the complex relationships of learning tasks.

The authenticity of the learning situations and tasks is assumed to be an important factor that can facilitate higher order learning (Brown, Collins, and Duguid 1989). This idea has been particularly stressed in the work of *The Cognition and Technology Group* at Vanderbilt (1996). The basic idea is to anchor the learning of knowledge and skills to meaningful situations and activities of everyday life. This has, however, appeared to be a very difficult task within the framework of institutional education. It is very difficult to bring meaningful activities of the external world to the teaching-learning process because of the restrictions of classroom teaching. It is also typical that practical projects carried out in the school context frequently fail to improve the learning of abstract knowledge and skills. Many learning scientists have assumed that information technology can be used to mediate real life problems to schools in a form that makes it possible to connect the practical problem solving with the learning of theoretical ideas and general thinking skills.

Instructional models based on peer co-operation or collaboration have been stressed in recent research of learning and instruction (Dillenbourg 1999; Littleton and Häkkinen 1999). In order to increase the possibilities for mutual understanding and task-related social interaction, interaction tools are needed that are adequately related both to the new concepts to be learned and to the previous experience and knowledge of the students. There should be flexible methods available for the students, to help them externalise their preliminary ideas and make their thinking processes transparent to other people. The tools available in an activity environment should permit students to follow one another's thinking processes, even in situations where one is not able to argue verbally. Furthermore, the environment and the working methods should encourage students towards mutual reflection.

Even in the late eighties most experiments on computer-supported learning were based on the so-called solo-learner model, and the opportunities to individualise learning processes were supposed to be the crucial feature of computers. This was especially true for CAI-programmes based on the ideas of programmed instruction, but the emphasis of individualistic models was also typical for many learning environments designed according to the constructivist principles (Crook 1994). It was, in particular, the omission of social interaction in computer-based learning environments which worried many educators in the eighties (Cuban 1986; Turkle 1984).

During the last ten years the situation has dramatically changed. Most of the recent research on the use of information and communication technology in education is more or less explicitly considering technology's possibilities to facilitate social interaction between teacher and students and among students (Lehtinen et al. 1999; Littleton and Light 1999). There are two research traditions that have powerfully contributed to the development of the ideas of computer-supported collaborative learning. The first source is co-operative learning, which was an important element already in the programmes of progressive pedagogics from the beginning of this century. According to Slavin (1997), research on co-operative learning can be considered as one of the greatest success stories in the history of educational research.

The other source of inspiration for developing computer-supported collaborative learning originates from the research on Computer-Supported Collaborative or Co-operative Work (CSCW). This research has revealed many issues about the co-operative nature of work in computerised work context (Baskerville et al. 1995). Some of the theoretical ideas and computer tools used in CSCL environments have originally been created and elaborated in modern work contexts.

Recent research on the role of collaboration in learning has tried to find deeper theoretical frameworks that could better guide the developing of technology-aided learning environments (Dillenbourg 1999; Lehtinen et al. 1999). A distinction between co-operation and collaboration is conceptually central in this approach. The distinction is based on different ideas of the role and participation of individual members in the activity. Co-operative work is accomplished by the division of labour among participants. It is an activity where each person is responsible for a portion of the problem solving whereas collaboration involves the mutual engagement of participants in a co-ordinated effort to solve the problem together.

Crook (1996) has widely analysed how computers can facilitate collaborative learning in schools. He makes a distinction between interacting *around* and *through* computers. The first perspective stresses the use of computers as tools to facilitate face-to-face communication between student pairs or in a small group. According to Crook (1996) technology may, in these situations, be serving to support collaboration by providing students with something he calls points of shared reference. He claims that a traditional classroom situation is too thinly resourced for successful collaboration. There are not enough available anchor points at which action and attention can be co-ordinated. The capabilities of computers can be used as mediating tools that help students to focus their attention to mutually shared objects (Järvelä, Bonk, Lehtinen, and Hämäläinen, in press). In Crook's (1996) distinction, interacting through computers refers to the use of networks. Local area networks (LAN) and wide area networks (WAN) and the global version of latter (Internet) provide education with a variety of mediating tools for collaboration (email, electronic bulletin boards, conferencing systems, and specialised groupware).

Appropriate representations are important elements in any learning and construction process, but the problem of relevant external representations is highlighted when complex concepts and skills are the content of learning (de Jong and Wouter 1998). Traditional teaching models do not directly consider the relationship between representations and concepts. On the contrary, it is typical that the concrete external representation used by the teacher is considered to be the complete concept. When students are not encouraged to pay attention to the abstract concepts and operations 'behind' the concrete facts and algorithmic routines, they try to learn the subject matter by imitation and memorisation of the mechanical procedures and symbolic expressions. Representational tools should help the students to externalise their idiosyncratic and informal hypothesis and to compare this hypothesis with scientific concepts and culturally shared definitions (de Jong and Wouter 1998; Reusser 1993; Collins and Brown, 1988).

3. THE IMPACT OF ICT ON LEARNING OUTCOMES: PROMISES OF MORE EFFECTIVE LEARNING

The first attempts to assess the educational use of information technology by compiling the results of several empirical studies were made in the early 1970's (e.g. Edwards et al. 1975; Vinsonhaler and Bass 1972). The first summary articles describing the experiences of the late 1960's and early 1970's concluded that computers seemed to help in training basic skills. Even the early summaries attempted to look analytically at the effects of different ways of using computers. For example, Edwards et al. (1975) started by making an interesting and still relevant distinction between two different kinds of experimental uses of information technology in teaching: one, where educational programmes were seen as substitutes for teachers, and the other, where educational software was used as an aid or supplement to the teacher's work. Their results supported the latter approach in particular, and many later studies have very consistently come up with this same finding.

Kulik and Kulik (1987) performed a meta-analysis on the 199 studies. The results of this meta-analysis can be summarised as follows:

1. Students generally learned more in classes when they received help from computers. The average effect of computers in all 199 studies used in our meta-analyses was to raise examination scores by 0.31 standard deviations, or from the 50th to the 61st percentile.

2. Students also learned their lessons with less instructional time. The average reduction in instructional time in 28 investigations of this point was 32%.
3. Students also liked their classes more when they received computer help. The average effect of computer-based instruction in 17 studies was to raise attitude-toward-instruction scores by 0.28 standard deviations.
4. Students developed more positive attitudes towards computers when they received help from them in school. The average effect size in 17 studies on attitude toward computers was 0.33.

The results of Kulik and Kulik's (1987) very extensive meta-analysis promise quite positive results from the use of computer-aided instruction. We must note, however, that the effects summarised above were average results. As a fifth point, they note that 29 of the studies analysed came to the conclusion that computer-aided instruction had no effects that would have differed from those achieved through traditional instruction.

A few years later Kulik and Kulik (1991) updated their extensive meta-analysis by adding to it all of the effectiveness studies carried out in the late 1980's. This study also showed that cognitive achievement was improved by computer-aided instruction (effect size 0.30). Later, Kulik (1994) published a summary of 12 previous meta-analyses, which turned out to have parallel results. The effect sizes found in these summaries reached all the way up to 0.50. Such large effect sizes already signify essential improvements in learning outcomes.

Khaili and Shashaani (1994) compiled studies from the late 1980's and early 1990's where the effectiveness of computer applications in teaching had been empirically studied. These studies were very extensive and looked at many aspects of learning. Based on them, a total of 151 different effect sizes could be examined. Among these, 138 (91%) turned out to be positive and 13 (9%) negative.

More interesting than the general effectiveness results are the specific results that the authors present based on the studies they compiled. Many interesting results emerge from these samples. One of the important features that clearly emerged in the meta-analysis of Khaili and Shashaani (1994) was the duration of the experiment: effects of very short-term computer-assisted instruction remained rather minimal. A crucial increase in the effect size resulted from increasing the duration of the experiment from a few days to four to seven weeks. On the other hand, for experiments that lasted even longer, the effectiveness began to decrease again. This simply means that there is some kind of novelty effect. A new method or technique brings new interest to the learning situation, which in and of itself increases motivation and improves achievement once, after a short period of practice, people learn to work with the new system. When the new method or technique has been in use in the classroom for somewhat longer, the novelty fades and what remains is the effectiveness created by the new activities and learning processes provided by the new system. Results on the duration of the experiment show us that with more long-term teaching/learning periods the effect stabilises and no longer decrease if the duration of the experiment is extended even further. Based on these results, we might argue that in the early 1990's studies of teaching effectiveness, the effect size 'purged' of the novelty effect would have been somewhere between 0.30 and 0.40.

There are interesting differences between the results of these studies done mainly in the 1990's and those done earlier. There is a clear difference in the level of education for which effects were obtained. In the studies from the 1970's and 1980's, it seemed that the largest effect sizes were found at the elementary level and that the effectiveness decreased towards the higher levels. More recent results draw a very different picture. Relatively good results are still obtained at the elementary level; they get worse at the lower secondary level; but at the upper secondary and tertiary level they are even better than at the elementary level.

Another clear difference between the earlier and the more recent studies is related to the effects of the type of applications used. The earlier studies suggested that the greatest effects came from the use of drill and practice programmes based on the ideas of programmed instruction. The recent studies show that the effects of using these programmes are very small when compared with applications that demand more autonomous active problem solving from the learner.

We can find at least two explanations for this large change. Firstly, computer-assisted learning environments based on a more modern constructivist learning theory were developed into workable applications only towards the end of 1980's and during the 1990's. The second explanation is based on a change in the assessment of learning outcomes. The earliest studies made clear that computer-assisted instruction had the greatest effects on simple memorisation and straightforward tasks, but that the programmes were not effective in teaching higher-level cognitive processes. With the shifts of emphasis in learning theory, from the early 1990's onwards these studies have also focused more on measuring problem solving skills. This has powerfully changed our attitudes about the kinds of learning environments that produce the best learning achievements.

Khaili and Shashaani (1994) made an additional important finding. Experiments done with very small student groups have produced extraordinarily high effect sizes, while the effects shrink significantly once the group sizes in the experiments increase. This result is related to an important theme which is presently being debated among scholars studying learning environments. How can we expand methods developed in small-scale experiments to cover the entire educational system?

Computer-supported collaborative learning (CSCL) is one of the most promising innovations to improve teaching and learning with the help of modern information and communication technology. Recently Lehtinen et al. (1999) finished a large review about the principles, tools, and effect of CSCL that was based on more than 200 published papers. According to these reviews the authors were able to conclude that a technologically sophisticated collaborative learning environment, designed following cognitive principles, could provide an advanced support for distributed process of inquiry, facilitate advancement of a learning community's knowledge as well as transformation of the participants' epistemic states through a socially distributed process of inquiry. Computer-supported collaborative learning appears to engage students to participate in in-depth inquiry over substantial periods of time and to provide socially distributed cognitive resources for comprehension monitoring and other metacognitive activities.

Many researchers have shown how very different technical applications can be used to facilitate collaborative and distributed teaching and learning including special network applications for CSCL, different multimedia/hypermedia applications and experiential simulations. It is not only the features of the applied technology but also the way of implementation of the technology that support student collaboration in particular. Local area networks and the Internet provide education with a variety of mediating tools for collaboration (email, electronic bulletin boards, conferencing systems, and specialised groupware). In research literature there are descriptions of several systems especially developed for various educational purposes (Lehtinen et al. 1999).

Several empirical experiments offer evidence that the well-known CSCL environments like CSILE (Lamon et al. 1996; Scardamalia and Bereiter, 1994) and Belvedere (Shutters 1998) have proved to be helpful for higher order social interaction and subsequently for better learning in terms of deep understanding. What is still lacking is the evidence that the same results could be achieved widely in normal classrooms. It is also possible that similar positive results could be reached in classrooms carrying out the same collaborative activities without computers (Lehtinen et al. 1999).

Although hundreds of papers on CSCL have been published during the last few years, the review of Lehtinen et al. (1999) shows that there are not too many well controlled experiments that could answer the questions concerning the wider applicability of CSCL in normal classrooms and the added value of computers and networks in comparison to collaborative learning environments without technology. In their review, the authors compared 18 studies in which controlled experimental designs were used. From these 18 studies, 16 showed positive effects on different cognitive or affective learning outcomes. Most of the publications studied for this review described the systems and conditions as well as the students' conversation processes, but presented no data of the learning outcomes.

Altogether, the reviews and meta-analyses of more than 1000 experiments show that ICT students have learned more and faster than students in control groups. In these experiments ICT has also improved student motivation and social interaction. The quality of learning depended on the type of ICT application.

4. ARE THERE ANY CHANGES IN REGULAR CLASSROOMS: OBSTACLES IN USING ICT IN EDUCATION

A large evaluation study in the Finnish educational system was conducted in 1998 aimed at investigating the impact of ICT on learning and instruction (Sinko and Lehtinen 1999). In the frames of this project, the main findings of the several recent national and international evaluation studies were also summarised. These results, describing the situation in regular classrooms, gave a somewhat different view on the impact of ICT than the one we could find from the experimental studies reviewed above.

In regular schools and classrooms there were a few examples in which ICT has been applied in a very innovative way. These spontaneous (not initiated by researchers) innovative implementations of ICT were often a part of a larger development project in which several teachers had networked with each other. The case studies also gave evidence that these applications have effectively created new kinds of teaching-learning processes and opportunities for deeper learning (Sinko and Lehtinen 1999).

However, in the majority of the schools, the researchers could not find any innovative use of ICT. Rather, there were many superficial activities aimed at acquainting students with the technology without any pedagogically ambitious attempt to reorganise the teaching-learning processes. In many technologically well-equipped schools, ICT was only sporadically applied in teaching-learning processes. Evaluations of the influence of ICT on teaching practices showed that only one quarter of the teachers agreed with the opinion that communication technology has essentially changed the teaching culture in their school. In general, teachers had embraced very progressive ideas of the possibilities of using ICT in reforming instruction but they had not been able to fulfil these ideas in their teaching practice. For example, when the use of ICT was examined as a tool for co-operative and collaborative learning, a conflict was noted between principles and practices. Sixty-three percent of the teachers agreed with the principle but only 22% had implemented it in practice (Sinko and Lehtinen 1999).

Most Finnish teachers have IT at their disposal either in their own classrooms or elsewhere in the school. IT is, however, not used very intensively. On the basis of the Finnish experiences it is possible to agree with Pelgrum (1996) who, after analysing the results of international assessment studies, concluded that for a majority of students the use of information technology in teaching and learning was still of very little significance.

5. CONCLUSIONS

Experimental research studies bring forward fairly promising results concerning impact of ICT on learning and instruction. According to the large assessment studies in regular schools and classrooms this positive effect cannot, however, be found in everyday teaching practices. How can this discrepancy between the two kinds of views be explained? One possibility is to question the accuracy of the experimental evidence based on the reviews and meta-analyses. When interpreting review articles and meta-analyses we must keep in mind that they might contain errors which give an overly positive picture of the effect of using information technology in education, as Kulik and Kulik (1987) point out. Another may be that although review articles are based on a large number of published studies, it is important to remember that before a research article is published, it goes through a critical evaluation process which usually screens out articles which present 'zero findings'. Articles that obtain results in accordance with their hypotheses have a much higher likelihood of getting published, and hence it might be possible that studies which hypothesised positive results but found none would simply not get published.

A second problem with analysing the effects of ICT on learning arises from experimental design. A new method (here, teaching with the help of ICT) is usually tried out by the most enthusiastic and committed teachers, which is not necessarily the case with the control groups. A third, often-cited potential source of over positive bias, is based on the possibility that in the experiments a great deal more effort might be put into planning the teaching that utilises information technology than into the teaching of the control group. It is possible that this planning effort alone, without the use of information technology, would bring about the effects shown (see for example, Kulik and Kulik 1987). It is therefore problematic that review studies usually look only at outcomes and pay little if any attention to investments. In many success stories described in experimental research literature there have been exceptional resources available to support the teacher in planning and fulfilling the treatment, concerning either pedagogical or technical questions. That is, however, not true in the everyday situations in regular classrooms.

The majority of teachers in the Finnish assessment study felt that their own technical skills are not good enough for effective use of ICT in their education. Even more frequently, teachers expressed that they lacked the sufficient pedagogical expertise to use ICT as a tool in their teaching. They also claimed that there is not enough technical support at their disposal when they try to apply ICT in their teaching.

It is also obvious that the pedagogical ideas used in small-scale experiments are not familiar to the regular teachers or are not easy to be adopted by them. For example, in an assessment study, Finnish teachers did not regard collaborative learning as an important application of computers although the scientific community has considered the principles of computer-supported collaborative learning highly promising for the development of future learning environments. These results are certainly partly due to the novelty of the theoretical ideas in schools, but they also indicate that the theoretical and practical principles presented by the researchers are often still too immature to be widely applied in practical educational reforms.

A school system is a complex social institution that has several significant social tasks and whose practices have developed little by little over a long period. This is why it is difficult to carry out rapid changes. It is to be assumed that the model of instruction and learning based on the extensive use of ICT presupposes such profound changes in traditional practices that the mere offering of technology to schools and the wish expressed by school administrations for its introduction do not yet ensure that purposeful practices are being developed. This observation highlights the importance of carefully analysing the presuppositions of application of technology-based instructional innovations in practical classroom situations, as well as the importance of adequate implementation and dissemination strategies.

REFERENCES

Achtenhagen, F. (1993) Learning, thinking and acting in complex economic situations. *Economia* 3 (1) 18-17.

Baskerville, R., Smithson, S., Ojelanki, N., and Degross, J. (1995) Information technology and new organisational forms: Choosing chaos over panaceas. *European Journal of Information Systems* 4 (2) 66-73.

Bereiter, C. and Scardamalia, M. (1993) *Surpassing Ourselves: An Inquiry into the Nature and Implications of Expertise.* Chicago, IL: Open Court.

Brown, J.S., Collins, A., and Duguid, P. (1989) Situated cognition and the culture of learning. *Educational Researcher* 18 (1) 32-42.

Cobb, P. (1994) Constructivism and learning. In T. Husen and T.N. Postlethwaite (eds.), *International Encyclopedia of Education.* Oxford: Pergamon.

Cognition and Technology Group at Vanderbilt (1996) Multimedia environments for enhancing learning in mathematics. In S. Vosniadou, E. De Corte and H. Mandl (eds.), *International Perspectives on Psychological Foundations of Technology-Based Learning Environments.* Hillsdale, NJ: Lawrence Erlbaum.

Collins, A. and Brown, J. S. (1988) Computer as a tool for learning through reflection. In: H. Mandl and A. Lesgold (eds.) *Learning Issues for Intelligent Tutoring Systems.* New York: Springer-Verlag.

Crook, C. (1994) *Computers and the Collaborative Experience of Learning.* London: Routledge.

Cuban, L. (1986) *Teachers and Machines.* New York: Teachers College Press.

Dillenbourg, P. (1999) Introduction; What do we mean by 'Collaborative Learning'? In P. Dillenbourg (ed.) *Collaborative learning: Cognitive and Computational Approaches.* Amsterdam: Pergamon.

Edwards, J., Norton, S, Taylor, S., Weiss, M., and Dusseldorp, R. (1975) How effective is CAI? A review of the research. *Research in Review.* 33, 147–153.

Järvelä, S., Bonk, C.J., Lehtinen, E., and Hämäläinen, S. (in press) A theoretical analysis of social interactions in computer-based learning environments: Evidence for reciprocal understandings. *Journal of Educational Computing Research.*

de Jong, T. and Wouter R. van Joolingen (1998) Scientific discovery learning with computer simulations of conceptual domains. *Review of Educational Research* 68 (2), 179-201.

Katz, S. and Lesgold, A. (1993) Collaborative problem-solving and reflection in Sherlock II. In *Proceedings of the Workshop on Collaborative Problem Solving: Theoretical frameworks and Innovative systems.* Edinburgh.

Khaili, A. and Shashaani, L. (1994) The effectiveness of computer applications: A meta-analysis. *Journal of Research on Computing in Education* 27, 48–61.

Kulik, C-L.C. and Kulik J.A. (1991) Effectiveness of computer-based instruction. An updated analysis. *Computers in Human Behaviour.* 7, 75–94.

Kulik, J.A. (1994) Meta-analytic studies of findings on computer-based instruction. In E.L. Baker and H.F. O'Neil (eds.) *Technology Assessment in Education and Training.* Hillsdale, NJ: Lawrence Erlbaum.

Kulik, J.A. and Kulik, C-L.C. (1987) Review of recent research literature on computer-based instruction. *Contemporary Educational Psychology.* 12 (3), 222–230.

Lajoie, A.P. and Lesgold, A.M. (1989) Apprenticeship training in the workplace: computer-coached practice environment as a new form of apprenticeship. *Machine-Mediated Learning.* 3, 7-28.

Lamon, M., Secules, T., Petrosino, A., Bransford, J., and Goldman, S. (1996) Schools for thought: Overview of the project and lessons learned from one of the sites. In L. Schauble and R. Glaser (eds.) *Innovations in Learning. New Environments for Education.* Mahwah, NJ: Erlbaum.

Lehtinen, E. and Rui, E. (1996) Computer supported complex learning: An environment for learning experimental methods and statistical inference. *Machine-Mediated Learning.*

Lehtinen, E. and Repo, S. (1996) Activity, social interaction and reflective abstraction: Learning advanced mathematics in a computer environment. In S. Vosniadou, E. De Corte, R. Glaser, and H. Mandl (eds.) *International Perspectives on the Design of Technology Supported Learning Environments.* Mahwah, NJ: Lawrence Erlbaum.

Lehtinen, E. , Hakkarainen, K., Lipponen, L., Rahikainen, M., and Muukkonen, H. (1999) *Computer Supported Collaborative Learning: A Review*. The J.H.G.I. Giesbers Reports on Education, No. 10. Department of Educational Sciences. University of Nijmegen.

Littleton, K. and Häkkinen, P. (1999) Learning together: Understanding the processes of computer-based collaborative learning. In P. Dillenbourg (ed.) *Collaborative Learning: Cognitive and Computational Approaches.* Amsterdam: Pergamon.

Littleton, K. and Light, P. (1999) *Learning with Computers: Analysing Productive Interaction.* London: Routledge.

Negroponte, N. (1995) *Being Digital*. New York. Vintage Books.

Pelgrum, W. J. (1996) The educational potential of new information technologies: Where are we now? In B. A. Collis (ed.) *Children and Computers in School*. Mahwah, NJ: Lawrence Erlbaum.

Reusser, K. (1993) Tutoring systems and pedagogical theory. In S. Lajoie & S. Derry (eds.) *Computers as Cognitive Tools.* Hillsdale, NJ: Lawrence Erlbaum Associates.

Rifkin, J. (1995) *The End of Work. The Decline of the Global Labour Force and the Dawn of the Post-Market Era.* New York: Putman Book.

Salomon. G. (1994) Differences in patterns: Studying computer enhanced learning environments. In S. Vosniadou, E. De Corte and H. Mandl (eds.), *Technology-Based Learning Environments: Psychological and Educational Foundations.* NATO ASI Series F: Computer and System Science, Vol. 137. Berlin: Springer.

Scardamalia, M., and Bereiter, C. (1994) Computer support for knowledge-building communities. *The Journal of the Learning Sciences*. 3, 265-283.

Suthers, D. D. (1998) *Computer aided education and training initiative.* Technical Report (12 January 1998)

Sinko, M. and Lehtinen, E. (1999) *The challenge of ICT in Finnish education.* Jyväskylä: Atena.

Slavin, R E. (1997) *Research on co-operative learning and achievement: A quarter century of research.* Paper presented at the Annual Meeting of Pedagogical Psychology, Frankfurt, September.

Tapscott, D. (1996) *The Digital Economy: Promise and Peril in the Age of Networked Intelligence.* New York. McGaw-Hill.

Vinsonhaler, J. F. and Bass, R. K. (1972) A summary of the major studies on CAI drill and practice. *Educational Technology*. 12, 29–32.

BIOGRAPHY

Erno Lehtinen is Professor of Education and Dean of the Faculty of Education at the University of Turku, Finland. In his work Erno Lehtinen has aimed at combining basic research on cognition and motivation with the practical development of diagnostic tools and learning environments. He has worked as a teacher and researcher in several universities including the Universities of Turku and Joensuu (Finland) University of Bern (Switzerland) and the Learning Research and Development Center at the University of Pittsburgh. In the mid-1980s he established The Centre for Learning Research with his colleagues at the University of Turku and in 1988, the Research and Development Center for Information Technology in Education at the University of Joensuu. He chaired an expert group carrying out a large evaluation for the Finnish Parliament on the impact of information technology on teaching and learning in Finland and currently he is a member of the research expert team in OECD planning a new large international evaluation study on effects of ICT based learning environments.

Index